NON OBVIOUS

NON OBVIOUS

How To Think Different, Curate Ideas & Predict The Future

ROHIT BHARGAVA

Best Selling Author of *Likeonomics*

IDEAPRESS
PUBLISHING

IDEAPRESS
PUBLISHING

Copyright ©2015, 2016 by Rohit Bhargava

All rights reserved.

Published in the United States by Ideapress Publishing.

IDEAPRESS PUBLISHING
www.ideapresspublishing.com

All trademarks are the property of their respective companies.

Cover Design by Jeff Miller/Faceout Studios
Cover Photo by Javier Pérez

Cataloging-in-Publication Data is on file with the Library of Congress.

ISBN: 978-1-940858-15-9
ISBN: 978-1-940858-16-6 (ebook)

PROUDLY PRINTED IN THE UNITED STATES OF AMERICA
By Selby Marketing Associates

SPECIAL SALES
Ideapress Books are available at a special discount for bulk purchases for
sales promotions and premiums, or for use in corporate training programs.
Special editions, including personalized covers, custom forewords, corporate
imprints and bonus content are also available. For more details, email
info@ideapresspublishing.com or contact the author directly.

*No animals were harmed in the writing, printing or distribution of this book.
The trees, unfortunately, were not so lucky.*

To my parents – for always giving me
a chance to see the world in my own way …
even if it wasn't always non-obvious.

CONTENTS

———

PART I
THE ART OF CURATING TRENDS

PART II
THE 2016 NON-OBVIOUS TREND REPORT

CULTURE & CONSUMER BEHAVIOR TRENDS

MARKETING & SOCIAL MEDIA TRENDS

MEDIA & EDUCATION TRENDS

TECHNOLOGY & DESIGN TRENDS

ECONOMICS & ENTREPRENEURSHIP TRENDS

PART III
THE 2015 NON-OBVIOUS TREND REPORT

CULTURE & CONSUMER BEHAVIOR TRENDS

MARKETING & SOCIAL MEDIA TRENDS

MEDIA & EDUCATION TRENDS

TECHNOLOGY & DESIGN TRENDS

ECONOMICS & ENTREPRENEURSHIP TRENDS

PART IV
THE TREND ACTION GUIDE

APPENDICES: THE PAST YEARS'
NON-OBVIOUS TREND REPORTS

AUTHOR'S NOTE:
THE 2016 NON-OBVIOUS TREND REPORT

When you write about the future, the last thing you would imagine doing on a regular basis is looking backwards. The future is new and sexy. The future is where money is made and culture is shaped. The past is boring and backward.

When I first actively started writing about predictions for the future a little over six years ago, my ambition was small. All I wanted to do was understand the world of marketing and how it was being changed by technology. Since then, my vision has changed. It is no longer small, but it is still contained.

Unlike other "Futurists," I don't focus on the long-term potential future, I focus on the short-term certain future. But how can any prediction of the future be offered with any certainty? I believe that the signs of the future are already here in the present. As I will share in this book, my definition of a trend is simply a curated observation of the accelerating present.

With new technology, innovation and behaviors, our *present* is certainly accelerating.

It has been a year since this book was originally published, and time for me to produce a new Trend Report for 2016 as I have done every year for the past five since 2011. Since this process happens every year you may be tempted to think that you are holding in your hands the ultimate expiring product – a book about fading trends destined to be obsolete every twelve months.

Yet the surprising truth I have uncovered about great trend predictions is that they don't get replaced or become invalid after some arbitrary period of time. New trends *don't* replace "old" trends. Instead, a trend will either continue to gain momentum ... or it won't.

Some of the biggest trends changing the world of business today are ideas that I first identified and wrote about more than three years ago. Trends like the "rise of curation" changing how content is created and shared, or "real time logistics" describing how organizations are using data to improve everything from supply chains to customer experiences.

Trends that I reasonably once described as "non-obvious," over time became perfectly obvious and even fundamental. In other words, they still matter. The problem is that they get pushed further down the page by what's new and perceived as more current. They get abandoned before their time.

For that reason, the book in your hands now will take a slight detour from my usual process. Rather than project forward 15 new trends, this book will feature 10 all new trends and 5 revisited trends from previous reports. Those previous trends are specifically selected for the impact that they are poised to have in the coming year and infused with new thinking and new examples I have not shared before.

In this way, it is my hope to add fresh thinking to trends that have become well established over years along with my usual research and insights about trends you are reading about for the very first time that will change the way business is done over the next 12 months.

Whether you happen to have read the first edition of this book or not, you will quickly realize as you get further into this book that it is about much more than a list of trends for 2016. It is also about a new way of thinking that helps you to see the patterns and connections that others miss. It is about learning to state your ideas with elegance and power. It is about appreciating the intersections between ideas and industries.

After reading, if your interest has been piqued to learn more about the trends for the coming year – then you are welcome to also join my reader's email list to receive infrequent updates about the trends (I will only email when I have something useful to share with you) and an exclusive sneak peek at the 2017 Edition a year from now before it is released to the general public.

To join the list, just visit www.rohitbhargava.com/nonobvious.

Finally, if the book sparks any new ideas for you or just gets you to think differently ... I would love to personally hear from you too!

I respond to all my emails, and I relish the chance to have a conversation with readers like you. You can reach me by email directly at rohit@trustimg.com or pick the social media platform of your choice (Twitter, Facebook, etc) to connect with me there instead.

Thanks for reading this and enjoy the book!

Rohit Bhargava
Washington DC
January 2016

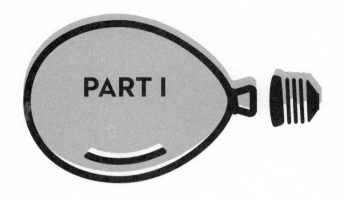

PART I

THE ART OF TREND CURATION

INTRODUCTION

.⸻.

"I AM NOT A SPEED READER, I AM A SPEED UNDERSTANDER."
—ISAAC ASIMOV, Author, Historian and Biochemist

Isaac Asimov was not just a science fiction writer.

In his prolific lifetime, he wrote nearly 500 books on topics ranging from his beloved science fiction series to a two-volume work explaining the collected literature of William Shakespeare. He even wrote a reader's guidebook to the Bible.

Even though he was celebrated for his science fiction work, Asimov never defined himself in one category. When asked which his favorite book was, he often joked, "The last one I've written." He wasn't a scientist or a theologian or a literary critic. He was simply a writer with an incredible curiosity for ideas.

Unlike other experts, he knew that the power of his thinking came from his ability to bring disparate bodies of knowledge together and add his own insight. In fact, he used to describe himself as a "speed understander," a skill he clearly relied on to help him maintain a grueling schedule of publishing more than 15 books a year at his peak.

What if each of us could become a "speed understander" like Asimov?

I believe we can.

The simple aim of this book is to teach you how to see the things that others miss. I call that "non-obvious" thinking, and learning how to do it can change your business and your career.

The context within which I'll talk about this type of thinking is business trends. For better or worse, most of us are fascinated by trends and those who predict them. We see these annual predictions as a glimpse into the future and they capture our imagination.

There's only one problem—most of them are based on guesswork or lazy thinking. They are *obvious* instead of *non-obvious*.

This book was inspired by the landslide of obvious ideas we see published today.

In a world where anyone is one button away from being a self-declared expert, learning to think differently is more important than ever. I believe that observing and curating ideas can lead to a unique understanding of why people choose to buy, sell or believe anything.

This book aims to teach you the skills to avoid the obvious and predict trends for yourself.

A great trend is a unique curated observation about the accelerating present.

Great trends are never predictions about the world 20 years from now. Those are most often guesses or wishful thinking. How many trend forecasters do you think predicted the rise of something like Twitter back in 1997? Exactly zero.

Yet this doesn't mean trends are useless. The most powerful trends offer predictions for the *short-term future* based on observing the present. And knowing the short-term future is more valuable than you may think.

Why Does Trend Curation Matter?

Most of our life decisions happen in the short term, though we may describe them differently. You choose to start a business in the short term. You choose whom to marry in the short term. You change careers from one role to the next, all in the short term.

Long-term decisions start in the short term, so understanding how the world is changing in real time is far more valuable immediately than trying to guess what will happen in the world 20 years from now.

When I speak on stage, I often describe myself first as a "trend curator." The reason I use that term is because it describes my passion for collecting ideas and taking the time to see the patterns in them to describe the world in new and interesting ways.

For the past five years, I have published a curated look at the 15 biggest trends that will shape the business world in the year to come. Each year it is called the *Non-Obvious Trend Report* and each edition is based on a year of research, conversation, thinking and writing.

Across that time, I have advised some of the largest brands in the world on business strategy, taught marketing courses at Georgetown University and spoken at events in 29 countries around the world.

All of this gives me the valuable chance to work in dozens of different industries and study media, culture, marketing, technology, design and economics with an unfiltered eye. Each year, I also read or review dozens of books, and buy magazines on everything from cloud computing to Amish farming methods.

I collect ideas the way frequent fliers collect miles—as momentary rewards to use for later redemption.

Why I Wrote This Book

Unlike many other trend forecasters, simply sharing my annual report is not enough. If I really believe in the value of curating trends, and that anyone can learn to do it, then it was important for me to share my process for how to do it.

So this book is divided into four simple sections.

Part I is dedicated to my methods of trend curation, which I have previously only shared in depth through private workshops or with my students in class. You will learn the greatest myths of trend prediction, five essential habits of trend curators and my own step-by-step approach to curating trends, which I call the Haystack Method.

Part II is the 2016 edition of the *Non-Obvious Trend Report*, featuring 15 new ideas that will shape business in the year to come. Each trend features supporting stories and research, as well as ideas for how to apply the trend to your own business or career.

Part III is a new look at the 15 trends I predicted would change business from last year. Each includes a new 2016 update on how they have shifted in the past year – and which will still matter over the next 12 months.

Part IV is filled with tips on making trends actionable, including a short description of workshops to bring trends to life. In this part, I also discuss the importance of anti-trends and how to use "intersection thinking" to see the patterns between industries and stories.

As a bonus, I have also included an extensive collection of appendices which include summaries from every one of my curated trends from four previous editions of the report (more than 60 total), along with new updated candid, honest "longevity ratings" of how accurate those trends still are in 2016.

You can choose to read this book in the order it was published or you can skip back and forth between trends and techniques. Whether you choose to focus on my predictions for 2016 and how to apply them, or learning the techniques of trend curation and non-obvious thinking for yourself, this book is written to be read in short bursts.

Like Asimov, you don't need to be a speed *reader*.

Being a speed *understander*, however, is a worthy aspiration. It is my hope that this book will help you get there.

THE NORWEGIAN BILLIONAIRE:
Why Most Trend Predictions Are Spectacularly Useless

In 1996 Christian Ringnes was a billionaire with the ultimate first-world problem – he was running out of space.

As one of the richest men in Norway, Ringnes is well known as a flamboyant businessman and art collector whose family started the country's largest brewery more than a hundred years ago. In his hometown of Oslo, Ringnes owns several restaurants and museums, and recently donated more than $70 million for the creation of a large sculpture and cultural park, which opened in 2013.

In his heart, Ringnes is a collector. Over decades he has built one of the largest private collections of art in the world. Yet his real legacy may come from something far more unique: his lifelong obsession with collecting mini liquor bottles.

This fixation on mini liquor bottles began for Ringnes at the age of seven when he received an unusual gift from his father: a half-empty miniature liquor bottle. It was this afterthought of a gift that led him on a path towards amassing what is recognized today as the largest independent mini-bottle collection in the world with over 52,000 miniature liquor bottles.

Unfortunately, his decades-long obsession eventually ran into an insurmountable opponent—his wife, Denise.

As the now legendary story goes, Denise wasn't too happy with the disorganization of having all these bottles around the house. After years of frustration, she offered him an ultimatum: either find something to do with all those bottles or start selling them.

Like any avid collector, Ringnes couldn't bear the thought of selling them, so he created a perfectly obvious solution based on his wealth and personality.

He commissioned a museum.

"To Collect Is Human"

Today the Mini Bottle Gallery in downtown Oslo is one of the world's top quirky museum destinations, routinely featured in irreverent travel guides and global lists of must-see Scandinavian tourist attractions. Beyond providing a place for Ringnes to put all of his mini bottles, the gallery is also a popular event venue with an in-house restaurant.

It was this event space and restaurant that offered me my first personal introduction to Ringnes and his story. I was in Oslo for an event and the conference team had organized a tour and dinner at the Mini Bottle Gallery.

It lived up to its quirky reputation.

The entrance to the museum was a bottle shaped hallway leading into an open lobby with a champagne waterfall. As you moved from room to room, each featured its own composed soundtrack, customized lighting and unique smells.

> *I have 52,500 different miniature bottles in a museum in Oslo. They're completely useless. But men, we like collecting. We like having things. That's human. Once you get fascinated by something, you want it and then you start collecting.*
> —Christian Ringnes
> (From interview in Arterritory.com magazine)

Only steps into the tour, it was clear the gallery was more than just stacks of bottles lined along the walls of a display case in random fashion. Like all great museum experiences, the rooms of the Mini Bottle Gallery had been carefully *curated*.

The mini bottles were grouped into intriguing themes ranging from a brothel themed Room of Sin with mini-bottles from the Dutch Red Light District, to a Horror Room featuring liquor bottles with trapped objects floating inside like mice and worms.

There was a Jungle Room, a Room of Famous Persons, and rooms themed around sports, fruits, birds, circus performers and the occult. There was even an entire room featuring the iconic porcelain series of the Delft Blue KLM houses, a series of tiny Dutch rowhouse-shaped liquor bottles given away to passengers by KLM Airlines for more than five decades.

Across all these rooms, the gallery typically has more than 12,000 bottles on display at any one time. The rest are stored in a bottle vault below the museum and available for display when needed.

Adding Meaning to Noise

The Mini Bottle Gallery only displays about 20% of Ringnes' full collection at any time, and carefully keeps the rest in storage. This thoughtful curation makes the experience of seeing them valuable.

If you consider the amount of media any of us is exposed to on an average day, the quest to find meaning amongst the noise is a familiar challenge. Navigating information overload requires a single important skill: curation.

Curation is the ultimate method of transforming noise into meaning.

Without curation, the meaning would be lost and the experience, meaningless.

An Accidental Trend Curator

It was only on my flight home from Oslo that I realized how important curation had become for my own work.

Just a few months earlier I had published the first edition of my *Non-Obvious Trend Report*, inspired by an idea to publish a blog post from the many ideas I had collected over the past year but never written about.

What I was already doing without realizing it was collecting intriguing ideas and saving them in perhaps the most disorganized way possible—by writing them down randomly, printing them out or ripping them out of magazines and keeping them in a folder on my desk.

In producing that first report, my ambition became to describe patterns in the stories I had collected that went beyond the typical obvious observations I was always reading online. My goal was to find and develop insights that others either hadn't yet noticed or that were not getting the attention they warranted.

To get a different output, sometimes you need a different input.

On that flight home from Norway, I realized that my accidental method for getting different input—collecting ideas for a year and waiting months before analyzing them—could actually be the very thing that would set my insights apart and make them truly non-obvious.

The *Non-Obvious Trend Report* (my annual list of 15 trends) was born from my desire to curate trends on a scale that others weren't.

Science's Dirty Little Secret

Now, if you happen to be an analytical person, this explanation will hardly seem rigorous enough to be believable. How can collecting ideas and waiting possibly be a recipe for developing genuine insights? What about proper research? What about trend panels and using a global army of spotters? What about the *science*?

Well, it turns out science isn't always done the way we think it is—and that may be a good thing.

In early 2013, a PhD candidate named Beckie Port gathered and published 75 examples of scientists using the hilariously viral hashtag #overlyhonestmethods to share some brutally honest truths about the realities of scientific research.

Among the compilation of tweets Port shared online were these entertaining sound bites:

- "Samples were prepared by our collaborators at MIT. We assumed no contamination because, well... they're MIT #overlyhonestmethods" (@paulcoxon)
- "Our representative device is representative of the ones which didn't immediately explode. #overlyhonestmethods" (@ajdecon)
- "Barbados was selected as a case study because the authors had a naive hope that it might justify some fieldwork there. #overlyhonestmethods" (@mlkubik)
- "We used jargon instead of plain English to prove that a decade of grad school and postdoc made us smart. #overly-honestmethods" (@eperlste)

When you think about the discipline that goes into scientific research and the many years of study that lead to a PhD, it is easy to see research as a task only performed by robot-like perfectionists. The truth of scientific research, just like the truth behind many equally complex areas of study, is that the people behind them are far more human than we tend to admit.

Trends, like science, are not always perfectly observed phenomena that fit neatly into a spreadsheet to be described. This doesn't mean they don't have immense value.

Great science always involves great observation. Scientists learn to observe the results of their experiments and then work to describe them with hypothesis and proof as best they can. Sometimes they do it and sometimes they don't.

There are many similarities between trends and science, but this is only half the story. Discovering trends takes a willingness to combine curiosity with observation and add insight to create valuable ideas that you can then test to ensure they are valid.

This is vastly different from the method we often mistakenly believe is behind most work with trends, "trend spotting." This phrase itself is a symbol of some of the many myths we tend to believe about those who predict or describe trends.

Let's explore the most common of these myths.

The 5 Myths of Trend Spotting

As a writer and speaker, I spend a lot of time seeking stories. When it comes to trends and predicting the future, the people who do this are often called "trend spotters."

Despite what you may have heard, there is no such thing as a trend spotter.

Unfortunately, this trend-spotter bias has created an unreasonable portrait of the type of person who can predict the future. Consider this lazy definition for what it takes to become a trend spotter:

> *To become a trend spotter, someone usually receives extensive education and training in the industry he or she is interested in working for. After receiving a thorough grounding in the mechanics and history of the industry, the trend spotter could start working in company departments which predicted trends, slowly working to the rank of an official trend spotter. (Wisegeek.com)*

The assumption that you need to be working in "company departments which predicted trends" is just plain idiotic.

Instead I believe that anyone can learn the right habits to train themselves on becoming better at curating trends and predicting the future for themselves.

The rest of this first part of the book is dedicated to teaching you to how to curate and uncover trends for yourself, but before we start, it is important to tackle each of the biggest myths surrounding trends so you know what to avoid reading (or trusting!) in case you happen to encounter it in the future.

MYTH #1: TRENDS ARE SPOTTED.

The idea of trend spotting suggests that there are trends simply sitting out there in plain sight ready to be observed and cataloged like avian species for bird watchers. The reality of trends is far different. Trend spotters typically find individual examples or stories. Calling the multitude of things they spot the same thing as trends is like calling eggs, flour and sugar sitting on a shelf the same thing as a cake. You can "spot" ingredients, but trends must be curated from these ingredients in order to have meaning.

MYTH #2: TRENDS ARE PREDICTED BY INDUSTRY GURUS/EXPERTS.

It is tempting to see industry expertise as a prerequisite to being good at curating trends, but there is also a predictable drawback: blind spots. Quite simply, the more you know about a particular topic, the more difficult it becomes to think outside your expertise and broaden your view. There is no single expertise required to curate trends, but those with a greater curiosity about the world beyond *any* industry will more easily avoid any danger of industry-based tunnel vision.

MYTH #3: TRENDS ARE BASED ON HARD DATA.

When it comes to any type of research, some people rely on numbers inserted into a spreadsheet as proof, and they conveniently forget that there are two methods to conducting research: the quantitative method *and* the qualitative method. Qualitative research involves using observation and experience to gather mainly verbal data instead of results from experiments. If you are uncovering the perfect pH balance for shampoo, you definitely want to use quantitative research. For curating trends, you need a mixture of both and the ability to remember that hard data can often be less important than really good observation.

MYTH #4: TRENDS ONLY REFLECT CURRENT POPULARITY.

The line between trends and fads can be tricky. Although some trends seem to spotlight a currently popular story, good ones need to describe something that happens over a span of time. Fads, in comparison, describe an idea that is popular in the short term. Great trends do reflect a moment in time, but they also need to describe something that is broader than a fleeting moment.

MYTH #5: TRENDS ARE HOPELESSLY BROAD PREDICTIONS.

Perhaps no other myth about trends is as fueled by reality as this one. The fact is, we encounter hopelessly broad trend predictions in the media all the time. The problem comes in treating those as indications that trends *should* be broad and all encompassing. Good trends tend to be more of the opposite. They define something that is concrete and distinct. Something that doesn't apply to everyone, but rather offers a point of view that you can easily grasp and describe in a unique way.

Now that I have shared five of the most common myths about trend predictions, we need to spend a brief moment talking about a final sad but true fact about many trend predictions you may read.

In our one-button world of publishing opinions online, many of trend predictions you might read are little more than self-indulgent guesswork or lazy thinking. At this point, you could be forgiven for wondering why I am so negative on so many other trend predictions out there. Why exactly do I dismiss them as useless?

In order to illustrate, let me tell you a little story.

Why (Most) Trend Predictions Are Useless

A few weeks ago I picked up the final edition of *Entrepreneur* magazine which promised to illuminate trends to watch in the coming year. Earlier that same week, a special double issue of *BusinessWeek* magazine arrived in the mail making a similar promise.

It was December and the trend season was in full swing.

Just like New Year's resolutions to lose weight, trend forecasting is what everyone starts talking about at the end of the year. Unfortunately, the side effect of this annual media ritual is an abundance of lazy predictions and vague declarations.

For entertainment over the years, I have started to collect them as standing memorials to the volume of pitiful predictions each of us have become used to confronting at the end of every year.

To illustrate my point, here are a few of the worst offending most obvious "trends" shared near the end of 2015. For the sake of kindness, I removed reference to which particular publication or writer a trend came from before listing them below:

- "It's all about the visuals."
- "Streaming entertainment."
- "The Year Of Drones has arrived. Really."
- "Content Marketing will continue to be the place to be."
- "Fantasy Sports"
- "Virtual Reality"
- "Change will be led by smart home technology."

Virtual Reality? Really?

Not to ruin the suspense, but I don't believe any of these are actually trends. Some are just random buzzwords or the names of platforms. Others are hopelessly broad, useless and, yes, obvious.

None is a unique idea describing the accelerating present.

Meanwhile, all of us as media consumers watch all of it unfold with varying levels of skepticism. Trend predictions have a believability problem, but I think it can be solved. In order to do that, a perfect place to start is by understanding the four reasons why most trend predictions fail so spectacularly.

REASON 1: NO OBJECTIVITY

If you sell smartphones, declaring 2016 the "Year of Smartphones" is clearly self-serving. Of course, most bias isn't this easy to spot and objectivity is notoriously difficult for any of us. Our biases are based on our expertise and the world we know. This is particularly true in business where we sometimes *need* to believe in industry or brand in order to succeed. The problem is, losing objectivity usually leads to wishful thinking. Just because we want something to be a trend doesn't make it one.

> *EXAMPLE: Near the end of last year, I received what seemed like dozens of emails about white papers and blog posts each forecasting that wearable technology or the "Internet of things" would be the hottest trend of the coming year. Unsurprisingly, the vast majority of them had some type of product or strategy to cash in on this hot trend—and were mostly dismissed by the media they were aiming to reach.*

REASON 2: NO CREATIVITY

Trends need to do more than repeat common knowledge. For example, saying that "more people will buy tablets this year" is obvious—and useless because it lacks creativity. The biggest reason that most trend predictions share these types of hopelessly obvious ideas is because it is easier to do so. Lazy thinking is always easier than creative and informed thinking. Great trends are never obvious declarations of fact that most people already know. They share new ideas in insightful ways while also describing the accelerating present.

> *EXAMPLE: The phrase "digital natives" was first coined nearly 15 years ago to describe a generation who would grow up never having known a world before the Internet. Despite its long history and relative ubiquity, several trend articles I reviewed last year shared the "emergence" of this group as if it were a brand new insight. That's just plain lazy.*

REASON 3: NO PROOF

Sharing a trend without specific examples is like declaring yourself a musician by simply buying a microphone and learning to sing one song. Unfortunately, many trend predictions coast on the power of a single story or example. Great examples and stories are powerful parts of illustrating why a trend matters. They are necessary elements of proving a trend. Only finding one (or none) and declaring something a trend without them is usually a sign that a so-called trend is based on little more than guesswork.

> *EXAMPLE: When publishing website Medium.com first became publicly available and increasing numbers of journalists and writers began using it to freely share extremely high-quality stories and articles, several early trend reports last year predicted the rise of a sort of anti-Twitter trend where people would begin flocking to longer-form content. Unfortunately, one popular website isn't enough to describe a trend, and most of these forecasts were predictable failures.*

REASON 4: NO APPLICATION

Perhaps the most common place where many trend predictions fall short is in the discussion of how to apply them. It is not enough to think about trends in the context of describing them. Aside from that being one of the myths behind finding trends, it also provides little value because it isn't clear what someone might do differently as a result of understanding a particular trend. The best trend predictions go further than just describing something that is happening. They also share insights on what it means and what you can do to use the trend in your own situation. In other words, their trends are actionable.

> EXAMPLE: In a beautiful piece of ironic content, a collaboration of top PR agencies published a sponsored editorial in Advertising Age magazine last year aimed at sharing predictions for the upcoming year to underscore the value of PR for big clients. Unfortunately, most of the top ten predictions featured plentiful buzzword babble, like "Big data is important, but big insights are critical" and was dramatically short on any real insights on how to apply the thinking or what to do about it. Not the PR industry's best work.

How to Think Different about Trends

Now that you've reached the end of this chapter, you are probably wondering what actually makes a great trend when there are so many myths and reasons for failure.

Here is my definition for what actually makes a "non-obvious" trend:

A non-obvious trend is an idea that describes the accelerating present in a new, unique way.

The next two chapters will dig further into the idea of non-obvious thinking by sharing a step-by-step approach to help you think differently about trends to improve your ideas, as well as your outlook on your business and your career as well.

So, let's get started.

THE CURATOR'S MINDSET:
Learning the 5 Essential Habits
of Trend Curators

In 2006, renowned Stanford psychology professor Carol Dweck wrote a book about an idea so simple it hardly seemed worth mentioning—much less devoting an entire book to exploring.

Across decades of research into motivation, achievement and success, Dweck had come upon a beautifully elegant idea to describe why some people succeeded while others failed: it all came down to *mindsets*.

After conducting experiments with grade school students, interviewing professional athletes and studying business leaders, Dweck proposed that most people had one of two types of mindsets: a fixed mindset or a growth mindset.

People with *fixed mindsets*, argued Dweck, believe that their skills and abilities are set. They see themselves as either being either good at something or not good at something, and therefore tend to focus their efforts on tasks and in careers where they feel they have a natural ability.

People with *growth mindsets* believe that success and achievement are the result of hard work and determination. They see their own (and others') true potential as something to be defined through effort. As a result, they thrive on challenges and often have a passion for learning.

It likely won't surprise you to learn that I believe in the power of the growth mindset and aspire to always maintain one for myself. When it comes to learning to predict the future, though, it is important to adopt that same mindset for yourself.

The beautiful thing about mindsets is that we all have the ability to change ours—we just need to make the choice to do it.

Seeing trends, like playing an instrument or being more observant, are skills within your grasp to learn and practice. Does this mean you can transform yourself into a professional flamenco guitarist or a full-time trend forecaster with enough practice? Not necessarily. Aptitude and natural talent do play an important part in succeeding at anything on a professional level.

Still, my work with thousands of executives and students at all levels of their careers has proved to me that the skills required for trend curation can be learned and practiced. When you learn them, they can inform your own view of the world and power your own future success.

> *As soon as children become able to evaluate themselves, some of them become afraid of challenges. They become afraid of not being smart. I have studied thousands of people ... and it's breathtaking how many reject an opportunity to learn.*
>
> —Carol Dweck (from *Mindset*)

Beyond adopting the growth mindset and having a willingness to learn, there are five core habits that will help you develop your trend-curation abilities. Let's explore them by starting with a story of the most famous art collector most people have never heard of—until he passed away.

The Unlikely Curator

By 2012, at the ripe old age of 89 years, a retired postal worker had quietly amassed one of the greatest collections of modern art in the world.

Herbert Vogel and his wife, Dorothy, were already legends in the world of art when Herbert passed away. News stories soon after his death told the story of five large moving vans showing up at the Vogel's rent-controlled, one-bedroom New York apartment to pick up more than 5000 pieces of art. This Vogel Collection, built over decades, would have a permanent home as part of the archives and collection at the National Gallery of Art.

The Vogels always said the only things they did were buy and collect art they loved.

This passion often led them to find new young artists to support before the rest of the world discovered them. The Vogels ultimately became more than collectors. They were tastemakers and their "fabled collection," as one critic later described it, which included art from hundreds of artists including pop artist Roy Lichtenstein and post-minimalist Richard Tuttle, was the envy of museums around the world.

The same qualities that drive art patrons like the Vogels to follow their instincts and collect beautiful things are the ones that make great curators of any kind.

The Rise Of "Curationism"

Museum curators organize collections into themes that tell stories. Whether they're quirky like those told in the Mini Bottle Gallery, or an expansive exhibit at the Metropolitan Museum of Art, the goal of curation is always to take individual items and examples and weave them together into a narrative.

Curators add meaning to isolated beautiful things.

I am inspired by curators—and I am clearly not alone. The business world has turned toward the longtime practice of curation with such growing frequency that even the world of artists and art critics has begun to notice.

In 2014, art critic and writer David Balzer published a book with the brilliant title *Curationism* (a play on creationism) to explore how "curating took over the art world and everything else." His book explores the evolution of the curator as the "imparter of value."

Along the way he shares the valuable caution that this rise in curationism can sometimes inspire a "constant cycle of grasping and display" where we never take the time to understand what all the pieces mean. In other words, curation is only valuable if you follow the act of collecting information with enough moments of "quiet contemplation" to truly understand what you are seeing and collecting.

This combination of collection and contemplation is central to being able to effectively curate ideas and learn to predict the future. To do it, there are five specific habits that I believe can help you utilize this type of thinking in a world that seldom seems to offer you the time for such a luxury.

Let's explore these five habits further.

The 5 Habits Of Trend Curators

Curators come from all types of backgrounds.

Some focus on art and design while others may look at history or anthropology. Some have professional training and degrees while others are driven by passion like Herbert and Dorothy Vogel. No matter their background, every one of them exhibits the same types of habits that help them to become masters at adding meaning to collected items.

Curation doesn't require you to be an expert or a researcher or an academic. Learning these five habits will help you put the power of curation to work to help you discover better ideas and use them to develop your own observations about the rapidly accelerating present.

THE 5 HABITS OF TREND CURATORS

1. **BEING CURIOUS –** always wanting to know why, seeking to learn more about the world and improving your knowledge by investigating and asking questions.

2. **BEING OBSERVANT –** learning to see the small details in stories and activities that others may ignore or fail to recognize as significant.

3. **BEING FICKLE** – moving from one idea to the next without becoming fixated, developing deep biases or overanalyzing each idea in the moment.

4. **BEING THOUGHTFUL** – taking enough time to develop a meaningful point of view and patiently considering alternative viewpoints before finalizing an idea.

5. **BEING ELEGANT** – seeking beautiful ways to describe ideas that bring together disparate concepts in a simple and understandable way.

For the past five years I have been sharing and teaching these habits through workshops and classes to business professionals, entrepreneurs and university students. I have learned one simple thing from that experience: we all have the aptitude to learn these skills. The challenge always comes from teaching yourself to apply them.

To do it, let's take a deeper look at each skill and some actionable ways to learn how to use them.

How to Be Curious

Bjarni Herjulfsson could have been one of the most famous explorers of his time.

Instead, his life has become a cautionary tale about the perils of lacking curiosity. In the year 986, he set off on a voyage from Norway with a crew to find Greenland. Blown off course by a storm, his ship became the first European vessel in recorded history to see North America.

Despite his crew pleading to stop and explore, Herjulfsson refused and guided his ship back on course to eventually find Greenland. Years later, he told this tale to a friend of his named Leif Eriksson who became inspired, purchased Herjulfsson has been mostly forgotten and his ship and took the journey for himself.

As many of us learned in grade school, Erikson is now widely remembered as the first European to land in North America—nearly 500 years before Christopher Columbus. Herjulfsson has been mostly forgotten and his story illustrates one of the most compelling facts about curiosity (or a lack of it): curiosity is a prerequisite to discovery.

Being more curious means asking questions about why things work the way they do and embracing unfamiliar situations or topics with a sense of wonder.

We as people are naturally curious. The challenge is to continually find ways to allow yourself to explore your curiosity without it feeling like an ongoing distraction.

When noted chef and food pioneer Ferran Adrià was once asked what he likes to have for breakfast, his reply was simple: "I like to eat a different fruit every day of the month."

Imagine if you were able to do that with ideas.

Part of being curious is wanting to consume different things all the time to earn greater knowledge of the world, even if that knowledge doesn't seem immediately useful. Here are some ways to do it:

REAL LIFE ADVICE (3 WAYS TO BE MORE CURIOUS TODAY)

- ✓ **Consume "Brainful Media"** – Sadly we are surrounded with what I like to call "brainless media," including reality shows featuring unlikeable people doing unlikeable things (sometimes on islands, sometimes in our backyards). While often entertaining, brainless media also encourages vegetation instead of curiosity. Curiosity is far better developed by consuming "brainful media," such as a short documentary film or inspirational 17-minute talk from TED.com.

- ✓ **Empathize with Magazines** – Curiosity can also help you see the world through someone else's eyes, even if it's uncomfortable. I often use niche magazines to learn about unfamiliar things. Simply walking into the magazine section of a bookstore or visiting www.magazines.com offers plenty of options. For example, *Modern Farmer*, *Model Railroader* and *House Beautiful* are three vastly different magazines. Flipping through the stories, advertisements and imagery in each will do more to take you outside of your own world than almost any other quick and easy activity.

- ✓ **Ask Bigger Questions** – Several months ago, I was invited to deliver a talk at an event for the paint industry. It is an industry I know very little about and so it was tempting to show up, deliver a canned talk and then leave. Instead, I stayed and walked around the exhibit hall asking questions. In less than 30 minutes I learned about how paint is mixed and what additives are typically used. I heard about the industry debate between all-plastic cans versus steel and the rise of computerized color matching systems. As a result my talk was farm more relevant because I chose to stay and ask more questions instead of taking the easy path.

WHAT TO READ

- ✓ **Historical Fiction** – Every great piece of historical fiction was inspired by a writer who found a story in history that was worth retelling and sharing with the world. This curiosity makes books like Erik Larsen's *The Devil In The White City* (about murder at the 1893 Chicago World's Fair) or Simon Winchester's *The Professor And the Madman* (about the creation of the *Oxford English Dictionary*) wonderful gateways to start thinking about the world in unexpected ways.

- ✓ **Curated Compilations** – There are many books that bring together real life stories or essays to help you think about new and interesting topics. A collection of shorter topics and stories is sometimes far easier to use for engaging your curiosity than a longer book. For example, the *This Will Make You Smarter* series edited by John Brockman or any book by *You Are Not So Smart* founder and psychology buff David McRaney are perfect, bite-sized ways to inspire your curiosity without requiring a huge time investment.

How to Be Observant

A few years ago I was invited to a formal dinner at an event in New York. The venue was a beautiful restaurant and after our meal the waiter came around to take our dessert orders from one of two set menu options. Less than 10 minutes later, a team of six people *not* including our waiter came and delivered all the desserts to our large table of 30 people, getting each order perfectly right without saying a word to anyone.

As they delivered the desserts, I started to wonder how that one waiter who took our orders had managed to relay all those choices perfectly to a team of six in such as short time?

By observing, I quickly figured out the simple trick our head waiter had used. If you had picked dessert option one, he had placed a dessert spoon *above* your plate. And if you picked option two, he had placed the spoon to the *right* of your plate.

So when that team of food runners came to the table, all they needed was the "code" to decipher the spoon positioning and they would be able to deliver the desserts perfectly. That little story of food delivery is a perfect example of why observation matters.

Being more observant means training yourself to see the details that most others often miss.

Perhaps you already knew that little spoon trick, but imagine you didn't. Simply observing it could teach you something fascinating about the little processes that we rarely pay attention to that keep the world moving along. Now imagine that moment multiplied by a hundred or a thousand.

Learning to be more observant isn't about seeing the big things. Instead, it is about training yourself to pay more attention to the little things.

By simply choosing to observe, what can you see about a situation that no one else notices?

What can that teach you about people, processes and companies that you didn't know before?

This is the power of making observation a habit, so let's explore three ways to help you do it.

REAL LIFE ADVICE
(3 WAYS TO BE MORE OBSERVANT TODAY)

✓ **Explain the World to Children** – If you are lucky enough to have children in your life, one of the best ways to train yourself to use observation more frequently is to get better about explaining the world around you to children. When my kids asked me recently why construction vehicles and traffic signs are orange but cars aren't, it forced me to think about something I would otherwise have easily ignored, even if I didn't have the perfect answer to the question.*

✓ **Watch Processes in Action** – Every situation is filled with processes, from how school buses drop off children at their stops to how coffee shops take and make orders every morning. When you look at these interactions, you'll notice that very little happens by accident. Pay attention and ask yourself what does a typical interaction look like? How does it differ when it involves a "regular" versus a "newbie"? Seeing these patterns in regular everyday life can help you train yourself to use this observational skill in other situations as well.

✓ **Don't Be Observationally Lazy** – It is easy to go through the mundane moments of life glued to your smartphone. Aside from being really good at capturing our attention (see Chapter 15 on *Engineered Addiction*), they also keep us from seeing the world around us. Rather than switching to auto-pilot to navigate daily tasks like commuting or buying groceries, train yourself to put your phone down and choose to be observant instead.

WHAT TO READ

✓ *What Every Body Is Saying* by **Joe Navarro** – If you need to learn the art of interpreting body language or detecting

---

* *In case you were wondering, they are orange because testing shows that is the color most visible from the greatest distance.*

lies, a former FBI agent like Joe Navarro is probably the ideal teacher. In this best-selling book from 2008, Navarro shares some of his best lessons on how to spot "tells" in body language and use them to interpret human behavior. His work on situational awareness and teaching people *how* to be more observant to assess people and situations for danger and comfort is a book that should be on your reading list no matter what you do. It also happens to be a perfect supporting book to teach you how to be more observant in general.

How to Be Fickle

Being fickle may seem like a bad thing, but that isn't always true.

When we hear the word, we tend to think of all the negative situations where we abandon people or ideas too quickly, but there is an upside to learning how to be purposefully fickle.

Being fickle means capturing ideas without needing to fully understand or analyze them in that same moment.

On the surface, this may seem counterintuitive. After all, when you find a great idea why wouldn't you take the time to analyze it and develop a point of view? There are certainly many situations when you will want to do that, and chances are you do it already.

But you probably *never* do the opposite. A part of becoming an idea curator is saving ideas for later digestion. Of course you can always think about them when you find them, but you don't always *need* to.

For example, here are three interesting stories which I recently saw and saved:

- Coca-Cola decided to disconnect voicemail for all employees at its corporate headquarters in Atlanta.
- Richard Branson allows Virgin staff to take as much holiday as they want.
- A Trader Joe's employee gave a gift of flowers to a flustered mom of adopted kids who was leaving the store after an

embarrassing toddler meltdown because the employee herself had been adopted and she just wanted to say thanks.

When I saved each of the stories above, I didn't make the broader connection to tie them together. Only when I reviewed them at the end of the year while researching trends did I realize that each of these stories says something unique about the state of employee relationships with their employers and empowerment.

There was a theme, but it was only by setting those stories aside and choosing to analyze them later that I had enough perspective to see that connection. Being fickle isn't about avoiding thought—it is about freeing yourself from the pressure you might feel around collecting ideas by making it easier to save an idea without necessarily analyzing it deeply in the moment.

To help you learn to do the same thing, here are some tips.

REAL LIFE ADVICE (3 WAYS TO BE MORE FICKLE TODAY)

✓ **Save Ideas Offline** – Thanks to wonderful productivity apps like Evernote and plenty of browser plugins, there are many ways to save information online, but they can sometimes be lost in collections you never return to and the connections between them are hard to visualize. Instead, I routinely print articles, rip stories out of magazines and put them into a *single* trend folder which sits on my desk. Saving ideas offline allows me to spread them out later to analyze more easily, but it also helps me avoid overanalyzing them in that moment when I find them.

✓ **Use a Timer** – If given the chance, most of us will naturally take the time to analyze something that we see or find in a moment. Being fickle is partially about intentionally delaying that process and using a timer can help. The other benefit of literally using a timer when you are consuming some type of new media is that it forces you to evaluate things more quickly and then leave them behind as you move to something else.

✓ **Take Notes with Sharpies** – Many of the articles and stories I find throughout the year are marked with just a few words about the theme of the article and story. I use the Sharpie because the thicker lettering stands out and encourages me subtly to write less because it takes up much more space. This same trick can help you to make only the most useful observations in the moment and save any other ones for later.

WHAT TO READ

✓ *The Laws Of Simplicity* **by John Maeda** – Maeda is a master of design and technology and his advice has guided many companies and entrepreneurs toward building more amazing products. In this exactly 100-page book, he shares some essential advice for learning to see the world like a designer and reduce the noise to see and think more clearly. "More appears like less by simply moving it far, far away," he writes when talking about the power of software as a service or the value of Google. I believe the same principle applies to information and ideas; sometimes you just need distance and time in order to fully appreciate them.

How to Be Thoughtful

In 2014 after 10 years of writing my personal blog, I decided to stop allowing comments. This seemed counter to the fundamental principle of blogging, which is to create a dialogue (as many of my readers emailed to tell me). Was it because I thought I was too important to answer comments, or was there something else at work?

The reason I stopped was simple. I had noticed a steady decline in the quality of comments over the 10 years that I had been blogging. What was once a robust discussion that involved thoughtfully worded responses had devolved into a combination of thumbs-up style comments and spam.

Thanks to anonymous commenting and the ease of sharing knee-jerk responses, comments had become *thoughtless* instead of *thoughtful*—and people were starting to notice. So I turned off the comments.

Unfortunately, the Internet is filled with this type of "conversation."

Being thoughtful means taking the time to reflect on a point of view and share it in a considered way.

Despite this general shift in online commenting, there is one platform that hopes to single-handedly change this landscape. In 2012 LinkedIn launched a pilot program called *LinkedIn Influencers* to feature insights from top business minds like Tom Peters and Bill Gates, who answered compelling questions like what advice they might offer to their 20-year-old selves.

These posts inspired amazingly detailed and well-thought-out comments from LinkedIn users. Every comment was linked to a professional profile, and the stature of the contributors led to better comments. After all, who would post an ill-informed stupid comment with their name attached to it if they thought Bill Gates might actually read it?

Online commenting might seem like a relatively frivolous way to illustrate the value of being thoughtful, but it is just a symbol of how important taking the time to consider an argument has become.

To help you be more thoughtful as you think about curating trends and understanding the media that you save and consume every day, here are some tips:

REAL LIFE ADVICE
(3 WAYS TO BE MORE THOUGHTFUL TODAY)

✓ **Wait a Moment** – The beauty and challenge of the Internet is that it occurs in real time. We have an idea, and we can share it immediately. It's easy to think that if you can't be the first person to comment on something, that your thoughts are too late. That is rarely true. "Real time" should not mean sharing a comment from the top of your head within seconds. Instead, you should aim to redefine it so your comment is still relevant beyond the particular moment you write it with social media. This means you might choose to take 15 minutes (or longer!) to think about *how* you want to share it.

✓ **Write and then Rewrite** – Anyone who has ever had to write for a long time will tell you that the ultimate way to get better is just to force yourself to do it even if whatever comes out isn't very usable. When it comes to being thoughtful with writing, even the most talented writers take the time to rewrite instead of simply sharing the first thing that they write down.

✓ **Embrace the Pauses** – One of the things speakers try to learn as soon as they spend any time standing in front of an audience is how to become comfortable with silence. It's not an easy thing to do. Yet when you can use pauses effectively, you can emphasize the things you really want people to hear or remember. This same principle works whether you are on stage or just engaged in a conversation. The trick is to use those pauses as times to find the right words so you *can* be more thoughtful when you eventually do share your point of view.

WHAT TO READ

✓ *Brain Pickings* **by Maria Popova** - Popova describes herself as an "interestingness hunter-gatherer" and she writes Brain Pickings, one of the most popular independently run blogs in the world. On the site she publishes articles combining lessons from literature, art and history on wide ranging topics like creative leadership and the gift of friendship. Every year she pores thousands of hours into publishing thoughtful pieces and her readers reward her by donating to support the continued ad-free operation of the site. The way she presents her thoughts is a perfect aspirational example of how to publish something thoughtful week after week.

How to Be Elegant

Jeff Karp is a scientist inspired by elegance ... and jellyfish.

As an associate professor at Harvard Medical School, Karp's research focuses on using bio-inspiration—inspiration from nature—to develop new solutions for all types of medical challenges. His self-named Karp Lab has developed innovations such as a device inspired by jellyfish tentacles to capture circulating tumor cells in cancer patients, and better surgical staples inspired by porcupine quills.

Nature is filled with elegant solutions, from the way that forest fires spread the seeds of certain plants to the way termites build porous structures with natural heating and cooling built in.

Ian Glynn, author of the book *Elegance In Science*, argues that elegant proofs or theories have most or all of the following features: they are simple, ingenious, concise and persuasive; they often have an unexpected quality, and they are very satisfying.

I believe it is this idea of simplicity that is fundamental to developing elegant ideas. As Einstein famously said, "make things as simple as possible, but not simpler."

Being elegant means developing your ability to describe a concept in a beautiful and simple way for easy understanding.

A good example of things described beautifully is in what talented poets do. If you are in the business world, chances are you don't spend much time with poetry. That is a missed opportunity. Great poetry has simplicity, emotion, and beauty *because* words are taken away. Poets are masters of elegance, obsess over language, and understand that less can mean more.

You don't need to become a poet overnight, but some of these principles can help you get better at creating more elegant descriptions of your own ideas.

For example, think back to the last time you encountered something that was poetically written. It may have been something you once read in school, or perhaps a Dr. Seuss book that you read to a child at bedtime.

Dr. Seuss in particular had a beautiful talent for sharing big ideas with a simplicity and elegance:

- "Today you are you, that is truer than true. There is no one alive who is youer than you."
- "A person's a person, no matter how small."
- "Everything stinks till it's finished."

We love to read or see elegant stories and we delight in their ability to help us get the big picture with ease, but they do not seem quite so simple to develop or write. If you have ever sat down with paper or in front of a computer screen and tried to tell a simple story you know that it is not an easy challenge.

But we all have the power to simplify our ideas and share them in more elegant ways. We just need to learn how. Here are a few ideas to help.

REAL LIFE ADVICE
(3 WAYS TO THINK MORE ELEGANTLY TODAY)

✓ **Start with the Obvious** – One of my favorite trends from my *2012 Non-Obvious Trend Report* was something I called "ChangeSourcing" to describe the idea that more and more people were turning to crowdfunding campaigns to inspire more movements for social change. At the time, crowdfunding was one of the hottest topics in the media. The idea of ChangeSourcing took something that people already knew in an unexpected new direction and used a simple and elegant title to do it. As a result, it was one of the most talked-about trends from the report that year.

✓ **Keep It Short** – One thing you will notice if you look back on any of my previous trend reports is that most trends are no longer than two words. Elegance often goes hand in hand with simplicity and this usually means using as few words as possible. When it comes to defining and curating trends, it is perfectly fine to start by describing the trend with as many words as you need. When you get to the point of trying to add more elegance, though, a necessary component will usually be reducing the words you use to name *and* describe it.

✓ **Use Poetic Principles** – There are some basic principles that poets use when writing that can also be helpful for anyone who is curating trends. One of them is to try and use metaphors and imagery instead of obvious ways of sharing something. Another is to rhyme words or use alliteration to add symmetry to an idea. If you flip to the Appendix of this book, you will see many places where I used these types of principles in the past to develop trends like "Branded Benevolence" or "Unperfection." A trend from my first report in 2011, Likeonomics, even inspired me to write a book with the same title a year later.

WHAT TO READ

✓ *Einstein's Dreams* **by Alan Lightman** – Lightman was the first professor at MIT to receive a joint appointment in the sciences and the humanities and is a trained physicist and a poet. His book *Einstein's Dreams* has been one of my favorites for years because of how it imagines what Einstein's dreams must have been like and explores them in a beautiful way through short chapters with interesting assumptions about time and space. This is not a book of poetry, but it will introduce you to the power of poetic writing while also offering the most elegant description of how time might actually work that you'll ever read.

Why *These* 5 Habits?

Looking back, the fact that I only chose 5 habits to help you learn the art of curating ideas may seem a bit random. What makes these five habits stand out? The fact is, the process of how I came to these five in particular was an interesting exercise of curation in itself.

Over the past year, I read interviews with professional art curators and how they learned their craft. I bought more than a dozen books written by trend forecasters, futurists and innovators. I carefully studied my own behavior, and (as I mentioned earlier in the chapter) I tested the effectiveness of these habits by teaching them to my students in classes and to business professionals in private workshops.

Ultimately, I selected the five habits presented in this chapter because they were the most helpful, descriptive, easy to learn and effective once you learn to put them into action.

So as a final recap before we get started with a step-by-step approach to curating trends, let's do a quick review of the five habits:

5 HABITS OF TREND CURATORS

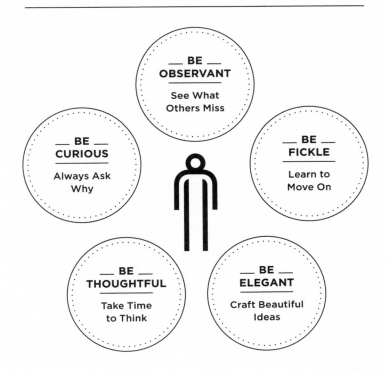

1. **Being *curious*** means asking questions about why things work the way they do, and embracing unfamiliar situations or topics with a sense of wonder.

2. **Being *observant*** means training yourself to see the details that most others often miss.

3. **Being *fickle*** means capturing ideas without feeling the need to fully understand or analyze them in that moment.

4. **Being *thoughtful*** means taking the time to reflect on a point of view and share it in a considered way.

5. **Being *elegant*** means developing your ability to describe a concept in a beautiful and simple way for easy understanding.

THE HAYSTACK METHOD:
How to Curate Trends for Fun and Profit

In 1982, a single book called *Megatrends* changed the way governments, businesses and people thought about the future.

In the book, author John Naisbitt was one of the first to predict our evolution from an industrial society to an information society, and he did so more than a decade before the Internet. He also predicted the shift from hierarchies to networks and the rise of the global economy.

Despite the book's unapologetic American-style optimism, most of the 10 major shifts described in the book were so far ahead of their time that when it was first released one reviewer glowingly described it as "the next best thing to a crystal ball." With over 14 million copies sold worldwide, it is still the single best-selling book about the future published in the last 40 years.

In the decades since the book came out, Naisbitt has been asked the same question in dozens of interviews with the media: how did he develop his ability to predict the future and could others learn to do it?

For his part, Naisbitt believed deeply in the power of observation to understand the present before trying to predict the future (as the opening quote to this chapter illustrates). In interviews, friends and family often described Naisbitt as having a "boundless curiosity about people, cultures and organizations."

A profile piece in *USA Today* back in 2006 even noted his penchant for scanning "hundreds of newspapers and magazines, from *Scientific American* to *Tricycle*, a Buddhism magazine" as a symbol of his incessant desire to learn.

John Naisbitt was and still is (at the age of 87!) a collector of ideas. His story has inspired me for years to think about the world with a similarly broad lens and to develop the method I use for my own trend work: the Haystack Method.

Inside the Haystack Method

It is tempting to describe the art of finding trends with the cliché of finding a "needle in a haystack." This common visual reference brings to mind the myth of trend spotting that I discounted earlier in this section. Uncovering trends hardly ever involves spotting them sitting neatly inside a so-called stack of hay waiting to be discovered.

The Haystack Method describes a process where you first focus on gathering stories and ideas (the hay) and *then* using them to define a trend (the needle) that gives meaning to them all collectively.

In the method, the work comes from assembling the information and curating it into groupings that make sense. The needle is the insight you apply to this collection of information in order to describe what it means—and to curate information and stories into a definable trend.

Trend curators don't seek needles, they gather the hay and then create the needle to put into the middle of it.

While that describes the method with metaphors, to truly learn how to do it for yourself, we must go much deeper. To do that for the Haystack Method, let's break it down into its five key components.

THE HAYSTACK METHOD

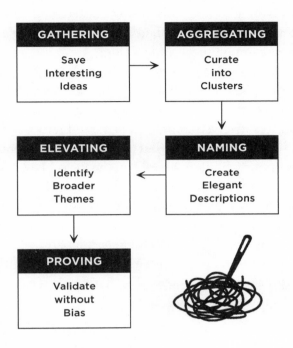

Why I Started Curating Ideas

The Haystick Method was born from frustration.

In 2004, I was part of a team that was starting one of the first social media–focused practices within a large marketing agency. The idea was that we would help big companies figure out how to use social media.

Back then "social media" mainly referred to blogging since it was before Facebook and Twitter. The real aim of our team was to help brands work with influential bloggers. There was only one problem with this well-intentioned plan—none of us knew very much about blogging.

So, we all did the only thing that seemed logical to do: each of us started blogging for ourselves.

In June of that year I started my "Influential Marketing Blog" with an aim to write about marketing, public relations and advertising strategy.

My first post was on the dull topic of optimal screen size for web design-ers. Within a few days I ran into my first major problem: I had no plan for what to write about next.

How was I going to keep this hastily created blog current with new ideas and stories when I already had a full time day job that didn't offi-cially involve spending time writing a blog?

I realized I had to change how I collected ideas.

At first it was just ideas for blog posts, scratched into a notebook or emailed to myself. Then, I started capturing concepts from the many brainstorms I was involved in on a daily basis. Pretty soon I was saving quotes from books, ripping pages out of magazines and generating plenty of blog posts (and client ideas!) based on the ideas I had collected.

These first four years of blogging led to my first book deal with McGraw-Hill. Several years later, the desire to write a blog post about trends based on ideas I had collected across the year led me to publish the first edition of my *Non-Obvious Trend Report* in 2011.

Collecting ideas led me to create a reputation and audience for myself through blogging, and this process of gathering ideas also happens to be the first step in the Haystack Method.

Step 1—Gathering

Gathering is the simple act of collecting stories and ideas from any interaction you have with people or with content in any form across multiple channels.

Do you read the same sources of media religiously every day? Or do you skim Twitter occasionally and sometimes follow the links to continue read-ing? Regardless of your media consumption, chances are you encounter plenty of interesting stories or ideas. The real question is, do you save them?

The key to gathering ideas is making a *habit* of saving interesting things in a way that allows you to find and explore them later.

My method involves always carrying a small Moleskine notebook in my bag and keeping a folder on my desk to save media clippings and printouts. By the time you read these words, that folder on my desk has changed color and already says "2017 Trends" on the outside of it.

In my process, I start the clock every January and complete it each December for my annual *Non-Obvious Trend Report*. Thanks to this deliverable, I have a clear starting and ending point for each new round of ideas that I collect.

You don't need to follow as rigid of a calendar timetable, but it is valuable to set yourself a specific time when you can go back and reflect on what you have gathered to uncover the bigger insights (a point we will explore in subsequent steps).

IDEA SOURCES—Where to Get Ideas

1. Personal conversations at events or meetings (ask lots of questions)

2. Listening to live speakers or TED Talks (write down memorable quotes)

3. Entertainment (TV shows and movies that actually make you think)

4. Books (Nonfiction and fiction)

5. Museums (the more obscure the better!)

6. Magazines and newspapers (as unexpected or outside your realm of knowledge as possible)

7. Travel! (even if it doesn't seem exotic or far away)

As you first read this list of sources, they might seem, well, obvious. It is rarely the *sources* of information themselves that will lead you toward a perfectly packaged idea or trend. Rather, mastering the art of gathering valuable ideas means training yourself to uncover interesting ideas across multiple sources and become diligent about collecting them.

TIPS & TRICKS: HOW TO GATHER IDEAS

- **Start a Folder** – A folder on my desk stores handwritten ideas, articles ripped out of magazines and newspapers, printouts of articles from the Internet, brochures from conferences, and just about any other paper-based ideas I find interesting. This folder lets me store things in a central and highly visible way. You might choose to create this folder digitally, or use both. Either way, the important thing is to have a centralized place where you can save ideas for later digestion.

- **Always Summarize** – When you are collecting ideas on an annual basis, it is easy to forget why it seemed significant in the first place. To help jog your own memory, get into the habit of highlighting a few sentences, or writing down a few notes about your thoughts on the idea. Later, when you are going through your gathered ideas, these notes will be useful in recalling what originally sparked your interest.

- **Seek Concepts, Not Conclusions** – As we learned in Chapter 2, a key habit of good curating is the ability to be fickle. In practice, this means not getting too hung up on the need to quantify or understand every idea you save in the moment. Many times, the best thing you can do is to gather something, save it, and then move on to the rest of your daily life. Perspective comes from taking time and having patience.

Step 2—Aggregating

Aggregating involves taking individual ideas and disconnected thoughts and grouping them together based on bigger ideas.

Once you have begun diligently gathering ideas, the next step is to choose a time to go and combine the early results of your observation and curiosity with thoughtful insights about what it means and how it fits together.

When you move from gathering to aggregating, you are taking the first step toward adding meaning to stories and ideas. One method to help you start is to use exploratory questions. Some of my favorites to try are listed in this "Aggregating Questions" box:

1. What broad group or demographic does this story describe?

2. What is the underlying human need or behavior that this idea is an example of?

3. What makes this story interesting as an example?

4. How is this same phenomenon affecting multiple unrelated industries?

5. What qualities or elements make me interested in this story?

At this stage it is important to remember that industries or categories don't matter for grouping. When sorting, don't fall into the obvious trap of putting all the financial examples together or putting every story related to Facebook together.

Aggregating involves sorting ideas based on insights and human motivations, not industries or demographics.

For example, when I was preparing my *2012 Non-Obvious Trend Report*, I collected marketing stories of new campaign strategies from three different companies, Domino's Pizza, Ally Bank (an online consumer bank) and Aviva (world's sixth largest insurance provider). The industries across these examples ranged from banking to food services to insurance.

The shared lesson behind each of their efforts though was how companies were finding new ways to avoid being faceless and find their humanity, so I aggregated them together in a group and wrote on an index card "companies being more human."

In this second step, it is not important to come up with a fancy name or even to do extensive research around any stories. Instead, you want to start building small clusters of ideas which bring together smaller concepts into broader groups to be analyzed later.

- **Focus on Human Needs** – Sometimes focusing on a bigger underlying human emotion can help you see the basis of the example and why it matters. For example, the basic human need for *belonging* fuels many of the activities people engage in online, from posting social comments to joining online communities. The more you are able to connect the ideas you have gathered with the basic human needs behind them—the more easily you can start to aggregate ideas.

- **Recognize the Obvious** – Along the path to uncovering non-obvious insights, there is some value in recognizing and even embracing the obvious. In a grouping exercise for example, you can often use the obvious ideas (like multiple stories about new wearable technology products) as a way of bringing things together and work later on finding the non-obvious insights in between them.

- **Follow Your Intuition** – When you train yourself to be more observant, you might also find that you start to develop a feeling for stories that somehow *feel* significant or fit together even though you may not be able to describe why. Embrace that intuition when it tries to surface a connection between ideas without the words to describe it. In later phases, you can think further about connecting these pieces into a more thoughtful trend concept.

Step 3—Elevating

Elevating trends means thinking about the underlying themes that relate one group of ideas to another to describe a single broader idea or shift.

If you have gone through gathering and aggregating ideas—this is the point where you will probably confront the same problem I do every year.

There are too many possibilities.

When I go through my annual exercise of curating trends, the first time I aggregate all of my ideas it usually yields between 70 and 100 possible trend topics. That is far too many for a book and a sign that there is more work to be done.

So, in this third step, the aim is to start to take a bigger view and aggregating multiple groupings of information together into something that might eventually be called a trend.

ELEVATING QUESTIONS—How to Think Bigger about Ideas

1. What interests me most about these ideas?
2. What elements could I have missed earlier?
3. What is below the surface?
4. What is the bigger picture?
5. Where is the connection between ideas?

This can be the most challenging phase of the Haystack Method as combining ideas can also lead you to unintentionally make them too broad (and obvious). Your aim in this step therefore must be *elevating* an idea to make it bigger and more encompassing of multiple examples.

For example, when I was producing my *2014 Non-Obvious Trend Report* I came across an interesting healthcare startup called GoodRx, which had a tool to help people find the best price for medications. It was simple, useful and the perfect example of an evolving shift toward empowering patients in healthcare, which I wrote about in my earlier book *ePatient 2015*.

At the same time, I was seeing retail stores like Macy's investing heavily in creating apps to improve their in-store shopping experience, and a suite of new fashion services like Rent the Runway designed to help people save time and money while shopping.

On the surface, a tool to save on prescriptions, an app for a department store and a crowdsourced tool for renting dresses don't seem to have much in common. I had therefore initially grouped them separately.

While elevating trends, though, I realized that all of them had the underlying intent of helping to *optimize* a shopping experience in some way. I put them together and ultimately called the trend *Shoptimization*, to describe how technology was helping consumers optimize the process of buying everything from fashion to medical prescriptions.

In the next step, we will talk about techniques for naming trends (and the backstory behind the term *Shoptimization*), but for now my point in sharing that example is that elevation is the step in the Haystack Method where you can start to make the connections across industries and ideas that may have initially seemed disconnected and fallen into different groups.

I realize the difference between aggregating ideas and elevating them may seem very slight. In fact, there are times when I manage to do both at the same time because the act of aggregating stories together may help you to broaden your conclusions about them.

In the Haystack Method, I chose to still present these steps separately because most of the time they do end up as distinct efforts. With practice though, you may get better at condensing these two steps together.

TIPS & TRICKS: *HOW TO ELEVATE AGGREGATED IDEAS INTO TRENDS*

- **Use Words to Elevate** – When you have groups of ideas, sometimes boiling them down to a couple of words to describe them can help you to see the common themes between them. When I was collecting ideas related to entrepreneurship for my 2014 report, for example, a word that kept emerging was "fast" to describe the growing ecosystem of on-demand services for entrepreneurs. It was the theme of speed that helped me to bring the pieces together to eventually call that trend *Instant Entrepreneurship*.

- **Combine Industry Verticals** – Despite my own cautions against aggregating ideas by industry sector, sometimes a particular trend ends up heavily focused in just one sector. When I see one of these clusters of ideas predominantly focused in one industry, I always try to find another batch of ideas I can combine it with. This often leads to bigger thinking and helps to remove any unintentional industry bias I may have had when first aggregating ideas together.

- **Follow the Money** – With business trends, sometimes the underlying driver of a particular trend is focused on revenue generation for the businesses using it. Following this trail can sometimes lead you to make connections you might not have considered before. This was exactly how studying a new all-you-can-read ebook subscription service and the growth of cloud-based software led me to my 2014 Non-Obvious Trend of *Subscription Commerce*. Both were examples of brands transforming their business models to rely on subscriptions instead of sales.

Step 4—Naming

Naming trends involves describing an elevated idea in an easily understandable and memorably branded way.

Naming trends is a bit like naming a child—you think of every way that the name might unintentionally be dooming your idea (or child) to a life of ridicule and then you try to balance that with a name that feels right.

Of course naming trends also involves the choice of sharing a specific point of view in a way that names for kids generally don't. Great trend names convey meaning with simplicity—and they are memorable.

For that reason, this is often my favorite part of the Haystack Method, but also the most creatively challenging. It is focused on that critical moment when you have the ability to craft an idea that will either stick in people's minds as non-obvious or be forgotten.

Sometimes this quest to share non-obvious ideas leads me to invent an entire concept.

My second book which focused on how likeability is the key to success in business is a perfect example of this. It was called *Likeonomics* and focused on exploring why we do business with people we like.

Back in 2006, I published a blog post on how content could be optimized for social media sharing. I called it *Social Media Optimization* and gave it the acronym of SMO. The idea spawned over a dozen SMO services companies still in business today and even has its own entry in Wikipedia.

Finding the right name for an idea can do that. It can help a smart idea to capture the right peoples' imaginations and help them to own and describe it for themselves. Of course, that doesn't make it easy to do.

In fact, naming trends can take just as long as any other aspect of defining or researching a trend. In my method, I try many possibilities. I jot down potential names on Post-It Notes and compare them side by side. I test them with early readers and clients. Only after doing all of that do I finalize the names for the trends in each of my reports.

NAMING QUESTIONS—
How to Ensure You Have an Effective Trend Name?

1. Is the name not widely used or already well understood?

2. Is it relatively simple to say out loud in conversation?

3. Does it make sense without too much additional explanation?

4. Could you imagine it as the title of a book?

5. Are you using words that are unique and not overused or cliché?

6. Does it build upon a popular theme or topic in an unexpected way?

So how do the names turn out? Of course, you could see the list of trends in Part II of this book to compare some of the trend names I developed for this year's report—but here are a few others from previous reports along with a little of the backstory behind the development and selection of each one:

- ***Brutal Transparency*** **(2011)** – Playing off the common phrase of being "brutally honest" the naming of this trend was meant to illustrate how brands were taking transparency to a new and unexpectedly extreme level as a way to build trust with their consumers.

- *Precious Print* (2013) – In an increasingly digital world, this trend was aimed at describing how more and more of us have come to place an even higher value on those things that we read or choose to print because we value them enough to bring them out of digital form. The word "precious" seemed like the perfect way to describe this sentiment, and also worked alliteratively together with "print" to complete this trend's name.

- *Obsessive Productivity* (2014) – As the life-hacking movement generated more and more stories of how to make every moment more productive, I started to feel that all of these tools and advice about helping each of us optimize every moment was bordering on an obsession. The naming of this trend was easy, but to me it worked because it combined a word most people associate as negative (obsessive) with a play on one that is usually discussed as a positive (productivity).

While there are literally dozens of ways to name trends, the following tips and tricks share a few of the techniques that I tend to use most often in naming and branding the trends in my reports.

TIPS & TRICKS: *HOW TO CREATE POWERFUL NAMES FOR TRENDS*

- **Mashup** – Mashups take two different words or concepts and put them together in a meaningful way. *Likeonomics* is a mashup between likeability and economics. *Shoptimization* is a mashup between shopping and optimization. Using this technique can make an idea immediately memorable and ownable, but can also feel forced and artificial if not done artfully. There is a reason I didn't call my book *Trustonomics*. The best mashups are easy to pronounce and as close to sounding like the original words as possible. Both

Likeonomics and *Shoptimization* sound like the words they are derived from, which makes them less likely to feel forced or over the top.

- **Alliteration** – When naming brands, this technique is commonly used by brands like Coca-Cola or Krispy Kreme. The idea of using two words beginning with the same consonant is one I have used for trends like *Partnership Publishing* or *Co-Curation*. Like mashups, it can feel forced if you put two words together that don't belong, but the technique can lead you toward a great trend name.

- **Twist** – The technique involves taking a common idea or obvious phrase and inserting a small change to make it different. My favorite 2015 example is a trend I called *Small Data*. This was inspired by the growing topic of "big data" used to describe how data and its collection is a major challenge and opportunity for success. The small data life trend was a way of using a term that was already commonly used and then giving it a little twist to help it stand out and get attention.

Step 5—Proving

Proving is the final step in ensuring that there are enough examples and concrete research to justify why an idea does indeed describe the accelerating present enough to be called a trend.

Up until this point in the process of developing and curating trends, you might be thinking there hasn't been much original research involved. In the process I have shared so far, that is true. But it doesn't mean that data or research isn't important.

The Haystack Method relies heavily on analyzing stories and ideas that have been collected over an extended period of time and spotting patterns in those ideas. When it comes to proving a trend idea, though, getting the right research and data is the a critical last step.

In part, the amount of data and original research you might require depends on how you are looking at using the trends. The more analytical or scientific your stakeholders and audience, the more likely it is you will need some more concrete data to support your curated trends.

Regardless of what type of supporting trend research you intend to use, the proving method I use is focused on making sure that every trend has proof in three critical areas: idea, impact and acceleration.

WHAT IS A TREND?

A trend is a unique curated observation
of the accelerating present.

3 ELEMENTS OF TRENDS

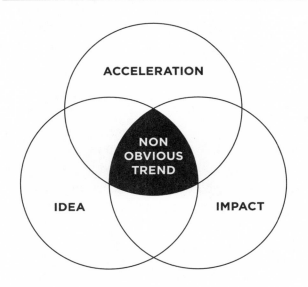

Let's look at each of these three elements.

1. **Idea** – Great trend ideas are unique descriptions of a shift in culture, business or behavior in a concise enough way to be meaningful without being over simplified.

2. **Impact** – A trend has impact when it causes people to start changing behavior, or companies to adapt what they are selling or how they are selling it.

3. **Acceleration** – The last critical element of great trends is how likely they are to continue affecting business and consumer behavior into the foreseeable future.

For the past five years, these three elements have been the central filter I have used to measure my trend ideas and ensure that I apply the right discipline to making sure they are proven. One element of consistently doing this is asking the same types of questions every year to finalize my annual short list of 15 trends.

PROVING QUESTIONS—How to Quantify a Trend

1. Is the trend idea unique enough to be described as new or fresh?
2. Has anyone published research related to this trend idea?
3. Is the media starting to uncover examples or focus on it?
4. Are there enough examples across industries to show adoption?
5. Is it likely to continue into the foreseeable future?

As you go through these questions, you may notice that some of the trend ideas that you have curated, analyzed, elevated and even created names for may not satisfy all these criteria. Unfortunately, you have now reached the toughest step in the Haystack Method: leaving behind trends that don't work.

Abandoning ideas is brutal—especially after you have become attached to them.

It probably won't help that in this chapter I have already advised you to name them before you prove them—which seems logically wrong. You never name something you're going to leave behind, right?

Well, as true as that may be, the problem is that you often *need* to name the trends before you can truly realize their importance. The process of naming helps you understand what a trend is and how you might prove it. Yet it also forces you to have discipline.

If you ultimately find that a trend doesn't work, you *must* abandon it and move on. Great trends always have the right proof to support them in front of the people they are meant to influence.

TIPS & TRICKS: *HOW TO PROVE YOUR TREND IDEAS*

- **Focus on Diversity** – One of the quickest ways to uncover that a trend idea may not actually be a trend is if you are only able to find examples of it in a single industry, category or situation. For example, I remember several years ago considering the idea of "Short-Form Communication" as a trend because of the rapid growth of Twitter and texting but I couldn't find enough diverse examples to prove the trend beyond social media, so I abandoned it.

- **Watch Your Biases** – Nothing will cloud your judgment more quickly than finding a trend that somehow helps your own industry, product or career. This is a tricky subject because part of the intention of curating your own trends may specifically be to support a product or belief. Yet it is also where many of the trends that are oversimplified or just plain wrong come from. Real trends, don't have apparent industry biases and are not gratuitously self-serving.

- **Use Authoritative Sources** – When it comes to the examples and research that you find to support a particular trend, the more authoritative sources you can find, the better. What this means in practice is using examples that people may recognize or finding research from reputable organizations or academic institutions. These sources can make the difference between selling your vision or having your audience question your conclusions because they don't believe your sources.

Whether your ideal method for proving trends involves relating them back to fundamental human needs or supporting your ideas with examples of successful businesses and quarterly revenue, there are many ways to prove a trend.

The trends you can predict with the Haystack Method are neither focused solely on consumer behavior, nor on global economies. Instead, this method can help you observe and identify patterns in media, culture, business or any other topic that may have particular relevance for you.

As a final step to help you put the Haystack Method into action, let's go through a step-by-step example of how it was applied, using one of the trends from last year's *Non-Obvious Trend Report*.

CASE STUDY:
How to Curate a Non-Obvious Trend

Last year while researching one of the trends for the trend report, I wrote this section simultaneously to illustrate my process.

The result is this section, which takes you through all five steps of the Haystack Method to gather, aggregate, elevate, name and prove a single trend from last year's *Non-Obvious Trend Report* which I called "Engineered Addiction."

THE TREND— ENGINEERED ADDICTION
STEP 1—Gathering

One of the earliest stories I saved, from February 2014, was about Dong Nguyen, the creator of mobile game Flappy Bird, which he suddenly pulled from the iTunes and Android stores after millions of downloads because he began to worry that the game was becoming too addictive.

His unexpected choice seemed significant—though I wasn't yet sure exactly why—so I saved it. Later that same year, I read a book called *Hooked* about how Silicon Valley product designers could build addictive "habit forming products" that seemed to describe perfectly what Nguyen had unintentionally done (and felt so guilty about)—so I saved that idea as well.

STEP 2—Aggregating

As I started the process of aggregating stories together from those I had gathered, I started seeing a pattern in stories that seemed to focus on some type of addictive behavior. The Flappy Bird story was about game design that seemed to lead to addiction. The book *Hooked*, by Nir Eyal, was about product design and using it to create habits in people.

To aggregate these together, I focused on the idea of design and the role that interface design seemed to be play in creating all these addictive experiences. I stapled these stories together to group them and put an index card on top with the simple description "Addictive Design" to describe what I guessed the trend might be.

STEP 3—Elevating

When I stepped back to look through my initial list of about 75 possible trends, there were several other trend concepts that stood out as possibly being related to this idea of Addictive Design. One in particular was an education-based trend I had started to track around the use of gamification techniques to aid in how people of all ages could learn new skills or knowledge.

I had used the relatively obvious term "Gamified Learning" on that index card to aggregate an article about the Khan Academy using badges to inspire learning and a startup called Curious that was making learning addictive by creating bite-sized pieces of learning on interesting topics.

The final piece to add to the puzzle as I was aggregating this trend was a book I had read called *Salt Sugar Fat* (by Michael Moss), which had also focused on the idea of addiction, but in the world of food manufacturing. The book exposed how foods like Oreos and Cheetos had been created to offer a "bliss point" that mimicked the sensations of addiction in most people. Along with the book, I also had several other articles on that topic saved under the term "Irresistible Food."

Adding the potential trend of Gamified Learning together with Addictive Design and considering the idea of Irresistible Food, I realized that there was an elevated trend that they all might be describing that went beyond popular apps or video games. This bigger trend described how all sorts of experiences and all sorts of products were being created as intentionally addictive based on more than just design or interfaces.

I put all the stories for each of these three aggregated concepts together and called the elevated grouping "Ubiquitous Addiction."

STEP 4—Naming

Now that I had plenty of examples as disparate as food manufacturing and online learning, it was time to put the pieces together with a name that would describe this bigger trend. For some trends, a name I develop during either aggregating or elevating the trends might work for the final trend name. Unfortunately, in this case "Addictive Design" seemed too small and "Gamified Learning" was too obvious and niche. The elevated name I had quickly assigned, "Ubiquitous Addiction," also didn't exactly roll off the tongue either.

I needed something better.

The final clue as to what the name of the trend could be came from another interview article I read which featured Eyal, the author of *Hooked*. In the article, he was specifically talking about his belief that his role was one which he liked to describe as a "behavioral engineer." This idea of engineering instead of just design immediately seemed far better suited to describing what I felt the trend actually was.

After testing a few versions of using the word "engineering" in the title of the trend, I settled on *Engineered Addiction* as the most descriptive and memorable way to describe this trend and all of its components.

STEP 5—Proving

The final step was to ensure that this was truly a trend that could be proven through more than stories across multiple industries. In this case, the proof was already done, in large part through the exercise of research because I had uncovered so many dimensions to the trend in different industries across the previous steps.

I still wanted more proof, though, so I started looking for more examples or evidence of intentionally addictive products and experiences. My research led me quickly to a recently published Harvard Study showing why social media had become so addictive for so many, and then to a book by noted MIT anthropologist Natasha Dow Schüll, who spent more than 15 years doing field research on slot machine design in Las Vegas.

Her book, *Addicted By Design*, exposed the many ways that casinos use the experience and design of slot machines to encourage addictive behavior. Together, these were the final elements of proof that would help tell the story completely.

Engineered Addiction made my *2015 Non-Obvious Trend Report*, and ultimately was one of the most talked about trends that year.

Avoiding Future Babble

Now that we have gone through my method used to build out, describe and prove a trend, there is only one final thing left to do—offer a word of advice against one of the biggest dangers of trend forecasting: sinking into nonsense.

Despite my love of trends and belief that any of us has the ability to learn to see trends—the fact is we live in a world frustrated with predictions, and for good reason.

Economists fail to predict activities that lead to global recessions. Television meteorologists predict rain that never comes. And business trend forecasters are perhaps the worst offenders, sharing glassy-eyed predictions about future industries that seem either glaringly obvious or naively impossible.

At least 50% of pundits seem wrong all the time. It's just hard to tell which 50%.

In 2011 journalist Dan Gardner wrote about this mistake-ridden obsession with the future in his entertainingly insightful book *Future Babble*. Part of his aim was to spotlight the many ways that experts have led us down mistaken paths and caused more harm than good.

In the book, he refers to the research of Philip Tetlock, a psychologist from the University of California's Haas School of Business. Over the span of years, Tetlock and his team interviewed all types of experts and collected 27,450 predictions and ideas about the future. They then analyzed these judgments from their many anonymous sources and concluded that "the simple and disturbing truth is that the experts' predictions were no more accurate than random guesses."

No matter how clever we are, no matter how sophisticated our thinking, the brain we use to make predictions is flawed and the world is fundamentally unpredictable.

Dan Gardner, *Future Babble*

The more interesting conclusion from Tetlock's research, which Gardner highlighted, was the wide disparity in how some experts reacted to the news of hearing their predictions were wrong.

The experts that fared worst were the ones who struggled with uncertainty. They were overconfident, described their mistaken predictions often as being *almost* right and generally had an unchanging worldview. In *Future Babble*, Gardner calls these experts "hedgehogs."

On the other side were experts who did not follow a set path. They were comfortable with being uncertain and accepted that some of their predictions could be wrong. Gardner called these experts "foxes" and described them as modest about their ability to predict the future, self-critical and willing to express doubt about their predictions.

His discussion of foxes versus hedgehogs gets to the heart of an important question that you might be wondering yourself at this point in the book. How can anyone know if your predictions are actually going to be accurate?

The Art of Getting Trends Right (and Wrong)

You already know that I believe anyone can learn to predict the future.

Yet I also shared Dan Gardner's caution about the dangers of false certainty and general skepticism around future predictions for a reason. If you are going to build your ability to curate trends, you also must simultaneously embrace the idea that sometimes you will be wrong.

In Part III and the appendices of this book, you will see a summary of every trend I have predicted in my last five annual editions of the

Non-Obvious Trend Report. Each trend also has a corresponding letter grade and a retrospective analysis of its longevity.

Some of them are embarrassingly off the mark.

The reason I share them candidly anyway is partly to illustrate Gardner's point. I want to be as honest with you as I try to be with myself after each year's report. Foxes are comfortable with uncertainty and know they may sometimes be wrong.

I *know* I am sometimes wrong, and I guarantee that you will be, too.

So, why write a book about predicting the trends and go through this entire process if we both might be wrong at the end of it?

A fear of failure is no excuse not to apply your best thinking and explore big ideas. That's the first reason. The second comes to my true purpose in writing this book—which is only *partially* about learning to predict trends.

Learning to predict the future has an even more valuable side effect: you will become more curious, observant and understanding of the world around you.

It is this mental shift that may ultimately be the greatest benefit of learning to see and curate trends.

Oscar Wilde once wrote that "to expect the unexpected shows a thoroughly modern intellect." *Non-Obvious* is about building this type of modern intellect through seeing the things that others miss, thinking differently and curating ideas describe the accelerating present in new and unique ways.

Now that I have shared the process and techniques I use to do that every year, let's focus on my predictions for the top trends that will be changing how we buy, sell or believe anything in 2016 with the sixth edition of the *Non-Obvious Trend Report.*

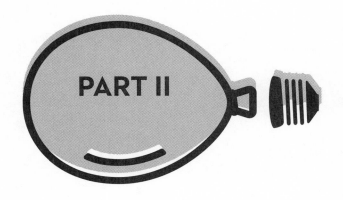

PART II

THE 2016 NON-OBVIOUS TREND REPORT

2016 NON-OBVIOUS TRENDS OVERVIEW – SUMMARY

WHAT IS A TREND?
A trend is a unique curated observation about the accelerating present

CULTURE & CONSUMER BEHAVIOR - Trends in how we see ourselves and patterns in popular culture

E-mpulse Buying

Strategic Downgrading

Optimistic Aging
(Originally Curated 2013)

MARKETING & SOCIAL MEDIA - Trends in how brands are trying to influence and engage consumers

B2Beyond

Personality Mapping

Branded Utility
(Originally Curated 2014)

MEDIA & EDUCATION - Trends in content and information impacting how we learn or are entertained

Mainstream Multiculturalism

Earned Consumption

Anti-Stereotyping
(Originally Curated 2014)

TECHNOLOGY & DESIGN - Trends in technology innovation and product design impacting our behavior

Virtual Empathy

Data Overflow

Heroic Design
(Originally Curated 2013)

ECONOMICS & ENTREPRENEURSHIP - Trends in business models, startups and careers affecting the future of work or money

Insourced Incubation

Automated Adulthood

Obsessive Productivity
(Originally Curated 2014)

Chapter 4

E-MPULSE BUYING

What's the Trend?

Despite fears that the ecommerce might kill impulse buying, the growing integration of mobile devices into the shopping experience is opening new possibilities for real time marketing to entice consumers to make split second emotional buying decisions once again.

Near the end of 2014 a story published in the *Wall Street Journal* predicted a doomsday scenario the article called "The End of the Impulse Shopper." and featured stories like that of interior designer Elizabeth Hoffman.

Her list-driven shopping style, the article argued, was becoming increasingly common among savvy price conscious consumers. Hoffman had trained herself to be immune to marketing displays and in-store suggestions. Her goal with any retail experience was to enter the store with a list and mission in mind. She practices the discipline of sticking to her list and doesn't engage in impulse buying.

Elizabeth Hoffman's shopping system is an example of "intentional shopping," but her story may be easy to dismiss as the predictable penny-pinching of consumers in austere times. It may be fairer, though, to assign more blame on another factor: that device in our pocket, always on and ready to entertain or distract us from any idle moment.

Do you remember standing in line at a grocery store or pharmacy, picking up a candy bar or pack of gum and adding to your basket or cart as an impulse buy? Those days may be over, thanks to the mobile phone. Today as most of us stand in line waiting to pay for items, we are checking our email or playing micro-addictive mobile games. What we *aren't* doing is looking at the displays for candy and gum.

Our phone provides "mobile blinders" shielding us from the things we once grabbed on a whim. When you add the rise of automated self-checkout kiosks and the new ability to pre-order products online and simply pick them up in store (or on the curbside outside the store) – you have the perfect storm that *should* kill impulse shopping.

Yet for all the pessimistic predictions about the end of impulse shopping, mobile devices have also opened up big new possibilities to create impulse shopping moments in ways that were never before possible. The new battleground for retail is "omnichannel" as brands try to reach consumers in multiple places. In 2016, this will lead to a new focus on *E-mpulse Buying* where the device which some blame for the demise of impulse shopping might single handedly resurrect it in a new format.

The mobile device itself is becoming central in how brands in all categories are now finding new ways to use real time engagement in the moment of purchase to entice more one click shopping, and perhaps bring lucrative impulse shopping back to retail.

Saving the Candy Bar

Perhaps no industry has more products on the front line of this assault on impulse buying than chocolate and confectionary brands. In a recent interview with the *Washington Post*, Hershey's senior director of retail evolution Frank Jiminez summed up the challenge this way: "Shopping is changing and impulse is under threat. What happens if and when the checkout goes away?"

It is an important question for The Hershey Company to ask, since it clearly has a lot at stake. The brand makes some of the most beloved chocolate products in the world including Kit Kat, York, and Reese's ... not to mention its own signature Kisses and namesake bars essential for any connoisseur of smores (an American treat featuring campfire heated marshmallows and melted chocolate sandwiched between two graham crackers).

In 2015, Hershey's piloted programs to test new types of vending machines in unexpected locations like next to gas pumps, candy dispensers as part of automated self-checkout kiosks, and even sponsored new research into the "Eight Human Truths Of Impulse."*

The brand is also experimenting with Amazon's new Dash Button program to allow consumers to instantly order packs of its Ice Breakers gum via a button placed in the home and connected to the Internet for instant one touch orders through Amazon.

Reimagining the impulse shopping experience is a priority for other brands in the industry as well. According to *Confectionary News*, both Mars and Wrigley will also launch significant pilot programs in 2016 designed to test new ways to capture consumer interest at the point of purchase and rethink how candy and chocolate is sold in retail environments as well.

Another example is Mondolez International (maker of household brands like Oreos and Ritz crackers), which is piloting integrations with Facebook to create new online "hot zones" to drive impulse buying the same way racks of items in the front of the store once did in real life.

The future will bring more seamless connections between mobile, social media and instant shopping – and it is already here in some countries.

Wallet-Free Shopping

The app that will change how we buy anything is already here – if you happen to live in China.

WeChat is a popular Chinese mobile app that is often mistakenly

---

* In case you're curious, they were delight, indulge, recharge, rescue, spoil, charm, aspire, and score (as in, get a good deal).

described by those outside the country as yet another messaging tool for hyper connected Millennials. While it may have started with messaging, in the span of less than five years the app has blossomed into a visionary mobile platform that is changing the way mainstream Chinese consumers live their daily lives.

In addition to messaging, the app lets consumers call a taxi, share the dinner tab with friends, check in for a flight, play bills, find music and access fitness tracker data. How can one app do all this? The platform allows businesses to create "official" accounts for the app and by the end of 2015, there will be more than 10 million of these types of accounts on the platform, which each use location and identity data users opt to share in order to provide services and tailored offers.

In Japan, the hottest mobile app of the year was Line – an app that provides free messaging and video and phone calls, and monetizes it through allowing users to buy and share "stickers" (tiny illustrations designed for texting and more detailed than animated emojis). In March of 2015, Line users sent an estimated 2 billion stickers each day from a library of more than 40,000 and these stickers generated an estimated $30 million in revenue from just their first seven months alone.

Line and WeChat are examples of dominant mobile platforms, but even more significantly, they offer an optimistic future vision of integrated always available payment options for consumers. Similar to how Amazon provides one-click ordering based on using stored customer data – WeChat and Line can offer the same to millions of brands and retailers that are using its platform.

Other mobile platforms are seeing this success and working hard to recreate it for themselves. Facebook, Twitter, Pinterest and Snapchat have all announced some version of "mobile wallets" in the past year, designed to enable one click buying and store a user's credit card.

Platforms like Apple Pay, Samsung Pay and Android Pay are all trying to entice consumers to do the same thing on the operating system or device level. Startups like Senanga are creating new tools for integrating check out enabled mobile and online advertising campaigns.

All this "mobile wallet" innovation is bringing the promise of one-click shopping closer and driving the potential of E-mpulse Buying as well. In a world where people can purchase something they see in real life or online without ever pulling out their wallet or signing anything – the only challenge is where to put the price tag.

Even that challenge has some interesting solutions already.

Scan To Buy ... Everywhere

Last year small Philippines-based airline Cebu Pacific created a unique sidewalk advertising campaign that only appeared when it started raining. Working with ad agency Ogilvy Asia, the campaign used water repellent spray stenciled onto the sidewalks in Hong Kong with the message "It's Sunny In The Philippines" along with a QR code that could be scanned for more information. The campaign resulted in a 37% increase in bookings as a result of the campaign.

Though decidedly low tech and mostly offline, the campaign is just one among plentiful examples of how the path from seeing or experiencing something and converting to purchase may be getting shorter and shorter.

UK based Powa Technologies makes "Powatags" to add scan-to-buy codes to any form of advertising and currently work with over 1000 brands. Visual search company Slyce has a solution to allow consumers to take a photo of a product and learn instantly who sells it and for how much. Home Depot's Project Color app lets consumers select any color and then virtually "see" how that color might look on their own walls at home – and instantly purchase the paint.

One startup called Delivery Agent is even working to add this capability for e-mpulse buying to how we watch television, aiming to offer "t-commerce" by allowing viewers to purchase products directly via their remote control. This past year Comcast also announced it would test instant buying via remote control as part of its new X1 next generation video streaming platform.

From out of home advertising to integrated advertising on mobile devices and television, the common theme among all these efforts is the potential for *anyone* to buy *anything* they see anywhere at the touch of a button or the scan of a code.

Why It Matters

Thanks to the rise of ecommerce and our addiction to our mobile devices, many have predicted that online shopping and automated checkouts would kill the highly profitable consumer behavior of impulse buying. In 2016, these fears will transform into hope and more innovative retailers and startups will focus on new ways to encourage *E-mpulse Buying* from consumers. As the mobile wallet becomes a reality, and brands get smarter about using location data to target more relevant offers, savvy shoppers will begin to take advantage of the time savings and ease of use to purchase more products in the moment they decide they want them. Whether consumers are walking down the street with the mobile device or sitting on the couch at home with the remote in their hand, this innovation will trigger resurgence of impulse buying – but only from those retailers smart enough to capitalize on the opportunity.

Who Should Use This Trend?

Though the trend in this chapter is most often discussed in the context of retailers – the lessons of this behavior apply to many industries far outside traditional retail. Business to business customers, for example, may be more informed by real time information as a part of their buying cycle even if it takes them far longer to purchase. Clearly anyone selling products on the more impulsive side of the purchasing scale, in terms of immediate use or low cost, could benefit greatly from leveraging this trend as well.

How To Use This Trend

✓ **Monetize your visuals** – Are people sharing visuals of the products you sell? Do you include visuals of services or products on your website? As visual search tools evolve, there will be new ad-tech players that offer the ability to monetize images through things like QR codes or hovering buy buttons. These are ripe opportunities to test how you might start to monetize content that was typically only used in a supporting way but may now become the highest converting content for sales as well.

✓ **Study global consumer behavior** - For anyone based in the US, there is a temptation to consider consumers close to home to be the most technically savvy and forward thinking. When it comes to mobile purchases and E-pulse Buying, this is far from the truth. Instead, consumers in Asian countries like China and Japan, or European consumers in Scandinavia (for example) are far ahead in their mobile buying habits. Studying their behavior today offers a valuable glimpse into what global consumers will be doing in the near future.

Chapter 5

STRATEGIC DOWNGRADING

What's the Trend?

As more products become Internet-enabled and digitally remastered, consumers start selectively rejecting these supposedly improved products and services – opting to strategically downgrade to simpler, cheaper and sometimes more functional versions instead.

Kyle Wiens is a modern day superman on a quest to save the world... one broken piece of technology at a time. His weapon of choice is a pentalobe screwdriver, mixed with an accidental journalist's talent for telling stories to inspire indignation. In the past several years, he has single-handedly become the voice of the "fixer movement" and a crusader for any consumer's right to fix the products they buy instead of being forced to throw them away.

Last year Apple insider website cultofmac.com described him as the "radical who wants the iPad banned." Boing Boing described him as "a culture hero of the 21st century" and he is a frequent contributor to some of the most influential publications in the world – including recent editorial pieces in *The Atlantic*, *Harvard Business Review*, *Wall Street Journal*, and *WIRED* (twice).

Why all this attention on a guy whose day job is running a cartoon-ishly titled company called iFixit? And what the heck is a pentalobe screwdriver?

The pentalobe screw is the "five-pointed Do Not Enter sign" used on most Apple devices. Shaped a bit like a five leaf clover, the proprietary screw is meant to prevent consumers from opening up Apple devices to fix or upgrade them. As a result, most older Apple devices end up in a landfill. According to Wiens, Apple is one of the biggest enemies of the fixer movement - making devices that are notoriously closed to tinkering or any sort of hacker upgrades. To fight back, iFixit was the first to develop its own pentalobe screwdriver and sell it on the Internet.

The move is emblematic of Wiens' personality. He lives to take on large brands and champions consumer's right to open up the things we own and fix or modify them as we choose. Though it seems like a logical mission, this "right to repair" has actually ballooned into a billion dollar legal debate. At stake is the very nature of ownership itself and whether we truly own the products we buy or not.

Who Owns Your Tractor?

The company propelled to the center of this debate thanks to a lawsuit in late 2015 was farm equipment manufacturer John Deere. At issue was its fervent legal argument that farmers, in fact, did not own their tractors but rather received "an implied license for the life of the vehicle to operate the vehicle."

Incensed by this particular bit of legalese, Wiens did what he does best and took to the media. In an op-ed published in WIRED magazine, he called this high tech farm equipment a "nightmare" for farmers. In an interview with NPR, he pointed out that that the problem comes down to the law. "Laws that govern the computer and the tractor were written by entertainment lawyers out of LA back in the 90s when they were trying to prevent DVD piracy ... it's just time to update some of these laws."

Governments worldwide are tackling exactly this problem with several pieces of legislation under deliberation right now. The problem for farmers is, they can't afford to wait for the outcome. So they are using the most logical workaround anyone might – they are seeking out older tractors with less technology. In other words, they are using *Strategic Downgrading*.

Writing about this downgrading behavior in late 2015, farm auction expert Greg Peterson noted that buyers were placing increasing value on older simpler models – and in a time of struggle for the agricultural sector due to low prices – the newest tractors with their built in technology limitations seemed to be the first item cut from the budget.

It turns out this desire for older products (instead of their supposedly better replacements) is affecting other categories beyond agriculture as well.

Desirably Dumb Devices

When it comes to technology, we generally assume that newer is better. Computers get faster, cameras add more megapixels, battery life gets longer, and old products aren't built to last - even if we do manage to open them up with pentalobe screwdrivers and learn to fix them.

Despite the appeal of shiny new devices, there have been growing signs over the past year that consumers overwhelmed by the frequent upgrade cycle of technology are actively seeking ways to press the pause button, or even rewind to simpler times with more basic devices.

For example, the "Blackphone" launched in 2015 was a stripped down mobile phone running a lighter version of Android that puts privacy first and foremost. Swiss startup Punkt built and released an "un-smartphone" that has no web browsing, no touchscreen and no camera – focusing instead on features like a multi-day battery life, high quality audio and built in noise cancellation.

Meanwhile a quick internet search yields dozens of recent stories and blog posts about over-connected consumers deciding to take a break, skip the "biennial fleecing" and downgrade their mobile devices to an older previously useless model usually sitting in a drawer somewhere at home.

With wearable devices, the "downgrading" is often due to a lack of usefulness. Watches replaced by wrist-worn fitness trackers are regaining their place. Clip on wearable trackers are being left at home. Succumbing to the problem of too much measurement and not enough meaning, a growing range of consumers are choosing to go back to the "dumb" unconnected jewelry that they preferred in the first place.

For many devices the downgrading to "dumb" devices is driven by consumer frustration with things like lower battery life or overly complicated functionality. In other cases, like with an interesting resurgence in the popularity of print books, this downgrading can be a matter of preference.

The Surprising Value Of Print Books

The death of print books is predicted every year with regularity. Since 2008 ebook sales have been on the rise consistently every quarter – until they seemed to hit a wall last year. Suddenly, the book industry was reporting a curious reversal, fueled by a series of new research reports that were coming out in 2015 with surprising findings.

Analysis from Neilsen's Books and Consumers Survey noted that "teens continue to express a preference for print that may seem to be at odds with their perceived digital know how." A study run by the University of Colorado on the evolution of the book industry found that college students preferred printed textbooks because they helped students concentrate and avoid distraction.

"Consumers have an emotional and visceral/sensory attachment to printed books," researchers wrote, "potentially elevating them to a luxury item."

Supporting this theory was the fact that the research showed the top three reasons consumers choose a printed book is because it is easier on the eyes, they prefer the look and feel of paper, and they want the ability to add the book to a personal library.

The most hopeful argument for the resurgence of print books came in September of 2015 courtesy of a *New York Times* article titled "The Plot Twist: E-book Sales Slip, and Print Is Far From Dead." The article cited a new study from the Association of American Publishers (AAP) which showed a decline in ebook sales of about 10% in the early part of the year, along with a rise in the number of independent booksellers of about 20% over the past five years (according to the American Booksellers Association).

Despite glossing over the nuance that only e-books among the AAP's member publishers were down while sales of ebooks overall, including independently published ebooks, were actually up – the evidence for a resurgence in print books was quite valid.

E-book subscription models like Oyster that aimed to pioneer an approach to reading modeled on the all-you-can-get Netflix style have come and gone within less than two years. Meanwhile, supposedly counterintuitive moves like Amazon opening its first physical bookstore in Seattle a few months ago are offering proof points that there may be more to the print vs. e-book debate than we once thought.

E-books may offer a superior experience when it comes to the gratification of reading them instantly, or the sometimes valuable feature of being able to see what other readers have highlighted or chosen to take notes on. Yet print books remain an indulgent (perhaps even luxurious) strategic downgrade. The ultimately retro reading choice of holding a print book in your hands still feels and smells and inspires … the same way it always has.

This focus on the immersive experience that strategic downgrading can offer is also at the core of some of the popularity of older music on vinyl and retro gaming as well.

Retro Media

At English retailer John Lewis, sales of record players have risen 240% in the past year alone.

Independent music stores across the world are now scrambling to make sure and carry enough record players to support growing demand. Meanwhile, vinyl sales are at a twenty year high. While some audiophiles may disagree with my categorization of this choice as a "downgrade" given their preference for the lovably imperfect sound of songs played on vinyl – the fact remains that choosing to listen to songs this way is a deliberately nostalgic choice, and one that an increasing number of people are making.

A similar resurgence in retro video games played on older consoles or mobile devices has taken hold over the past year as well. The low resolution retro design of Candy Crush has not slowed down the popularity of the mobile game which has an unbelievable estimated 93 million people playing it *every day*, spending an estimated $800,000 daily.

Popular 80s video game maker Coleco has plans to launch a new game controller and console in 2016 that will offer players the chance to enjoy old 8-bit, 16-bit and 32-bit games once again – as well as use actual game cartridges … just like they once did 20+ years ago.

All this focus on retro experiences in gaming and music are not just for the older and more prone to nostalgia either. People of all ages are discovering joy in leaving insanely realistic third person shooter games, or algorithmically balanced digitally remastered music behind and opting for an older, less perfect, but still thoroughly awesome experience.

Sometimes this desire for better experiences is based less on nostalgia and more on time – or a lack thereof – like is has been for a growing number of sports that are being played or experienced in shortened timeframes than in the past.

Abbreviated Sports

By even the most optimistic numbers, the decline of golf has been pronounced. Down from a high of 30.6 million golfers in 2003 – just over a decade later the National Golf Foundation reports only about 24.7 million. Even more worrying for the industry is the fact that there has been a 30% decline in new golfers under the age of 34 playing the game.

The price and time commitment (often up to six hours for a full 18 rounds) are often cited as the most common barriers – but there is a movement within the industry to try and appeal to this younger demographic by addressing the time barrier with initiatives like the industry's "Time For Nine" campaign focused on enticing younger golfers to come and play an abbreviated half round of nine holes.

This invitation to enjoy a downgraded and less time intensive version of sport also explains the increasingly popular Twenty20 version of short form cricket, which features each team batting for only 20 overs as opposed to the usual 50 overs for a standard one day match. Twenty20 matches can be completed in 2-3 hours versus 7-8 hours for a one day match and a full five day for a Test match.

Each of these traditionally long sports are adapting to the fragmented media landscape of today and offering younger and older people with shrinking attention spans new ways to downgrade their experiences into shorter and more palatable chunks of time for participating or watching.

Rejecting GMOs

The final example of strategic downgrading comes from the food industry, and the story of one the most awe-inspiring ideas of the modern era – whose very existence is based on a scenario that all humankind hopes will never happen.

Situated on a tiny remote Norwegian island near the Artic Ocean, the Svalbard Global Seed Vault holds more than 100 million seeds for nearly 1 million food-crops from around the world. Often called the "Doomsday Vault," its mission is to keep the world's seeds save in the event of global catastrophe, so the survivors might replant the planet.

While the vault and scenario it was created for may seem far-fetched – the challenge of increasing our planet's food supply to account for our growing human population is a fierce global debate. In the center of the debate is the use of genetically modified organisms (GMOs) in food production. In America, they are commonly used in food production and deemed safe thanks to media education and government lobbying from the companies that produce them.

In Europe, as recently as a few months ago, two thirds of all countries upheld a ban on all GMOs. Despite the disagreements about the safety of GMOs, the debate itself is leading many people in food secure countries towards selecting older and presumably safer products. For example, there are "seed swaps" taking place among farmers and home gardeners to keep non-gmo crops alive. New diets continue to pop up advocating for simpler food like the "paleo diet."

All of it points to the increasing fear that the role of technology in our food may be causing health dangers we don't quite understand. The natural reaction is people choosing to strategically downgrade to food grown with more simple and human methods, without growth hormones and free from the genetic engineering.

Why It Matters

The fundamental shift described in this wide ranging trend is the idea that we as individuals and consumers are often choosing "downgraded" product and experiences that were once described as sub-optimal. Over the past year, the value of these supposedly outdated experiences is multi-faceted and causing a reevaluation of what features really matter.

Technology can be too smart, sports can take too long and crops can be too engineered. Driven by the underlying expectation of empowerment and choice, a greater number of consumers will choose to selectively opt out of innovation they don't value and instead return to the comfortable past where food seemed safer, books were tactile and things just worked.

Who Should Use This Trend?

As many companies struggle with finding the right kind of innovation to keep up to date in their industry, this idea of strategic downgrading represents the ultimate counter-trend. The organizations who will find the most value in it, therefore are the ones working hardest to evolve their products or industry into the future. Along with the desire to integrate more technology and improve a product must also come the understanding that sometimes people won't want anything to change or see more value from the older version they are already used to.

How To Use This Trend

✓ **Offer a "classic mode"** – When Microsoft launches a new operating system, there is usually a way change your interface to use the "classic view" you were used to from the previous version. In the newest Samsung Galaxy mobile phone, you can use "ultra power saving mode" – which turns off almost all phone functionality and switches to a black and white screen, quickly dumbing down your phone to save battery. What both Microsoft and Samsung know is that sometimes "downgrading" is exactly what consumers want. So how could you offer a "classic mode" for your own products or services?

✓ **Respond to zeitgiest** – The word zeitgeist refers to a prevailing thought that captures the culture of a particular time, and it is often used when talking about new cultural trends. Media seek it out, researchers report on it – and it offers valuable advice for leveraging this trend as well. When record players started generating buzz, for example, it created a big opportunity for a certain type of store to begin carrying and selling them. Zeitgeist can be like that – an early predictor of what people will care about. Brands must learn to watch and respond to this zeitgeist.

Chapter 6

OPTIMISTIC AGING

What's the Trend?

After years of being sold anti-aging solutions – a generation of newly aging adults are embracing the upside of getting older and finding cause for optimism in the growing opportunities, financial freedom, respect and time that their "third lifetime" can offer.

In 2015, the winner of the prestigious Academy Award for Best Picture was a quirky, beautiful, vaguely biographical comeback story from an actor that many people remembered but had not watched on the silver screen for years. Michael Keaton resurrected his career with that film and jump started his second act to a career that seemed at one point like it was fading away.

His story is becoming surprisingly common.

Despite all hovering around their sixties, the latest cadre of action hero leads in films is virtually unchanged from the 1990s – including Sylvester Stallone, Arnold Schwarzenegger, Liam Neeson, Bruce Willis and Kevin Costner. After years between high profile projects, actress Robin Wright has won accolades for her co-starring role in the popular Netflix drama House of Cards opposite Kevin Spacey. There are dozens more stories of older actors coming back to prominence and finding new roles.

One explanation is that the volume of scripted series has grown 75% from 2009 to 2014 (according to research from cable network FX), fueled partially by the efforts of streaming networks like Amazon, Netflix and Hulu commissioning new programs. Many of these new programs are creating opportunities for aging but still recognizable actors with niche audiences to find new roles.

"It's never been a better time to be a middle aged actor making a comeback," *Businessweek* wrote in a profile of former TV star Paul Rieser. "In a previous era, these actors might have disappeared completely, but with such a glut of entertainment now, there's more than enough work to go around."

While this opportunity boom is clearly a sign of hope if you happen to be an aging actor – it also represents the increasingly central role that aging and older people are likely to take in our culture and the opportunities that will be offered to them. This is resulting in an interestingly and somewhat surprising trend affecting how we age: *Optimistic Aging*.

The Case For Optimism

In 2015, a survey from the National Council on Aging found that 89% of older adults were confident they could maintain a high quality of life throughout their senior years. In a recent article for the *New York Times,* author and Columbia journalism Professor Paula Span noted "social scientists have known for years that older people, freed from the midlife stresses of work and child rearing, become happier. They call it the U-shaped curve: life satisfaction is greatest in people's youth and then again in old age."

Outside the US, however, this optimism is not quite as pronounced. In Japan, for example, nine in ten people surveyed in a 2014 Pew Research Center described aging as a major problem for their country. Concerns were similarly high across South Korea and China. In Europe, more than half of the public surveyed in Germany and Spain said it was a major problem as well. This difference of opinion globally makes sense if you consider the facts of demographics.

By 2050 the population of people over 65 years old is expected to surge to 1.5 billion people, nearly three times the current level measured in 2010 (530.5 million). Thanks to our increased life expectancy, this trend means that several countries will soon be in the challenging position of having more adults aged 65 and older than they have children younger than 15. As the Pew Report notes, this is not a favorable demographic trend for growth.

Yet the upside of this gradual growth is that it is fueling innovation and the people who are poised to benefit from this innovation over the next 30 years are exactly the ones creating it today. New technology is improving quality of living, changing healthcare, enabling easier social connections, and allowing greater mobility.

It is also inspiring a reevaluation of how older workers are treated in the workplace. The Center on Aging & Work at Boston College recently predicted that workers 55 and older will make up 25% of the workforce by 2019.

In 2016, a combination of these factors will lead to a renewal of a trend I first wrote about back in 2013: *Optimistic Aging*. As the quest to provide better treatment and mobility for these seniors grows into a multi-billion dollar business, a string of investment will result in growing optimism even from the nations contending with the highest numbers of elderly citizens by sparking innovations that help improve their lives.

While this innovation will do little to address the concern that younger people express about the burden older citizens will represent to society, the elderly themselves show a relatively consistent optimism about how they will be taken care of and kept productive members of society.

While the original trend back in 2013 first described greater ability for older citizens to connect with one another through social networks and remain engaged in the workplace, the coming year will see more tools for everything from fostering better social relationships to transforming the healthcare, careers, leisure activities and home of seniors.

Smart Homes & Aging In Place

Several years ago, concept homes were the most popular method for researchers to test smart home technology for the aging. The Gator Tech smart house, for example, was originally developed by University of Florida researchers more than decade ago as an early step on the journey to offer more smart home technology for older people.

Today, this smart technology is more integrated, smaller, cheaper and more available for anyone. Washington State University's Center for Advanced Studies in Adaptive Systems (CASAS), for example, has built a "Smart Home in a Box" – a network of about 30 sensors that can "watch" a home for movement and activity like doors opening or using the kitchen.

The range of this new technology is equally nimble. Fast cooling stoves will allow safer cooking and minimize the potential for burns. Sleep trackers will monitor resting activity. Smart medication trackers can provide alerts, increase adherence and provide reminders. Live connected web cams can allow care givers and adult children to easily check in with aging parents and quickly be alerted about any changes to normal routines.

A recent AARP survey found that over 90% of seniors would prefer to remain at home and "age in place" without having to move into senior living facilities or with family. The market to help them do exactly that is poised to explode in the coming years, giving seniors even more cause for optimism about aging because aging in place is already a reality.

Beyond The Wheelchair

Aside from where to live, one of the biggest challenges with aging is how it forces many to remain in one place – foregoing the ability to easily move around or even to travel the world. As journalists write dreamily about how the self-driving car may transform morning commutes or help Google complete its mapping of the Earth – the far greater impact of this technology may be in the mobility it offers to those no longer able to drive, such as the elderly.

In addition to automated vehicles, new personal mobility devices like Honda's recently announced UNI-CUB or the fast selling IO Hawk (described as part skateboard, part Segway) are popularizing the idea of smaller devices designed to be used by individuals to move around more easily and rapidly. Larger products like the GOOD DESIGN award winning WHILL personal mobility device (described as the "Tesla for sidewalks") are reimagining the traditional motorized wheelchair into something more functional and beautiful.

The market is ready for products like this. A recent study from Grand View Research estimates the market will grow to be worth $8 billion by 2020. As an increasing range of products offer safer methods for older people to continue leading active lives – this ability to leave their homes with relative ease will help more of them to continue making productive contributions to the workplace as well.

Legacy Careers

In the past year, plenty of companies have started thinking differently about retaining or attracting older workers. Brands like Barclays, IDEO, Intel and others have built or launched pilot programs to keep older workers engaged or even to attract workers past 50 years of age. BMW recently launched ergonomic changes to its factory assembly line such as wooden floors and magnifying glasses to aide productivity among aging workers.

The idea of having seniors rejoin the workforce in new and unexpected roles was also featured in the popular 2015 film *The Intern* starring Robert De Niro and Anne Hathaway where De Niro's character was hired as an assistant and intern for a rising fashion etailer's young alpha-founder played by Hathaway. His character in the story ended up bringing a new viewpoint and a much needed rigor and maturity to help the fledgling startup tackle its growth related challenges.

In a perfect example of art mirroring reality, those interested in continuing or reentering the workforce after a break will also encounter a growing range of companies new and old which are ready to help.

Leading "career reentry" company iRelaunch, for example, support and job placement for relaunchers (those who want to restart a career), returnships (mid-career internships) and strategic volunteering (using unpaid volunteering as a means to paid work). Their website lists dozens of large brands who are ready to engage older workers seeking meaningful work.

This quest for meaning has also driven the popularity of Encore.org, a company dedicated to helping older workers use their skills and expertise to make world changing impact on a social level. As brand consultant Tom Agan wrote in a *New York Times* piece about how innovators get better with age, "if an organization wants innovation to flourish, the conversation needs to change from severance packages to retention bonuses. Instead of managing the average age downward, companies should be managing it upward."

Silver Entrepreneurs

Aside from working with established organizations, there is also a parallel growing trend towards those over 50 embracing entrepreneurial challenges as well. In traditionally risk averse German culture, for example, the idea of starting a company later in life seems like it should be out of character ... but in a country second only to Japan in contending with an aging population, one in ten new startups in Germany has a founder over 55 years old (according to German research institute KFW).

In 2014 the US Senate offered validation for this emerging trend as well by hosting its first ever hearing on the topic of Senior Entrepreneurship, inviting a panel of experts such as *Senior Entrepreneurship Works* founder Elizabeth Isele. When asked by a Senator what her one recommendation to the committee would be, Isele responded "it's time to stop the prevalent gloom and doom attitude ... [and recognize] that seniors are assets not liabilities ... they represent a 'silver lining,' yielding golden dividends."

Her message was about seeing aging not as a societal problem but rather as an opportunity. In other words, to see hope instead of fear – and for plenty of aging workers, this range of opportunities to work or become entrepreneurs later in life is offering them exactly that.

Achieving The Bucket List

Of course, one of the benefits many people look forward to with aging is *not* having to work anymore – and instead to enjoy other pursuits, such as travel.

In its annual report on travel trends of Baby Boomers, the AARP estimates that 2016 will bring a "travel boom" as older travelers take more international "bucket list" trips and plan their trips further ahead – and primarily online. In a survey of top travel agents, wellness travel emerged as a rapidly growing category of travel among older travelers as people increasingly were seeking experiences that allow them to come back from a vacation feeling mentally *and* physically refreshed.

Luxury travel has long been seen as a category dominated by older adults who have the financial resources to spend on travel. These same travelers often organize (and pay for) family trips where large groups travel together to a destination.

Medical tourism, too, is a booming industry driven partially by a more active older generation wanting to optimize their finances and vacation time, while getting better or more luxurious treatment in the process.

All this travel, and the ability to connect with family through social media to share their experiences is contributing to this widespread optimism around aging as well. When you have the time and resources to enjoy experiential travel, work on your own schedule, use technology to offer ongoing mobility and have the chance to age in your own home – a rise in optimism around aging is an understandable result.

Why It Matters

There is no doubt a global demographic shift is underway as the worldwide population grows and people live longer than ever before. Whether you call it a second act, or a legacy career, or life past halftime – the point is that the expectations of the next generation of older people (and what younger generations expect *from* them) will be vastly different than in the past.

Thanks to growing technological help, renewed interest and focus on finding ways to use their unique skills in the workforce, an growth in "silver entrepreneurship" and a world that will need their individual skills and talents to help solve big societal challenges ... there is plenty of cause for optimistic aging leading into 2016 and beyond.

Who Should Use This Trend?

For years businesses have thought of their products as being promoted either to older people or not. In the coming year, this form of thinking will finally get left behind as more businesses realize these older people may already be their best underappreciated customers. No matter whether you are in the product or services side of business, this trend is first and foremost a valuable reminder not to forget about what could be a critical demographic filled with opportunity for your business.

The secondarily lesson from this chapter is that older consumers are likely to bring a new optimism to any interaction and will expect to see this optimism reflected back at them in communications and marketing. Understanding this sentiment, respecting it, and being strategic about how to use it (and when to depart from it) will be critical.

How To Use This Trend

✓ **Create programs to embrace older workers** – One of the subtrends this chapter mentioned was the practice of young startup companies hiring an Intern who had "life experience" to offer mentorship to younger less experienced workers. Embracing and finding ways to tap real life expertise from older workers can have a transformative effect on how an organization thinks, how younger workers mature and how the benefit of experience can provide reminders of long forgotten but still valuable legacy solutions to age old problems.

✓ **Avoid visual age bias** – Several years ago, a big priority among companies became making sure they were not unintentionally disrespecting diversity in imagery. Today, most stock images of groups feature people from multi-ethnic backgrounds and having diversity in images is a given. Unfortunately, this same lesson is woefully forgotten when it comes to age diversity. Using images of older consumers are not just for pharmaceutical ads or for typecasting them as doting grandparents. Brands in all industries need to work harder to be more inclusive in everyday imagery – featuring older adults alongside younger ones.

✓ **Listen more** – Something curious happens to most of us in our thirties and continues into our forties and fifties – we become more confident doers and less capable listeners. As we achieve more seniority, we are expected to offer answers instead of asking better questions. We all have something to learn if we can get better at listening. A good place to start is in any interactions the older generation. Taking time to benefit from someone else's life journey and earned wisdom is never a waste of time.

Chapter 7

B2BEYOND
MARKETING

What's the Trend?

Brands used to promoting their products or services to other businesses embrace their humanity, take inspiration from other sectors and think more broadly about effectively marketing to decision makers as people first and buyers second.

Sysco is the perfect example of a dominant B2B business in its industry. Since 1970, the company has been a preferred supplier of food to restaurants, healthcare facilities and other out of home food service providers. In 2014, the company had over $46 billion in sales and had more than 50,000 employees working to provide services to more than 425,000 customers around the world.

If they operated like most B2B businesses, you would expect that most of Sysco's marketing would focus on sponsoring trade shows, running print ads in food industry magazines and using a dedicated sales force to call upon restaurants on a regional basis. Like most other B2B brands, you would expect them to focus on being where the influencers were and targeting their message.

In fact, the brand has done all these things – until 2013 when it tried something different.

In that year, Sysco started a relationship with the *Food Network* which included having Chef Robert Irvine (star of the restaurant makeover show *Restaurant Impossible*) become an official Sysco brand ambassador. Since that time, he has spotlighted the quality of their ingredients and the importance of those ingredients in running a quality restaurant in nearly every episode.

The format of the show features "before" stories of everything from fridges filled with rotten milk and brown old produce to disorganized owners making convenience store trips to pick up ingredients they failed to order in advance. Each time, Chef Robert transforms this process by bringing in his preferred food supply partner – Sysco Corporation.

The integration of their services onto his show is one of the best examples of brand integration you are likely to see on network television today – but it may seem like an odd place to do it. After all, the vast majority of people watching *Restaurant Impossible* don't own restaurants and will never buy a single thing directly from Sysco. Yet *Food Network* ratings data shows that one of the most popular times of the day for viewing is the usually dead midnight to 4am time slot.

One possible explanation for the popularity of this time is that it overlaps with when restaurant owners working long shifts are getting home and decompressing. The numbers support this theory, as network data shows that more than 70% of independent restaurant owners watch the *Food Network* at least once a week.

For most consumers, the only "brand experience" they are likely to have with Sysco is driving alongside one of their trucks on the highway. Yet rather than limiting their marketing to trade media – Sysco is a perfect example of a new philosophy of *B2Beyond Marketing* where brands are focusing more on *humans* instead of *buyers* and the way they communicate.

Imagination Comes To Life

For years B2B marketers aimed to solve the same fundamental question: how can we best reach our extremely targeted niche audience at exactly the right time with the right information? Industry publications promised a straightforward solution to this challenge through print (and more recently digital) advertising. Industry events promised a solution through networking and bringing buyers and sellers together through trade shows and conferences.

General Electric is a brand that invests in both tactics – but across 2015 the brand won attention and praise for consistently thinking beyond these limitations to pioneer a new way of thinking about reaching business buyers. The shift is based on a simple but frequently forgotten insight: *B2B buyers are people first and buyers second.*

Years of B2B marketing has consistently obscured this fact.

Most of the time, B2B brands justify this choice as a strategic one, based on the reality that they are charged with promoting more "serious" products to professional audiences. Real time tweets about "dunking in the dark" during the Super Bowl or funny YouTube videos are fine if you're selling a cookie – but enterprise software (for example), is an entirely different story.

Over the past several years, GE has changed this script. Last year I rated the brand as the "most strategic brand in social media" and shared lessons from a session I fortunate to host at an event alongside GE CMO Beth Comstock about the role of storytelling in B2B marketing (see the article "How To Create A Brand Story" in Bonus Content section at the back of this book for a full recap of this session).

Today the brand is has a suite of marketing all designed to tell stories about the people behind the brand. A new set of TV spots launched in 2015, for example, focus on the human side of GE. One called "Childlike Imagination" features a little girl talking about what her mom does at GE and was launched alongside an emotional employee engagement effort which featured kids of real employees doing the same thing.

Another ad series called "What's the matter with Owen?" features an excited millennial-aged developer talking about getting a programming job with GE, while his incredulous developer friends ask "so, you'll be working on a train?" The tagline at the end sums up the message: "GE – The digital company. That's also an industrial company."

Moving into 2016 the brand will continue to focus on being more human by creating stories that, as GE global creative director Andy

Goldberg puts it, "capture the wonder and magic of what we do." The ambition is big for GE, as are the resources they are committing to the effort. Though they are one of the most prominent leaders, they are not the only B2B brand thinking creatively about how to tell their story in a human way. Other unexpected brands are trying the same strategy as well.

Making Construction Equipment Fun

Last year construction equipment manufacturer Caterpillar launched a video featuring a collection of industrial moving equipment with "names" like Cat 320E and Cat M316D set in a place called the Caterpillar Testing Facility facing off in an epic Jenga game with the object of removing 700 pound wooden blocks one by one from a tall stack until eventually the entire stack collapsed. The video rapidly went viral and has racked up more than 3 million views to date.

The point, says Caterpillar global brand creative director Archie Lyons, is "to take the Cat brand on the offensive. We are a large, Fortune 50 company … we want to go from cold, corporate and conservative to human, relevant and approachable."

The video series clearly does that – but the campaign has also faced common B2B industry criticism. How valuable are branded videos like this, skeptics ask, when they are most likely to be seen and shared by people who are *not* prospective buyers or qualified leads?

To answer, one analysis of the campaign described the potential value this way: "Caterpillar scored valuable sales points with prospective buyers without hitting them over the head with a sales pitch. And they built credibility for the brand by demonstrating the capabilities in a dramatic and very memorable manner."

A follow up quote from Lyons, when speaking about the potential value of these efforts, points to a similar theory – "the campaign is designed to reach people outside of our normal scope of customers. The viewer for these videos could be a teenage boy who likes to play Jenga, and he might show his mom and dad, or uncles, who may work in construction." The value, in other words, comes from starting conversations from person to person – which may eventually lead to consideration, growing reputation, and eventually purchase. Of course, these types of anecdotes also illustrate that being more human is a notoriously difficult business strategy to assign value against or measure quantifiably.

ROI of Epic Content

In a recent talk, Content Marketing Institute (CMI) founder Joe Pulizzi shared a telling insight from an upcoming 2016 research study: only 30 percent of B2B marketers rated their own organizations as using content marketing effectively – down eight percent from the previous year. Yet 83% of those same marketers admitted to having *some* strategy for content marketing and investing dollars into it. With all of these marketers investing in figuring out the power of content, why were so many admitting failure so early?

A big part of the reason stems from the temptation to look at an audience in terms of two distinct groups – people who are prospective customers … and everyone else. The problem with this point of view is that it leaves out nuanced audiences like business influencers and also fails to make the connection that B2B audiences are also consumers themselves.

When Volvo took the unusual step of launching an ad for the "dynamic steering" available on commercial trucks during the Super Bowl in 2014 – the mission was to get consumers of all kinds to reevaluate the brand through the highly impactful visual of aging action star Jean Claude Van Damme doing an "epic split" while balancing between two moving trucks.

The ad treated its business consumers as people first, and buyers second – a perfect example of *B2Beyond* thinking.

B2Beyond In Building

One industry that has dealt with this dual audience challenge since its inception is the building industry. When construction industry media firm Hanley Wood announced their top marketing brands of 2015, Marvin Windows and Doors was selected as the *2015 Brand Builder Awards*

Marketer of the Year. Citing the "cohesiveness of their campaigns, the platforms used and the results of this transformation," Hanley Wood CEO Peter Goldstone praised their brand reinvigoration and innovation.

Like most brands in the competitive residential, commercial design and construction industry – Marvin Windows' "Built Around You" campaign featured communications directly to consumers as well as targeted information to dealers. Like many other industries, in building trade industry buyers can be influenced by retail customer preferences and vice versa.

Dealing with this same truth, glass supplier PPG launched a series of explainer videos about glass and windows featuring a consumer friendly character called "Glenn the Glass Guy" explaining how to select the right type of window and comparing the thermal performance of different windows with different technology inside them. The videos are simultaneously detailed and basic – making the complexity of buying a product with which many non-trade consumers would have limited experience far less daunting.

Across the home building industry, this trend is leading to a new evolved model of thinking about the consumer and creating integrated content and messages that are appealing both to the trade professional and the residential consumer as well. Over time, this dual challenge for industries like this will lead to more of this B2Beyond thinking – and continued crossover of communications.

Why It Matters

In an opening presentation for the 2015 Business Marketing Association conference, Google exec Jim Lecinski shared insights from recent Millward Brown research, including a key finding that 46% of B2B buyers are now millennials – up from 27% when the survey was last conducted just two years ago.

In addition, the research online product searches had doubled in the past two years, yet the number of brands buyers were actively considering had dropped. In other words, online content was being used to allow buyers to be more selective and narrow their consideration lists earlier.

The implication is that B2B brands will need to do more to get on the radar of potential customers before those customers even identify a need – and they will have to do it using more untraditional forms of media that appeal to younger audiences. As a result the future of B2B marketing will be about creating better content, leveraging tactics and ideas that were once considered solely the realm of B2C brands, and ultimately building credibility by being more human.

Who Should Use This Trend?

Any B2B brand will be able to use the lessons in this trend to think more broadly about how they can create marketing and communications that engages people on a human level and then adds the detail and nuance afterwards to answer questions and provide value as part of the ongoing sales process.

How To Use This Trend

✓ **Make it fundamental** – When it comes to changing how we think about B2B marketing, much of the resistance comes from getting mired in the complexity of the message. How will an "ordinary" person understand what you want to say when they don't know your industry? Yet Volvo didn't fret over whether people would know what "dynamic steering" was, or even whether they would care. Their fundamental message was that Volvo technology can make driving surprisingly smooth – even if the driving experience happens to be two 18 wheeler trucks going backward with an action superstar balanced between them. People got the message.

✓ **Get over the fear of wastage** – It is easy to think that making your content and marketing available to a more broad audience will simply be irrelevant because people won't be interested. The reason most B2B advertising gets placed in trade media is because of fear that it won't be as relevant to anyone else. When Sysco partnered with the Food Network, they didn't worry about how many non-restaurant owners might see their message. Instead, they focused on the fact that if they told their story simply (we can get you fresh food!) – their target audience would get it, and act on it when they had a need.

Chapter 8

PERSONALITY MAPPING

What's the Trend?

As behavioral measurement tools like gaze tracking build a detailed map of our personalities, multiple industries will be able to use this information to bring likeminded people together and provide more transformative learning and bonding experiences.

For over 70 years the most popular method for assessing personalities was based off a vocational test for children to determine their potential future careers. The Myers-Briggs Type Indicator (MBTI) uses four pairs of temperament categories to define everyone with some nuanced version of 16 possible personality combinations. Despite routine criticism, the test has stood the test of time and is still widely used today.

This past year, a new method that started capturing the attention of the business world was developed by former ad agency executive Sally Hogshead based on the seven keys to holding attention from her book *Fascinate* (passion, power, prestige, mystique, alert, innovation, trust). Using these seven principles as the foundation, her latest book *How The World Sees You* uses your responses to a detailed questionnaire to assign one of 49 different "personality archetypes."

Each one uses a "primary and secondary advantage" along with an aspirational personality descriptor such as "The Artisan" or "The Trendsetter" to describe a person's best self, as well as offer tips on how to leverage your archetype. The early popularity of the model is a sign of our longstanding desire to better understand our own motivations and those of the people around us.

As the range of social data on our relationships online grows, and online behavior trackers measure every interaction – we are coming closer to taking the next step in understanding personality that goes far beyond how we might answer questions in a survey in order to have an algorithm place us into a predefined personality category.

This emerging promise of this increasingly detailed *Personality Mapping* will allow us to more deeply understand ourselves, and also allow companies to more efficiently target messages not by demographics or sociographics, but by personality types and behavioral tendencies.

This is not about personalization to the individual – but rather understanding and catering to our personality *type*, which might be very similar to thousands or even millions of others.

Driven by this trend, education will become more valuable as learning is more tailored by personality to maximize its efficiency. Travel and experiences will be built to connect us with like minded individuals who love what we love. And the workplace will see a shift as organizations get better about using personality mapping as a part of motivating teams and the recruiting and hiring process.

So if this map of personality could actually be done – a natural first question to ask is: how close are we to truly mapping anyone's personality in a deeper way than a four letter descriptor of who we are? To answer that, let's start with the technology behind this mapping itself and the one thing that much of it is focused on tracking … our faces.

The Windows To Personality

Thanks to the Hollywood film *Minority Report* – many consumers believe that the main reason for gaze tracking technology is so manipulative brands of the future can create ads that use your gaze to customize intrusive billboards with eerily personalized offers. Actually, the earliest efforts of gaze tracking had a far more noble ambition.

For example, a 2009 eye tracking study from Scotland on how people perceive threats confirmed the "fight or flight" theory that people's eyes naturally move more quickly to towards threatening faces and body postures. More recent studies have learned that consistent telltale patterns of eye movements can be used to diagnose conditions like autism or dyslexia in young children. Of course, since that early heritage, the tracking of our gaze and facial features has started to see plenty of commercial applications.

The most well-known example of this came in 2012 when Microsoft patented eye tracking in its Kinect gaming system – and later announced facial tracking advancements that could allow it to target ads by mood and emotion. As this research evolves, the combination of eye tracking and what is now being termed "facial coding" is leading to an interesting potential future where such technology could be used to determine more detailed aspects of our behavior and even to recognize us individually in a crowd based on our facial features or moods.

Of course, this potential for a true Interpol-style big brother execution of facial tracking that could recognize any of us raises plenty of ethical concerns. The real promise of this technology, however, goes beyond fears government monitoring.

If it were really possible to create a full map of personality in any moment, it could open innovation in many industries. Perhaps the most hopeful of them all is the education and learning space ... which could use personality mapping to reinvent the way any child or adult learns a new skill in the future.

The Most Advanced Schools on Earth

In the past several years, one of the fastest growing spaces in education has been massively open online courses (MOOCs), which are helping to augment or replace traditional learning models. As more people go through these courses, the data they are generating about learning is huge.

On educational website edX, for example, over a million people engaged with one of nearly 70 courses across the past two years and all these students generated more than a billion clicks through their activities. On the Coursera platform, the most popular calculus class (lovingly called MOOCulus) features Ohio State math professor Jim Fowler teaching calculus using props like a blow up balloon or stick figure puppets.

But how do we know any of these courses are working? Rather than relying on periodic knowledge testing, the future of learning involves factoring a student's learning personality more heavily into the experience.

The AltSchool in San Francisco is one experiment designed to do exactly that. Founded a year and a half ago by former Google head of personalization Max Ventilla, these set of four schools now use data gathering technology to measure all aspects of student interactions and use the data to make teachers and their lessons more effective.

The school has already raised more than $133 million in funding and aims to open several more schools in 2016. Another example from the same region is generating even more interest thanks mainly to the man behind it: Salman Khan, founder of Khan Academy.

While it may seem like an odd choice for the creator of the largest and most successful online library for learning to create a real life school – this was always Khan's big ambition. Online learning can only take you so far. And it is no replacement for face to face real life learning. So Khan's new school also uses new open techniques and sophisticated analytics to track each students progress and let them work at their own pace as well.

As quantified learning tools and online classrooms give the ability to collect more data on learning styles, students can continually be segmented into personality based groups that go beyond the usual categories of visual, aural or verbal learners. This new model of learning involves using personality mapping as a critical part of helping education itself to become more useful around any topic.

The same method is also being used to create more opportunities to have travel experiences with people who share similar things based on their personality.

Nerds, Elephant Safaris & Personalized Travel

Just over a year ago, *WIRED* magazine Articles Editor Adam Rogers shared the story of a memorable trip he took on the "nerd cruise" – an annual fan cruise called the JoCo Cruise Crazy, organized by singer-songwriter Jonathan Coulton. The six-year-old cruise is described as a "summer camp for nerds" and attracts passionate fans, geek celebrities like Wil Wheaton and John Hodgman, and over 800 people each year.

Baked into the experience is a powerful trend that is tilting the future of travel towards more memorable experiences tailored perfectly to their personality – no matter how quirky. In fact, brands and professional consultants alike are making this type of travel a commonplace reality.

Leading bespoke travel advisory firm Brown + Hudson is one example. The group redefines what travel can be for their clients by mapping travel experiences to the personalities of the travelers and creating some of the world's most unique experiences. The world renowned Oberoi Hotels & Resorts group features exotic vacation packages that are customized for a traveler's personality with everything from elephant safaris to textile printing classes.

In addition to being a conduit to amazing regional experiences like the Oberoi, hotel brands are also stepping up their efforts to become personality-driven creative hubs for travelers seeking more unique and authentic travel experiences. The W hotel brand from Starwood Hotels was one of the earliest pioneers of the modern boutique hotel trend en masse with its runaway success that landed the brand in *Fast Company* magazine recently as one of the "20 moments from the past 20 years that moved the whole world forward."

More recently over the past year, there has been an explosion in growth among both independent and large hotel group funded boutique properties. The newly launched Proper Hotels group aims to create "hotels that [are] proud emblems of the local culture." Marriott's new Moxy brand features 24 hour communal areas and board games, and its EDITION brand aims to create "cultural epicenters" – with early properties planned in New York, London and Istanbul. Hilton has its Curio brand as well as its upcoming Canopy brand dedicated to incorporating local culture at a lower price tier.

This personality driven trend with boutique hotels is also moving outside of the usual big cities as well. Destination Hotels, for example, opened its first Quirk Hotel in the unexpected market of Richmond, Virginia to early accolades for offering something different in that traditional southern city. Even the W hotel, after introducing the boutique style to large cities, has plans in the coming year to nearly double its properties from a current 47 worldwide to add another 40-plus in development – many of which will be outside of the largest cities and create landmarks of their own.

All of these efforts are driven by a single insight about the business and leisure traveler alike. In a world where consumers are increasingly being tailored to on a more personal level (see my 2015 trend *Everyday Stardom* for more on this point), the travel brands that stand out are the ones that bring their own personality and match it to the personalities of their ideal customers.

The more the industry learns about the personalities of guests and of the cities themselves, the more these experiences will be tailored to bring out the best and most interesting of each.

Programmatic Advertising & The Perfect Pet

The final place where the trend of Personality Mapping also figures prominently is with one of the hottest topics of the past year in the world of marketing – programmatic advertising. The term refers to growing use of automated tools to ensure messages can hit the right people at the right time.

In one recent example, an animal shelter from California used digital targeting to find the perfect pet-owner matches. If you were a single woman who was an avid reader, you saw an ad for a cute cuddly cat. If you were athletic guy who loved hiking, you saw an ad for an energetic Jack Russell Terrier. The campaign was billed as the world's first pet adoption drive driven by programmatic media. It is also a sign of how mapping our personalities through the content we share online will be increasingly valuable for marketers.

Facial coding software from startups like Affectiva and Emotient are offering even more ability to customize messages to personalities. Both are currently used to test potential ad effectiveness and to compare different creative executions.

All this innovation in ad-tech will bring plenty more crossover battles, consolidation, acquisition and the occasional smart integration in the coming year. Over time the industry will eventually see the value in sharing data, consumers will see more messages tailored perfectly to their personality and enticing them to act based on exactly what they love or already want.

Why It Matters

The enormous side effect of all the programmatic efforts at personalization in marketing is the fact that all this data we are collecting on human behavior will finally allow us to create richer and more meaningful maps of human personality – and see ourselves beautifully quantified within them. As Personality Mapping draws complex, nuanced, specific conclusions about the sort of person we are and aspire to be, how we learn and what we believe – industries of all kinds will find new ways to use this data to architect more impactful experiences of all kinds.

Learning will be more effective catered to individual personalities. Travel will be more immersive and powerful when it takes passions and triggers into account. Marketing can become more uplifting and effective when personality mapping is layered on top. With the positive potential, though, also comes the danger of manipulation.

As organizations of all kinds gain the ability to mine our personality data, publishers could use it to exploit us by creating more sensational media to prey on our worst fears. Marketers could use these insights to push our triggers around insecurities we already have and entice us to spend money to "fix" them. Yet this potential for misuse will not overcome the vast potential for this trend and the brands that use it for good will find new loyal connections to be made with consumers who feel validated by the personal touch offered to them.

Who Should Use This Trend?

Any organization struggling with the potential for how to leverage data to better understand their consumers will find value in this new way of thinking. For brands used to thinking about consumers not in terms of demographics but in terms of personas – this type of thinking will make perfect intuitive sense. For others, the act of thinking in terms of how to group consumers by personality drivers will lead them toward a more nuanced view of their consumers that will inspire more personal messages and effective communications.

How To Use This Trend

✓ **Map your audience personality segments** – One of the most valuable ways to think about this trend is in relation to how you can start to segment your audience with personality. As you do, you can start to take a persona driven view where you see the people you most want to reach not in terms of relatively meaningless numbers like age or post code, but in terms of the things they are most passion about and would themselves describe as the beliefs that define them.

✓ **Be a convener of personality** – There is a powerful role that organizations can often take as conveners to bring likeminded people together. The up side of having more data on the personality drivers of your audience is that you can decide what common interest or shared belief they all hold and then convene your own gathering based on that. Not only will you be providing a chance for people who share interests and passions to gather (which everyone loves) – but you'll also have a chance to build a deeper connection with the most loyal and engaged personalities who show up as well.

Chapter 9

BRANDED UTILITY

What's the Trend?

Brands use a combination of content marketing and greater integration between marketing and operations to augment promotions with real ways to add value to customers' lives..

If there is one brand engineered to profit from every question you ask online, it is Google. In September of 2015, the brand published a blog post on "micro-moments"—proposing four common moments of need when consumers seek information via its search engine. The key to successful marketing for any brand, according to Google, is to find a way to provide relevant useful information in any of these moments.

The moments were described through a matching set of simple phrases: I want to go; I want to do; I want to know; and I want to buy. Each described a different trigger based on what the consumer was looking for, but Google's advice for reaching them in each micro-moment came down to one fundamental principle—be useful.

This quest to provide value through usefulness is at the heart of the rise in interest among brands over the past several years in content marketing. To describe this trend, *Branded Utility* was the phrase I first used two years ago in the 2014 Non-Obvious Trend Report. In that year, a series of bestselling books from well-known marketing authors like Jay Baer (*Youtility*), Mitch Joel (*Ctrl Alt Delete*), and Ann Handley (*Everybody Writes*) also offered insights into how to create content that consistently provides value and utility.

In the two years since, this ambition to create valuable marketing has exploded in importance as empowered consumers continually get savvier and the technology to filter out traditional interruptive forms of advertising gets better and more predictive.

My original description of this trend included the stories of several brands like Charmin and KLM creating smart but short-lived promotions to offer instant value to consumers in exchange for fleeting brand engagement. Over time, this focus on quick and flashy promotional campaigns has shifted to something deeper.

In industries from consumer electronics to financial services, the idea of creating "brand channels" for content to be delivered on a longer timeframe and a corresponding focus on integration versus sponsorships is transforming what *Branded Utility* means for the future of marketing.

Brand Magazines

Intel is a brand that has spent the past decade rethinking the role of content in its overall marketing strategy. For years the brand has been a pioneer with social media, enticing employees to start well-read internal and public blogs, and routinely investing in bigger content initiatives. The iQ by Intel web magazine, for example, is a tech culture hub with the mission of "bringing you deeper into the lives of people and the technologies they are using to change the world." The magazine has a team of internal content creators focused on building top-quality stories and continually updating it with new articles on fashion, sports, gaming, lifestyles, and many other diverse topics.

Another high-profile example that has become the gold standard on producing valuable, business-oriented content for a professional audience is American Express' long-standing Open Forum online magazine dedicated to offering advice for entrepreneurs and small-business owners. While Intel and American Express' examples are multiyear efforts focused on the web, there are also several brands investing in producing content and creating engagement through print magazines as well.

One such effort with the longest tenure is *The Furrow*—a 120-year-old magazine focused on the farming industry and published by John Deere. Most airlines also produce monthly branded magazines, including mainstream publications that are placed into every seat-back pocket and more exclusive efforts like United Airlines' first-class–only publication, *Rhapsody*.

Even mobile-first brands launched for the sharing economy are finding strategic uses for magazines. Airbnb created its 100+-page glossy magazine, called *Pineapple*, specifically for insiders who host or stay at Airbnb properties. Uber has a far less professional 15-page printed magazine/newsletter for its drivers, called *Momentum*, which inspired viral online ridicule for its lack of quality and its promotional nature.

Whether mocked or appreciated, the past year brought many such new efforts from brands to make a bigger commitment to long-term content initiatives like branded magazines as opposed to attention-grabbing content schemes focused on short-lived social media posts.

The "Appquisition" Spree

If you were the creator of a popular app in the fitness, financial, or productivity space, 2015 might have been a very good year.

Under Armour spent $560 million in 2015 to buy MyFitnessPal and Endomondo, after spending $150 million in 2013 to acquire the MapMyFitness app. Matching these moves, Adidas spent an estimated $240 million to acquire Austrian fitness app Runtastic. The presumed intent of this acquisition frenzy among sports clothing makers was to add a layer of utility to each brand's clothing and footwear in an industry where consumer expectations are rapidly evolving beyond fashion or fit and more into performance and integrated technology.

In the financial services industry, the past year has also seen a similar string of "appquisitions" as plenty of long-standing bank and credit card brands aim to augment the basic functionality of their own apps, which offer necessary features, like balance reviews and check scanning, with more visual dashboard tools and advice to help customers better manage their money.

Early in 2015, for example, Capital One acquired startup Level Money, which included its smart spending and financial literary tools. The past year also saw plenty of controversy and debate in the financial services industry over the growing role of "robo-advisors" and how automated financial advice based on dispassionate assessments of algorithms and financial trends might pose a threat to the livelihood of traditional (human) financial advisors.

Apps have always been used for productivity tools as well, and Microsoft was among the technology brands investing in effectively buying more utility by acquiring calendar app Sunrise to add more valuable functionality to the Outlook app.

In 2016 these appquisitions will add more functionality, get integrated, and start to factor into the overall experience for customers.

Teaching the World to Grill

Before content marketing was en vogue, outdoor grill maker Weber was quietly implementing a masterful book-publishing strategy to own the market by being the brand that helps educate consumers on how to grill.

To accomplish this vision, for more than a decade, Weber has been producing a string of cookbooks under its own brand or in partnership with celebrity chefs, all designed to inform and educate home cooks and grill masters on how to marinate, cook, and serve amazing grilled food for any occasion.

Today, the brand's content marketing reach extends far beyond printed books and into useful recipe apps, video tutorials, online tools, and even a robust online community known as Weber Nation. All of these content features allow the dialogue about grilling to extend far outside of books alone. All of this learning material combined offers the best value in the world to anyone trying to cook a great meal. It is also a perfect example of the potential *Branded Utility* has when it is done right.

If you can answer consumer questions and continually create valuable content, it is possible to own an entire educational category and promote your brand in the process.

Why It Matters

The underlying reason why consumers respond so well to content is because much of it provides value in the form of utility. While there will always be a place for great branded entertainment like a sponsored film or an entertaining, 30-second spot that tugs at the heartstrings, Branded Utility is where the most powerful opportunity for using content to connect with consumers exists. The brands that find ways to create more of this utility—either with smart branded investments into online or print magazines, or through appquisitions to build a foundation for offering mobile utility—will be the biggest winners in 2016.

Who Should Use This Trend?

The companies that can benefit most directly from branded utility are the same ones that offer products and services where significant education has value. Learning how to use a grill or manage your finances, for example, are categories where educational content has a high value for customers. Anytime a brand can take this role of educator or help solve a problem through functionality that is immediately useful, they can eventually stand out.

How to Use This Trend

✓ **Address Bigger Issues** – It is often said that the best products solve a problem for consumers. The only downside of this assumption is that it can lead many brands and teams to become so focused on finding and solving one specific problem that they forget to think more broadly about their customers' world outside that problem. Sometimes the most valuable content and utility you can provide focuses on being helpful rather than just solving a problem simply because you want to sell the solution.

✓ **Answer Unexpected Questions** – One of the most important elements of utility is providing an answer to customers' questions, particularly those they don't expect you to answer. One brand that uses this principle to its benefit is Hilton, which has spent the last few years building the Twitter handle @HiltonSuggests to answer travel-related questions from anyone, regardless of whether they happen to be staying in a Hilton property or not. The brand has used the handle to tweet nearly 40,000 times already, with the vast majority being direct tweets to individuals. Imagine the response from potential consumers and word-of-mouth from surprised people if you could offer a similar level of unexpected utility.

Chapter 10

MAINSTREAM MULTICULTURALISM

What's the Trend?

After years of being ignored niche demographics, multicultural citizens and their cultures find new widespread acceptance through growing integration of diverse ideas and people in entertainment, products and politics.

If the Kardashians get replaced as reality television's family to watch in 2016 ... it may be the Keswanis that do it.

On the most basic prerequisite level, the California based Indian family has plenty of natural family drama to pull from. The heads of the family are "doctor dad" Anil and "momager" Vaishali who left a career as an optometrist to manage the exploding social media popularity of her son "Big Nik." Nik, who suffers from a rare form of dwarfism, has managed to build a loyal following of more than 2.5 million fans for his Vine videos. Rounding out the made-for-reality-TV family are his 15 year old aspiring beauty pageant star sister Sarina and 6 year old "transgender princess" sister Devina (originally born Dev).

Riding a strategic marketing wave generated by People magazine's prediction that they will become "America's new obsession" – their popular new web series launched in 2015 (on People.com) and was called *The Keswanis: A Most Modern Family.*

The Keswanis seem perfectly scripted to challenge our long standing beliefs and stereotypes about multiculturalism in entertainment, but if you watch several of the short pilot webisodes even their story is surprisingly, well, normal. And that is the truth at the heart of this trend of *Mainstream Multiculturalism.*

When AdAge magazine interviewed NBC Entertainment President Jennifer Salke about this rise in diversity on TV, she shared what she had heard reflected back in focus groups from their audience: "I am so sick of the word 'diverse' ... our kids don't think about words like 'diverse.' Instead it's all just 'mainstream.'" What is now called "mainstream" took years to arrive at this point.

Outsiders Get Inside

Multiculturalism in the past was a favorite device used in television and films to tell outsider "fish out of water" style stories (like the 2002 film *My Big Fat Greek Wedding*). The bias still seems evident in popular programs like *Blackish* and *Fresh Off The Boat*, which both feature central characters struggling to fit into the world around them – yet the stories have also shifted dramatically.

In *Blackish*, Anthony Anderson's main character of Andre (Dre) is an African American advertising executive in an industry that has traditionally lacked diverse leaders. His antics in the show, and its title of "Blackish," are based on the challenges he encounters in embracing his new culturally blended family and his own evolving identity as a black man.

Fresh Off The Boat takes a nostalgic look at the immigrant struggle to fit in back in the 90s from the modern perspective of a first generation Chinese teenager played by Hudson Yang. The show is narrated by the grown up version of this character, who represents the Millenial/GenXer of today who has grown up with a far more blended cultural identity.

The theme in both stories is that diverse stories about outsiders are no longer about the hilarity of being outsiders, but rather about the hilarity of being insiders. In other words, diversity in entertainment is going thoroughly mainstream. Even *My Big Fat Greek Wedding* is getting a newly integrated update in March 2016 with a sequel produced nearly 15 years after the original, featuring the same characters dealing with a troubled teenage daughter who typifies this new "blended" generation.

This mainstreaming of the outsider may be evident in entertainment, and it is a logical place to start with discussing this trend – but Mainstream Multiculturalism extends far beyond movies and television. Far reaching parts of our lives, from eating to elections, are now reflecting this new reality and businesses of all kinds will need to have a strategy to react in 2016.

Cultural Condiments

When Huy Fong Foods, maker of the popular Sriracha hot sauce, finally opened their factory doors in April of 2014 – it was dubbed by some media as a "Willy Wonka" moment. Rather than being inspired by finding his successor, though, the 69 year old founder David Tran was trying to make a point.

Just a few months earlier, local council representatives in Irwindale, California had filed a lawsuit declaring the factory a "public nuisance" after a handful of residents had complained about "stinging fumes" causing asthma, heartburn and teary eyes. The move caused a partial shut down of the factory and triggered worldwide attention.

Tran's decision to invite the media in to see the factory (and its environmentally safe processes) was a shrewd PR strategy which eventually led to the lawsuit being dropped just over a month later. Yet the case also led to an unexpected side effect – a US-wide panic from consumers over the fear that their beloved sriracha sauce may no longer be available.

The panic led thousands of consumers to horde bottles of their precious sauce, and cemented the cult popularity of Sriracha that had been growing for more than a decade. Though Tran keeps sales figures secret, it is estimated that the company is now worth more than $60 million and that they sell more than 20 million bottles a year. The brand has also become a centerpiece in the dialogue happening in food circles today about the growing multicultural influence on the consumer palate of the future.

In November of 2015, *Fast Company* chronicled this multicultural evolution of the condiment aisle, sharing that "exotic flavors have quietly crept into restaurants and supermarkets ... resulting in an explosion in hot sauce sales, which have grown by more than 150% since 2000—more than ketchup, mayonnaise, mustard and barbecue sauce combined. The fiery condiment is now the foundation of a billion-dollar industry."

Desperate to retain their market share, even the traditional mainstays of the grocery aisle are fighting back with new exotic creations of their own. The nearly 150 year old Tabasco brand has launched their own sriracha, chipotle and habanero flavored versions. Heinz has sriracha and jalapeno flavored ketchup and A1 Steak Sauce comes a spicy chipotle flavor. Spice maker McCormick even named Japanese 7 Spice as a flavor trend to watch for 2015.

The evolution of our palates is one symbol of mainstream multiculturalism – but it is only a small slice of the overall shift. There is also a shift taking place in politics in business, brought to life most recently by the early moves of the charismatic young prime minister of Canada.

"Because it's 2015"

For most politicians, their most memorable tag lines will typically come as part of their campaigning efforts or on the debate stage when confronting their opponents. For newly elected Canadian Prime Minister Justin Trudeau, that line came less than a week into his administration when he introduced his 30 person cabinet – the first ever to include a gender balanced 15 men and 15 women.

When asked by the media why gender equality was so important, he answered simply "because it's 2015." The words struck a chord and his press conference and simple answer quickly went viral online. In the process, he became a champion for diversity and the symbol of a new kind of politician who would be willing to do more than simply talk about creating more diversity.

This model of team diversity is one that some forward thinking businesses are trying hard to match as well.

Almost every Fortune 500 large brand has some type of diversity and inclusive hiring initiative aimed at attracting a more diverse workforce. Carnival, the parent company for nine different cruise lines is one recent example. In the past two years, seven of the nine heads of the different lines have been replaced. Among the newcomers, *BusinessWeek* reports, "four are now women, one is black and one is gay, a big change in a business that was an offshoot of the European, male-dominated shipping industry."

The strategy at Carnival was to intentionally a way to foster a "diversity of thinking," as CEO Arnold Donald described it. "I guarantee if you get a diverse group of people aligned around a common objective with a process to work together, they will out-engineer, out-solution a homogeneous team 90 percent of the time and created things none of them alone would have created." The strategy has been working as Carnival's share price rose 53% during Arnold's first year on the job, and net income during that period rose 15% as well.

Over the past year this connection between diversity of hiring and success has created pressure to change in many other industries as well. In one example from the world of higher education, Yale University administrators responded to student demands by pledging to do more to encourage faculty diversity through a $50 million dollar initiative.

The point of view they all routinely share is to remind the world that the demographics of the next generation are slowly shifting and our culture is becoming more and more blended with multiple ethnicities mixing together. This blending is causing a dramatic shift in the $200 billion beauty industry as well.

Ethnic Beauty

In the early 1990s, Somali born supermodel Iman was approaching the peak of her career. Once described by fashion icon Yves Saint-Laurent as his "dream woman" – she appeared on dozens of magazine covers, in feature films and was even invited to play the queen Cleopatra in Michael Jackson's iconic music video for the song Remember The Times.

Iman was also a pioneer in the world of ethnic beauty, founding her own self branded cosmetics firm in 1994 focusing on difficult to find shades for women. For most of the two decades since that time, the world of ethnic beauty products was driven by niche companies like Iman's – mostly created by entrepreneurs dissatisfied with the limited selection of mainstream beauty products.

M·A·C Cosmetics, for example, was founded by a photographer and a beauty salon owner in Canada frustrated by the lack of colors that would shoot well with photography. Fashion Fair was a cosmetics brand created for women of color by the late Eunice W. Johnson and eventually became the largest Black-owned cosmetics company in the world.

Meanwhile large brands like Lancôme, Avon and Cover Girl experimented for years with reaching more diverse audiences through creative advertising and spokesmodel deals with "ethnic" celebrities like Salma Hayek (Avon) or Lupita Nyong'o (Lancôme).

So what is different today? In 2016, the longtime separated niche of ethnic beauty will no longer be seen as separate.

Oru Mohiuddin, a senior analyst at the Euromonitor International beauty desk, sees this trend clearly supported by the numbers. In a prescient blog post from 2013, she predicted that "ethnic beauty is poised for a boom," citing examples of increased R&D spending on developing lines for a wider range of consumers.

There are plenty of industry examples to support her theory. Yves Saint-Laurent's Le Teint Touche Éclat foundation reportedly spent nine years researching over 7000 global skin tones before finally launching their "perfect" 22 shades to reflect the full range of skin tones from around the world. L'Oréal recently relocated its multicultural beauty research to its main innovation hub in New Jersey. The brand also acquired Niely Cosméticos in Brazil and is opening an innovation center in Rio by the end of 2016.

The shift is even affecting brands founded to offer options to ethnic women in the first place. Brands from Cover FX, Fashion Fair and Carol's Daughter (all brands first started to cater to ethnic customers) are now expanding to target a broader audience regardless of ethnicity. Even Iman Cosmetics has noticed the shift, recently using more Asian,

Latina, Middle Eastern and Native American models in their ads and testing products on a broader range of women.

As Iman told *Women's Wear Daily*, "I was admittedly comfortable with Iman Cosmetics being identified as a beauty brand that filled the gap for black women because it was deeply personal for me. However, as we gathered more information about the game we were in, we started to shift into the more holistic vision that we are known for now throughout our positioning and advertising: Women of all skin tones want to look good when they rule the world."

Why It Matters

In 2015 the world saw a range of pioneers like Canadian Prime Minister Justin Trudeau and Somali-American supermodel Iman commit to the idea that multiculturalism was no longer something that describes the outsiders in our culture. Through evolving entertainment, food and culture – we are now starting to see the influence of ethnicity change the way that we see our world today. It is powering a shift in how the younger generations view themselves and a far more inclusive view of those who they consider part of their culture ... no matter how different they look. Over 2016, this blending of culture will continue to offer new opportunities for fresh thinking when it comes to diversity in marketing messages, the range of new mashup-style products and services people will crave, and what it truly means to belong to any group or culture.

Who Should Use This Trend?

For years multiculturalism and diversity have been seen as something to worry about for the future. Audiences were changing, customers were evolving and cities were getting more blended. This point of view is officially outdated. Audiences have *already* changed. The implications of this are important for anyone in an industry that still holds onto the older assumptions about who a target audience is or where they come from. If you are in an industry has longstanding biases about the demographics of common customers, this trend should be a more urgent call to change your thinking and prepare for a future where those old assumptions break down and shift profoundly.

How To Use This Trend

✓ **Rethink your imagery** – One of the areas that is most easy to reveal unintended bias is in the imagery we choose to use for describing what we do and who we do it for. A key way to start thinking about this trend on a very small level is to run an audit of all the communications materials you use and what types of people are illustrated in them. Across print materials, websites, advertising and anywhere else – the question to ask is whether the diversity reflected there truly reflects the diversity in the world around your business. If not, focus on changing it.

✓ **Hire for unexpected diversity** – It is one thing to decide that you will hire someone with a different background than the rest of your team. It is another to give someone a chance who comes from outside your industry or has a diverging point of view shaped by having a cultural background unlike your own. Part of the challenge with building a more diverse work-force is seeing that diversity not as a checkbox to be marked – but rather as a unique element of someone's overall qualifications to be a valuable member of your team.

Chapter 11

EARNED CONSUMPTION

What's the Trend?

The desire for authentic experiences leads to a willingness from consumers to earn their right to consume, and offers businesses the chance to build more loyalty and engagement by letting consumers "pay" for products or services with more than money.

When a highly anticipated mobile app launches – there is a predictable frenzy that has now become commonplace among early adopters. People clamor to be first to get access and become "alpha" or "beta" users. Gaining access has become an achievement worth sharing with friends. And in the past several years, several iconic app launches have perfected the roadmap for how to incite this frenzy.

When Google launches products now, they often provide extremely limited access and give every user only a few invites to selectively invite others. The strategy is a masterful way to build a network of close connections by ensuring the first wave is only made up of close friends.

When the now shuttered *Mailbox* app launched several years ago – they landed on a strategy of creating a counter on their homepage for the nearly 400,000 users who signed up. Everyone was assigned a number and could watch the counter tick downwards to their number. People knew exactly how long until they had access and shared their anticipation and excitement online.

What each of these launches illustrated was that there could be a strange power in giving consumers a chance to "earn" their access. Dozens of subsequent app launches started promising to put people on the waitlist and took it one step further by allowing them to even faster early access in exchange for activities like tweeting about the launch or inviting 5 friends to join the list. One app called Trak.io even charged users $29 to jump their beta waiting list.

While this might easily be dismissed as the odd behavior of app-addicted technophiles wanting in on the next big thing – the practice of letting consumers *earn* the right to buy and consume a product or experience has been growing for years.

A decade ago, consumers were lining up outside Apple stores the night before an iPod release in order to earn their chance to purchase a $500 device. For even longer people have accepted waiting as the necessary price for access to everything from country club memberships to season tickets for popular sports teams.

Yet today the big change is that this act of earning our consumption is increasingly seen as a badge of honor rather than an inconvenience. The earning process is part of the joy of the experience itself. In some cases, it is even giving us a chance to make a greater impact on the world at the same time.

Voluntourist Pride

Fathom is unique new cruising brand from industry leader Carnival Cruise Lines. The vision for the brand is to puts social impact at the heart of everything it does. Tailored for twenty to thirty somethings who aspire to do more good in the world, the cruise eschews luxury excursions in favor of seven day trips with "voluntourism" stops in countries like the Dominican Republic and Cuba (one destination is chosen per cruise) to work alongside locals and non-profits on activities like planting trees or making ceramic water filters.

The ship is one of the most prominent examples of multiple travel industry experiences catering to this emerging desire among conscientious travelers to make an impact in some way beyond simply spending money in a local economy.

In Scotland, for example, a tiny independent bookstore called The Open Book in Scotland offers an Airbnb listing for a room above the retail establishment that comes with a forty hour per week job in the bookstore itself – literally allowing you to earn your consumption of the room.

On the more extravagant side, a luxury tour to Africa with the hefty price tag of $250,000 allows travelers to partake in a once in a lifetime experience of helping a group called Rhinos Without Borders to sedate and move a live Rhino from high risk areas in South Africa to the relatively safer bush in Botswana.

While many of these "voluntourism" experiences have their fair share of detractors who criticize that they marginalize causes and people, or don't generate as much true impact as they promise … the fact is their prevalence is rising and the consumer desire for travel with social purpose is on the rise.

There are also growing examples of how consumers can earn their experiences by "paying" in the form of charitable work or monetary contributions outside the travel industry as well. One of the more surprising passion areas with increasing examples of charitable integration is gaming.

Gaming and Coding For Good

Among gaming fans, "speedrunning" is the standard term to describe the practice of expert gamers using skill and masterful tricks to make it through every level of a game in as little time as possible. The Awesome Games Done Quick (AGDQ) Conference is an annual gathering of several hundred of these expert and aspiring speedrunners to celebrate the craft and share tips and techniques. The event is also an unlikely example of earned consumption.

As gamers rapidly make their way through games, tasks and challenges are imagined for them and bid on in real time – encouraging them to take a detour, or save trapped animals or accomplish some other in game task. The bids and results are tallied in real time and the frenzy from those in the room as well as those interacting with the community online is electric. And it is profitable.

This past year, that single event raised more than $1.57 million to donate to charity. Why for charity instead of for profit? As founder Andrew Schroeder explains it, "without charity you would come away feeling happy you met new friends but you would not have an overwhelming sense of accomplishment and community pride."

Another interesting example comes from Free Code Camp, an organization that allows newly educated programmers to test their real life coding skills and team work ethic by collaborating with others to build apps and tools for nonprofits. The project teams are offered plenty of support through online training videos and tutorials and the experience allows them to earn experience which they can showcase as part of a job search.

It is this sense of accomplishment that explains one of the most powerful emotional drivers behind the trend of Earned Consumption itself – namely, that you simply feel better about an experience if you believe you *earned* your chance to be part it.

This sense of accomplishment and the emotional payoff of earned consumption is also a surprisingly common strategy baked into some of the most sought after dining experiences in the world.

How To Dine At Secret Restaurants

Totoraku is one of the most curious five star dining experiences you have never heard of.

The menu is made up almost entirely of beef served as a multicourse experience, and the not-so-secret method for landing a reservation typically involves either a personal invitation from chef Kaz Oyama, or an invitation from a previous diner who is lucky enough to have Oyama's personal contact details. The rules for obtaining these details are as elaborate as the meal itself.

Diners are requested to bring a bottle of wine – which will be sampled by the chef himself. If the wine is deemed up to par, you may be lucky enough to earn access to make a future reservation via a secret phone number hand written on a white business card by the chef himself. Totoraku gives diners a chance to earn the chance to dine, and it is far from the only exclusive restaurant to use this strategy.

Noma in Amsterdam has an estimated 20,000 people vying for a spot when online reservations open on the 6th of every month. Sukiyabashi Jiro is nearly impossible to get into without a Japanese host joining you and a good deal of persistence. Minibar, a tiny restaurant from celebrity chef Jose Andres serving a 30 course meal with only 12 spots per seating, opens reservations for any date one month ahead of time and typically sells out within 15 minutes.

Aside from making reservations hard to get, some restaurants are also making diners earn their consumption *experience* as well. The Dans le Noir restaurant in Paris is famous for its practice of requiring all diners to eat in absolute pitch black – so they can encounter the flavors in the food completely and without the distraction of sight. "The Rock" is a destination restaurant in Zanzibar which requires a boat (or extremely low tide) in order to reach.

On the surface, all this manufactured difficulty might seem like needless hubris. Why put diners through such angst simply in the name of fueling a reputation for exclusivity? This, however, is only part of the intent. As the restaurant industry mostly knows, and other industries are slowly discovering – earned consumption can make the payoff much bigger. In a world where gratification is instant and it seems everything has its price, the idea of being a disempowered consumer has a reverse appeal.

Sometimes we are delighted to work for the right to consume.

Other times, however, earned consumption can become just an alternative form of currency or a method for paying with our time and attention instead of our money. To explore further how this model is most commonly used, let's turn to the world of media and publishing.

The Online Earnwall

Media disruption in recent years has led publishers and producers to generally adopt one of two strategies to monetize their content: put valuable content behind a "paywall," or find more creative ways to capture advertising dollars through publishing "native advertising" created with editorial style and placed alongside non-advertising content.

A little over a year ago, a UK based startup launched a platform called Sharewall realized that there could be a third method for monetizing content based on users completing desirable actions to "earn" their right to consume and unlock premium content without subscribing or paying in hard cash.

This same concept of earned access to content is common with popular gaming apps that integrate advertising and give users some type of incentive in the form of loyalty points or unlocked features in exchange for watching content that the app charges advertisers to place. The most well known example of this is Perk, a platform that offers users loyalty points in exchange for watching videos or other advertiser sponsored content.

As the media and mobile gaming industries continue to evolve new models for monetizing their content and experiences, this idea of an "earnwall" where consumers can engage in desirable online activities or respond to challenges in order to earn their consumption of paid content will become increasingly common.

Why It Matters

Earned Consumption is a trend that lies at the center of several big cultural shifts which by now are perfectly obvious to anyone reading this book. Consumers are seeking more meaningful and authentic experiences. They want to be part of something that offers them social capital to share with friends and family online and offline. And they are increasingly influenced by purpose and want to engage with companies that offer something positive into the world.

In 2016, each of these observations above have become so ubiquitously discussed that it's not a stretch to call them truisms – statements that describe our world in ways that we have already heard many times before. What is different this year is the trend they have sparked amongst consumers who have increasingly become used to and even willfully seeking out chances to earn their consumption in multiple ways.

From welcoming charitable work programs into their travel experiences, to using their social capital to promote new technology or navigate "earnwalls," to chasing impossible reservations at elite restaurants – consumers are assigning the most value to the experiences they are forced to work hardest to access and increasingly wear that access as a badge of honor.

Who Should Use This Trend?

This trend could easily be misconstrued as an invitation to make an experience worthlessly complex. Just because consumers want to earn their experiences more frequently doesn't mean you should intentionally break something that is already working well simply in the name of trying to creating more intrigue and work for your customers. Instead, the best organizations to leverage this trend are those which already have (or are working towards building) an experience that consumers rave about. Once you have that, then allowing those same consumers more ways to earn their place in the experience and celebrate their achievement once they do can work extremely well.

How To Use This Trend

✓ **Create a secret room** – The not-so-sexy secret about many of the most unique and exclusive dining experiences in the world is that they are embedded as part of another experience. When Jose Andres first opened his minibar concept restaurant, for example, it was located in a mini bar area (literally) on the top floor of another of his restaurants – Café Atlantico. Over time, he eventually moved it, but initially the idea started as a secret room and experience that only some diners knew to ask for. When you think about how to use earned consumption in your own business, this same mindset may help. Creating something new and secret can be a great draw. Putting it inside of an existing experience – at least at first – can help to make it more manageable.

✓ **Don't forget the purpose** – As you can see from the majority of examples shared in this chapter, the idea of using earned consumption often works best when there is a bigger purpose attached to it. There is a reason why gamers who have been to AGDQ rave about the experience and why travelers who have integrated some form of voluntourism into their travels feel more enriched as a result. When we earn our right to consume, we want to believe it is for a bigger purpose. The more this sort of purpose can be built into what you offer, the more likely it is that people will want to share that with everyone else they know.

Chapter 12

ANTI-STEREOTYPING

What's the Trend?

Across media and culture, traditional gender roles are being reversed, assumptions about alternative lifestyles are challenged, and perceptions of what makes someone belong to a particular gender, ethnicity, or category are being fundamentally changed.

Karl Stefanovic is an Australian TV personality who spends his mornings on air as co-host of the Aussie morning news show *Today.* In 2015, he achieved global notoriety after confessing to a secret experiment he had conducted over the past year in an attempt to shine a spotlight on a bias most women take for granted: heightened expectations for their fashion choices and physical appearance in contrast to the lower expectations for their male counterparts.

After seeing the constant criticism his co-host Lisa Wilkinson faced about her clothing and appearance, Stefanovic decided to do something to visualize it. For a year, he wore the same suit on air with a few small variations just to see if anyone would notice. No one did.

As the story about his experiment came out, most people saw it as further proof that women in media and entertainment are judged by different criteria. The fact that this double standard exists is not all that surprising. What is more interesting is just how common it has become for men like Stefanovic to decide to shine light on this kind of unfairness.

For years, gender-based battles for equality were seen as "women's issues," causes tailor made for women to band together to fight against the men holding them down. Gender and other equality issues are no longer considered one-sided. In the coming year, as these complex problems continue to evolve beyond stereotypes, forward thinkers will join together against backward thinkers, regardless of gender, race, ethnicity, or other categories. The widespread rejection of categorizing entire groups based on assumptions is the shift at the heart of *Anti-Stereotyping*, and it is changing everything from how we see men versus women, and the lines dividing them as well.

While I first described this trend two years ago, the time since then has brought plenty more stories of how women and men are shifting traditional roles, how genders are becoming less rigid, and the idea of looking at gender as a distinctive identifier or divider of capability is fading as well.

Masculinity Makeover

Many years ago, the idea of men steadily embracing their softer sides was unfavorably described as "metrosexual" behavior. The term was popularized in the nineties as a way to describe men who cared about their physical appearance, got manicures regularly, and carried around "man-bags" instead of wallets. A generation later, the new stereotypical description for men is to call them "lumbersexuals" –a term describing the growing number of men returning to long-standing masculine choices, like wearing flannel shirts and growing unkempt beards.

Yet both of these descriptors focus on short-lived fashion trends, or minutia such as how long the average man's beard happens to be at a particular time. The more interesting evolution of masculinity over time has been how the familial qualities of being a nurturing caregiver, enjoying time with children, and loving being a parent have shifted to renewed importance. The new face of masculinity has little to do with what material your shirts are made of or when you last shaved.

Instead, a new generation of dads is abandoning old stereotypes of fathers working long hours to support the household in lieu of spending time with kids and family. Some quit day jobs to become entrepreneurs, while others start or choose to work at organizations willing to offer equal time off to men for everything from paternity leave to attending more kid's activities.

A greater number of companies such as Virgin, Microsoft, Johnson & Johnson, and others offer generous parental leave for dads as well as moms—a practice common in many European countries (especially Scandinavia) but uncommon in other regions. Profiling an expansion in the types of people choosing to become parents in the first place, *Pacific Standard* magazine recently profiled a growing trend among single, straight men using fertility clinics and gestational carriers to finally have children and become caregivers, without requiring a female partner.

Longtime doll maker Mattel also made waves in 2015 by featuring a boy in its TV spot for the Moschino Barbie doll, responding to years of criticism about its role in perpetuating gender stereotypes. In the original description of this trend, another example of this shift was a petition from a 13-year-old girl which led toy maker Hasbro to create a gender-neutral version of its iconic Easy-Bake Oven for girls and boys.

This shift towards a kinder and more well-rounded portrait of men has also been reflected directly in imagery through leading stock-photo provider Getty Images. In 2015, the brand launched a popular new curated collection of images of men as part of its popular "Lean In Together" , which showed men doing formerly unexpected things like changing diapers. (In fact, global searches for the phrase "dad changing diaper" increased sevenfold from 2007 to 2015.)

Why is this imagery so important? As Getty Images director of visual trends Pam Grossman shares, "we believe the more images that a person ingests which are gender-forward and which break gender stereotypes and clichés, the more normalized that becomes. Not only does that help make them much more comfortable with images of women leading or men caretaking, but they are much more comfortable with adopting that kind of behavior in their actual lives and aspiring to that behavior."

Clearly, the imagery shift is also reflecting what advertisers and others seeking stock imagery are searching for as well. In 2007, for example, the top-selling fatherhood image was a relatively typical scene of a dad playing football with his son. In 2015, the top image was a dad reading to his daughter.

Fierce Femininity

The biggest box-office opening of any film in Hollywood history officially belongs to *Star Wars: The Force Awakens,* which premiered in December 2015 and amassed more than $1 billion in just its first 12 days—the fastest film to the $1 billion mark ever.

The original *Star Wars Trilogy,* as most people will remember, featured the far-from-helpless Princess Leia as a central character. She had a quiet strength and was a hero to an entire generation of women. Aside from being the latest installment in one of the best-loved science-fiction franchises of all times, this new addition to the Star Wars film franchise also reimagines gender roles for a new generation, featuring two new young stars, Rey (played by Daisy Ridley) and Finn (played by John Boyega).

In the film, the young Finn is routinely saved by his female co-star Rey—a story model that has been repeated through some of the most popular action films of the past two years, including *The Hunger Games, Divergent,* and many others.

This flip of gender roles has become common in television as well. *Bella and the Bulldogs,* for example, is a Nickelodeon teen show featuring a central character who is quarterback for the middle-school football team (and just happens to also be female). *Quantico* is a terrorist-story thriller starring Priyanka Chopra—an actress best known for her roles as a dancing diva in Bollywood films—as a fierce FBI agent on the run.

This changing model of strong female characters as role models is happening outside the world of entertainment as well. In the business world, there are a growing number of top female executives at some of the largest companies in the world, including top executives at Facebook, Pepsi, GM, Xerox, Oracle, HP, Mondelez International, and Lockheed Martin.

Former child star Danica McKellar (*The Wonder Years*) is now the bestselling author of a series of books all about geometry and algebra designed to get girls interested and excited in math, a longtime passion for McKellar who also describes herself as a lifelong "math nerd."

In the world of sports, two professional hockey leagues for women in the United States and Canada are both growing. Even the NFL, long dominated by men, saw its first female coach in 2015 when the Arizona Cardinals hired Jen Welter as a training camp and preseason intern.

In sports, business, media, and entertainment combined, the past year brought plenty of examples of the continuing shift in gender roles and stereotypes. We are moving toward a new model for how women are being appreciated as more than side characters, and judged on more than traditionally feminine qualities.

Gender Blend

In late 2015 Wesley Morris, critic-at-large covering all things cultural for The New York Times, wrote a recap of the year titled "The Year We Obsessed Over Identity." The article explored our shifting cultural understanding of gender and just how confused and blended it has become. He wrote "gender roles are merging. Races are being shed ... we've been made to see how trans and bi and poly-ambi-omni we are."

This same merging was at the heart of what Getty Images declared as one of the prevailing trends of the past year in imagery, the growing "gender blend" where identities are being reimagined. This blend was partially explained and showcased in their "Lean In Together" collection, referenced earlier in this chapter, and also through the imagery sought out and used by a growing number of advertisers, which makes gender a more neutral quality.

Billboards in Toronto, for example, from fashion retailer Desigual showed two models of non-specific gender in an embrace right above the words "gender neutral." This focus of the neutrality of gender is also at the heart of a multi-year shift among toy stores around the world to reimagine the concept of having separate boys' and girls' sections and instead simply showcasing products by category and letting kids choose based on their passions rather than their gender.

As we move into the coming year, this blending of gender identities will continue to influence marketing, media, retail store design, and many other unexpected categories.

Why It Matters

For years the idea of gender was at the heart of how we saw ourselves and our identities. In 2016, this focus on gender will transform into more content and experiences being driven by passion and personality. People will be encouraged to like what they like and find others who like it as well. The younger generation of boys and girls are already seeing dominant and collaborative role models who reflect any identity they relate to.

Ultimately, this balancing of genders will lead to a new view of typically stereotypical assumptions of others. We will personally see more exceptions to the "rules" and have more firsthand experiences of those situations where stereotypes are proven untrue by the existence of their opposites. The result of this change will be more people willing to take risks outside of traditional roles and the expectation that the experiences they are offered reflect that same desire for something new and unexpected.

Who Should Use This Trend?

This trend will be particularly useful if you happen to be in an industry that has typically been dominated by one type of person or one gender. Harley-Davidson motorcycles, for example, has seen tremendous growth over the past several years thanks in part to its ability to successfully reimagine its target audience from predominantly male to now a more even mix of men and women. The brand has made the shift so deeply that it is now routinely used as an example of how to promote an unexpected brand to women and succeed. The lesson from their example is clear: Your audience may be broader than you think—and in a world where people are rediscovering what role identity plays in the experiences they love, you have an ability to open your business to new audiences and drive new revenue as well.

How To Use This Trend

✓ **Search for Accidental Stereotyping** – The biggest theme from this trend is that there are plenty of ways that we put gender bias into the messages that we share without even thinking about them. Do you always refer to CEOs as "he," nurses as "she," or use dated imagery on your website? These may seem like small things, but a growing number of customers and business professionals alike are paying attention to these subtle cues and may actually be influenced by them more than you think. As a result, finding and removing these biases will be critical.

✓ **Appreciate Dads!** – As a dad who once worked in a full-time role before starting his own company, I remember how tough it could be to find time to meet work demands and commitments to my family. Some businesses make it easier than others, but there are more and more that create a double standard by allowing more free time and flexible schedules for moms, and finding subtle ways to avoid or create a cultural bias against offering the same thing to dads. Don't be one of those companies. Learn to appreciate and support new dads at least as much as you support new moms.

Chapter 13

VIRTUAL EMPATHY

—.——

What's the Trend?

The decreasing cost and growing quality of virtual reality is allowing creators tell more immersive stories and people see the world from another point of view – growing their empathy in the process.

It would be hard to read any prediction about the future of the entertainment industry without enduring yet another breathless description of how virtual reality (VR) is a game changer. In a recent interview 20th Century Fox Home Entertainment President Mike Dunn illustrated the point perfectly. "VR is not a gimmick or a marketing addendum to a film," he said "but the studio's No. 1 priority in home entertainment."

Dunn's comments may reflect and overload of optimism, but there have been plenty of signs over the past year that virtual reality is on the edge of becoming widely available and perhaps even mainstream.

In mid-2015, the "Cardboard" device released by Google allowed consumers to experience a crude version of VR directly from their smartphones with a simple viewing device built out of cardboard. Several months later, Samsung released its first consumer Virtual Reality Headset called the Gear VR at the consumer friendly price under $100 USD and designed to work with existing Samsung mobile phones.

Oculus Rift, the pioneer in virtual reality technology that was acquired by Facebook in 2014 for an estimated $2 billion, continues to pioneer new content experiences and also to power the forces of many efforts from brands like Fox, Lionsgate and Samsung.

With all this investment, it is tempting to see Virtual Reality only as a technology with the potential to transform how we are entertained – and it will certainly do that. The wider implications of the technology, though, are far more ... human. When the technology for experiencing the world through someone else's eyes is within arm's reach of the masses – then empathy too can become easier to enable.

More than one enthusiast has referred to Virtual Reality as the world's greatest empathy machine, with the potential to help each of us better understand people not like ourselves, sympathize with those in the world who live in poverty or under threat of war, better appreciate and protect our environment and maybe even make ourselves into better humans. Sound like a dream? In this chapter, we will see just how much of this utopian vision for *Virtual Empathy* is already on the way to coming true.

If You Chop a Tree in a Forest, Do You Use Less Paper?

At the Stanford University Virtual Human Interaction Lab, one of the world's foremost research teams studying how virtual reality impacts human behavior have uncovered some surprising insights. As lab director Jeremy Bailenson shares "we are entering an era that is unprecedented in human history, where you can transform the self and experience anything the animator can fathom." These experiences are already taking an unexpected turn.

In one experiment, for example, Bailenson and his team invited participants to wear a headset and crawl around on their hands and knees while the simulator created a virtual mirror in which the participants saw themselves as a cow. The intriguing question the research posed was, "if you know how a cow feels, will you eat less meat?"

To find out, participants were prodded with a stick while experiencing the same treatment in the virtual reality headset as a cow being led to its own slaughter. After the experiment, one participant summarized the experience by writing "once I got used to it I began to feel like I was the cow. I truly felt like I was going to the slaughter house towards the end and I felt sad that I (as a cow) was going to die. That last prod felt really sad."

Far from starting with an agenda of converting people to become vegetarians or build their capacity for bovine sympathy, though, Bailenson was simply interested in whether experiencing a situation *virtually* was enough to alter behavior in *reality.*

No matter what experiment he devised, the answer always turned out the same. Does seeing a 65-year-old avatar of yourself inspire you to save more for retirement? Yes. Does virtually chopping down a tree (and hearing it fall) make you more likely to use less paper? Yes.

The implication of his team's research is significant. We as humans can learn to have more empathy toward others, animals and the environment through immersive virtual reality experiences. Particularly when those experiences are crafted into a powerful story of a part of the world most of us would never get to see otherwise.

The Rise Of Immersive Journalism

In February of 2015 at the World Economic Forum in Davos, more than 120 top diplomats waited patiently in line to wear a Samsung Gear VR headset and experience a war zone first hand. The "film" they were waiting to see was in fact a collaboration dreamed up by filmmaker and virtual reality pioneer Chris Milk with UN senior advisor and self-described "bureaucratic ninja" Gabo Arora.

After first being introduced by U2 guitarist the Edge at a music album launch party, the two quickly dreamed up a collaboration to develop an eight minute short film called *Clouds Over Sidra* that would generate more understanding for the Syrian refugee crisis by letting the viewer experience the world through the eyes of a twelve year old girl named Sidra living amongst 80,000 fellow refugees from the Za'atari camp in Jordan.

Efforts like this are leading to a growing renaissance of what many are starting to describe as "immersive journalism" – a new form where journalists can do things like sharing the untold plight of marginalized groups through a combination of investigative reporting and on the ground humanitarianism.

Other powerful efforts launched in the past year take you into what it feels like to be a perpetrator of a sexual assault crime (*The Party*), experience the strange sensation of swapping your gender (*Machine To Be Another*) and even engage in a virtual reality business negotiation scenario where you are forced to play both roles in order to illustrate the importance of compassion in effective negotiations (*Harvard University*).

The New York Times even launched a large scale experiment with Google Cardboard where the newspaper shipped the cardboard lenses to subscribers and invited them to download a custom app in order to "simulate richly immersive scenes from across the globe."

Outside of immersive journalism and telling important stories, virtual reality is also changing how we deliver quality healthcare and also the role of empathy in the business world.

Empathetic Health

Back in 2005 when Dr. Albert Rizzo first developed his virtual reality software designed to help soldiers experiencing PTSD (post traumatic stress disorder) symptoms, he had a device problem. The virtual reality headsets he was using at the time cost nearly $1600 apiece. Today, these costs have come down dramatically as VR headsets like the Samsung Gear take advantage of the complex gyroscope and accelerometer that you have already paid for inside your mobile phone.

Now that cost is no longer the biggest barrier, Dr. Rizzo is among a growing range of clinicians and healthcare professionals who believe that VR will fundamentally transform many elements of how health care is delivered today.

There are plenty of signs that their belief is well on its way to coming true. Loyola University is using virtual reality to test a game called "Snow World" which allows burn victims to play a mental game shooting snowballs at penguins and snowmen while undergoing extremely painful treatments like skin stretching therapy.

In San Francisco, a virtual reality startup called Psious is pioneering a new virtual reality based version of exposure therapy designed to help individuals conquer all sorts of fears – from public speaking to an anxiety when flying. Researchers are using similar methods to help children with autism more easily learn social cues and interaction.

On the other side of healthcare, medical students like surgery residents and dental surgeons also now have the ability to learn and practice techniques through virtual simulations – even allowing them to navigate tricky complications in a safe learning environment or even to see a procedure from a patient's point of view.

Other industries are finding new value from testing VR as well.

Focus Groups of the Future

For the past 15 years, Ford Motor Company has been using virtual reality technology without much fanfare to develop and test designs before they are built. As Ford technical specialist Elizabeth Baron explained in a recent *Forbes* interview, "what we're looking for is the perceived quality of vehicles as a customer would see them. We want to be able to see the cars and our designs and experience them before we have actually produced them." Baron estimates in the past year that the technology has been used to examine more than 135,000 details on 193 virtual vehicle prototypes in a variety of lighting situations, positions and shapes.

In January at the Detroit auto show, the brand unveiled plans for the new Ford GT – a "supercar" with a top speed of 200 miles per hour meant to challenge the offerings from top exotic car makers like Ferrari and McLaren. The project was one of the first to come from the secretive Ford Performance team, a small group of engineers and designers nestled in an intentionally separate facility in Ford's Dearborn, Michigan headquarters. The majority of early conception of the car, as well understanding how the car would interact with the driver was largely created digitally through VR.

In the business world, this type of simulation using VR in order to empathize with how real people will interact with multi-million dollar structures is becoming commonplace. A virtual reality studio called Third Fate is one example – in 2015 the firm opened a B2B practice designed specifically to work with architects and businesses to create VR renderings of spaces that could be imagined and explored prior to ever starting construction.

Virtual reality software company WorldViz has one of the most popular platforms for businesses to develop these types of renderings of spaces and products. The company's VR software development platform Vizard is used by architects and designers to imagine spaces, create safe equipment maintenance training scenarios for oil and gas industry workers and even given surgeons and nurses the chance to criticize planned hospital room designs before those rooms are completed. Each offers the chance for those designing spaces for professionals to build their empathy towards their end users and actually take the input of the users in real time and use it to make their designs more functional.

Outside of designing spaces or products, virtual reality is also starting to find its way into more social aspects of business as well. New programs are coming up to allow directors to use VR as a part of the recruiting and interviewing process. Others are using VR headsets to enable better collaboration and understanding between remotely dispersed teams and even to teach interpersonal communications by helping workers build empathy for understanding different points of view.

Why It Matters

As Oculus Rift, Samsung and others challengers continue to bring more consumer friendly and lower priced devices to market, virtual reality will continue to give us all more ways to step outside ourselves and experience the world from another point of view. Entertainment and gaming will likely continue to get the biggest share of attention and excitement, however the transformative nature of virtual reality will continue to hinge on its ability to allow each of us as humans to empathize with more people and situations than ever before. At the very least – we will continue to enjoy more immersive entertainment experiences throughout 2016.

More promisingly, the growth of virtual reality has the potential to even make us into better humans in the process.

Who Should Use This Trend?

If you happen to work for a smaller brand or one without a secret in house lab then this trend focused on using virtual reality to build empathy may seem like its nice to know about but out of touch in reality. While the simulation usages of VR for things like testing prototypes of architectural plans or automotive designs certainly are more extreme models, you don't need to be prototyping innovation in order to potentially use this trend. One of the most powerful and transformative effects of the technology is in the way that it challenges each of us to see outside our own biases and limited viewpoints of the world.

To that end, any business that wants to encourage its workers to reduce industry-induced tunnel vision, to have more empathy for customers or one that just wants to give workers a chance to open their minds to new innovative possibilities could benefit from using VR. The good news is, there are plenty of readily available new programs and tools that are being built for VR that reduce the necessity for you to have to build something yourself. While many offerings for VR today might be quite entertainment driven, the lessons they offer can be useful for businesses of all kinds … and the near future will see more specific programs to encourage more empathy in business during tasks like hiring, firing, negotiations, sales and plenty more.

How To Use This Trend

✓ **Invest in your own VR micro-lab** – The word "lab" typically conjures up images of expensive pristine rooms filled with scientists, but today with a minimal investment of $500 to $1000 – you can purchase a range of interesting and new gear to try out, and then encourage your teams to just come in and play. The value of new technology often comes from the ideas it might spark for doing businesses differently in your industry. And at the very least, playing with new tech toys can offer an always appreciated jolt of energy and excitement to a routine day.

✓ **Make it a priority to personally test out "real" VR** – Aside from playing with the small limited VR experiences currently available for home use, there are plenty of new showcases of the full power of VR that are happening in places like co-working or incubator spaces in large cities, expo halls at tech trade shows or on University campuses. VR, like many different new technologies, is best understood by actually donning a headset and traveling into the experience yourself.

Chapter 14

DATA
OVERFLOW

What's the Trend?

The combination of growing personal and corporate owned data mixed with open data creates an new challenge to go beyond algorithms to manage this data and rely instead on better artificial intelligence, smarter curation, and more startup investment.

Big data is getting bigger, small data is getting smaller – and the intersection of both is starting to cause some serious problems.

Despite the continual business conversation on big data and how to collect more information, last year I introduced the idea of "Small Data" to capture the growing practice of consumers using their *own* data collected by smart devices and social platforms and learning to leverage it for better service, pricing or outcomes. The future, I argued, would belong to the brands that could find ways to entice consumers to share this *small data* and combine it with the big data that they were already collecting.

In the coming year, this blend of big and small data will lead to a new related problem of *Data Overflow* – where any company collecting data will struggle with the fact that they will soon be buried by its sheer volume. On first glance, it may seem you've heard about this overflow before.

Sometimes termed "data overload" – much has been written about the dangers of collecting too much data or the futile journey individuals and organizations sometimes take to make sense of it once they have it. The trend of Data Overflow describes the next level of this chaos, where the intersection of self-collected consumer "small data" and corporate collected "big data" will be rendered even more confusing by a third collection of frequently useless "open data" often lacking structure or metadata and dumped online publicly by companies and governments in the name of transparency or regulatory compliance.

As one example of this rapidly growing data deluge, the GovLab Index tracks open data trends and publishes annual reports on the state of open data adoption by governments worldwide. In the most recent update, the Index report included some sobering data points:

- Over 1 million datasets have been made open by governments worldwide.

- Less than 7% of these datasets are published in both machine-readable forms and under open licenses.

- 96% of countries are sharing datasets that are not regularly updated.

- In 2015, there were nearly 400 open government data portals worldwide (up from only two just six years earlier).

While it is clear that the volume of this open data is growing exponentially year after year, the problem is that much of it may not be that inherently useful. In an interview with *The Economist*, Joel Gurin of the Centre for Open Data Enterprise estimates that perhaps four fifths of the data that has been released is *not* particularly useful due to missing the metadata or consistent standardization that would provide much needed context.

So how can we best tackle this disarray of data? And is there a cure for data overflow? To find out, let's explore the story of how one group of scientists are trying to solve a piece of challenge ... from inside of one of the most dangerous and scientifically advanced locations on Earth.

Deciphering Super Collider Data

The Large Hadron Collider (LHC) is like an experiment straight from the pages of science fiction. The largest single machine in the world, the LHC was built by the European Organization for Nuclear Research (CERN) in collaboration with 10,000 scientists from 100 countries and sits in a 17 mile long tunnel underneath the France-Switzerland border. Its purpose is to allow physicists to test how particles collide and further our understanding of the physical world.

The main challenge of this technological feat is not making the collisions happen, but rather how to decode the terabytes of data the collisions generate. The volume is far too high for even the most sophisticated algorithms and too nuanced for even the smartest scientists using the fastest computers. And it turns out the team at the LHC is not the only group of scientists facing this problem.

In an article in late 2015 from the journal eLife, for example, cell biologist Robert Insall sparked an industry wide debate when he shared that the majority of senior researchers he interviewed feared a crushing volume of new biomedical research papers released each year was leading to a decline in trustworthiness for their field overall.

In the past year, both Google and IBM made big announcements to promote more development on their AI platforms (TensorFlow and Watson, respectively) by creating more open source libraries, tools and tutorials for the technical community. The aim of each is to inspire more developers to create initiatives using "deep learning," an aspect of machine learning that describes the quest to make machines more intuitive and closer to true artificial intelligence.

Over time, AI and deep learning can automatically go through a glut of research or questionably valuable open data and help make the connections that lead to real discovery. AI holds the promise to give the scientists at the LHC and the overwhelmed biomedical researchers help in their quest to make sense of all the data.

As the world of science tests new AI-driven solutions to this data challenge, their example will be watched by many other global industries – including several that are suffering from a data overflow of their own.

TECHNOLOGY & DESIGN

AgTech: Growing Data For Farmers

The agriculture industry offers the perfect example of some on the ground challenges that data overflow can cause. The industry is overrun with data. A single farm can now provide mountains of data from sensors in the soil, wearable trackers on farm animals and aerial drones for crop monitoring.

Drones in particular hold great promise and peril for the farming industry, as the Association for Unmanned Vehicle Systems International estimates that agriculture drones may make up 80 percent of the future commercial market.

All the data generated by this agricultural technology (often called "AgTech") is ushering in a new evolution of what is increasingly being described as precision farming – the ability to plant the right crop in the right spot and harvest it at the right time. Consistently achieving this precision isn't easy … and doing it takes an integration of technology into farming on a scale that has rarely been tried, or even discussed.

One of the biggest chances to have that discussion came in July of 2015 at the AgTech Summit in Salinas, California hosted by Forbes. The event was aimed at bringing agriculture industry insiders together with Silicon Valley innovators to talk about the future of the farming industry and how technology could play a role. At the event, real farmers shared the one big challenge they faced from all this new data – how to make meaning from it all.

Data was overflowing and farmers on the ground were finding it nearly impossible to make sense of it all.

Farmers are usually not scientists with PhDs in advanced particle physics trained to parse and analyze data. They are rarely doing their day's work from a comfortable chair in front of a laptop. They are mobile, savvy, time strapped and usually need data in a format that they can act on immediately.

Most agree that the solution will come not from new innovative tools to collect even more data, but by putting technologists in the same room as farmers and encouraging them to create more innovation that is actually useful at solving the data overflow. Thanks to the AgTech Summit and events like it, there are more initiatives than ever focused on tackling this challenge.

In the agriculture driven nation of New Zealand, for example, a local business incubator has launched a 20 week accelerator program for agtech called Sprout Agritech. AgTech initiatives across the world are seeing more investment as well. By the end of 2014, industry site AgFunder tracked over $2.36 billion of investment across 264 deals – which outpaces sectors with far more hype such as financial technology ($2.1 billion) and clean technology ($2 billion).

Meanwhile many of the open data sets released by governments around the world relate to data that is highly valuable for farmers – such as regional weather data and data on regional food consumption. As this public data intersects with traditional farm data (like crop yields and soil metrics) and nontraditional new farm data (like drone based measurements) – the same data overflow challenge common in other industries is hitting agriculture as well.

Yet noted venture capitalist Randy Komisar believes this is going to inspire a golden age of investment and innovation in agtech. As a partner at noted venture capitalist firm Kleiner Perkins Caufield & Byers, Komisar is used to looking farther into the future than most. In late 2015 he shared some of his insights in an interview with *National Geographic* – predicting a more open future for agriculture where farmers could take back control from the biggest players that run the agricultural industry with a near monopoly today. This would enable them to remove themselves from being mere vendors to the big agriculture companies and instead own and share their own data more openly with one another.

In farming – innovators and new startups companies funded by growing investment are the hope for solving data overflow and creating more meaning from the intersection of data from all directions.

Curated Health Data

In the health sector, privacy is always the most important concern when it comes to sharing any data online. The first topic innovators tackle, regulators ask and patients worry about is how individual data will be used.

The health industry, though, faces the exact same data overflow issues as other industries profiled in this chapter ... fueled by the same set of circumstances.

Hospitals collect data on patients and outcomes. Patients collect their own data through wearable fitness trackers and technology designed to help them manage conditions they may have such as diabetes or asthma. And, of course, there is plenty of public health data launched openly onto the Internet by governments for anyone to access.

Rather than turning primarily to AI as scientific researchers have, or inspiring more startups to tackle the challenge as in the agricultural industry – healthcare is poised to see an explosion in a different coping strategy inspired mainly by individual curators and the power of the human eye to see and solve problems that algorithms of even artificial intelligence might still struggle with.

One of the most powerful examples of this process comes from an app often described as "Instagram for doctors" called Figure1. It is a simple app that allows medical professionals to share anonymized images of patients struggling with some type of condition in order to get feedback and comments from other medical professionals. It turns out this behavior of sharing images of patient afflictions without personal details is already surprisingly common.

When Figure1 founder Josh Landy, an intensive care specialist at Scarborough Hospital in Toronto, Canada, first developed the idea his ambition was to take what he was seeing people do already in terms of sharing images individually, and transform it into "a global knowledge notebook." Today the app has more than 150,000 active users, is perfectly tailored for visual learners as many doctors happen to be, and was described by one third year medical resident in Texas as her "medical guilty pleasure."

The app offers far more than a chance for medical voyeurism though. It is also using the power of the crowd to help medical practitioners gain insight and support from those in other parts of the world to diagnose and treat conditions that may be common in one place but rare in another. In this case the data and the usefulness of it stems from a person to person interaction on a human level.

When it comes to huge data sets shared more publicly, though, the challenge gets different.

Cedric Hutchings is the co-Founder and CEO of Withings – a company that makes a suite of wearable tech and quantified self products. He is also a believer in the power of anonymous data to be useful on a regional and global level to incite change.

For the past several years, Hutchings has been driving his company to make more use of the aggregated anonymous data from all the users that they collect. Thanks to this data, he has been able to pinpoint, for example, that a tiny city on the outskirts of Paris called Argenteuil has the notorious distinction of being the most obese city – and communications around this in 2015 motivated the mayor and people of the city to issue a comprehensive plan to change school lunches and lose that dubious distinction.

Not surprisingly, Hutchings believes in the power of open data and has committed his organization to its own open data initiative, called the Withings Health Observatory. More significantly, in order to make meaning from this dataset instead of just dumping it online as many have done, Withings committed resources to helping make sense of the data.

The brand now creates content featuring key statistics, insights, and community reports. It also partners with researchers and academics to publish scientific papers through the Withings Health Institute and now offers this content as a toolkit to help researchers and other scientists to make sense of their data and to make it more valuable for everyone it is shared with.

Why It Matters

In 2016, the intersection of big data, small data and open data led to the consistently big challenge of Data Overflow. Rather than relying on algorithms alone – industry sectors from scientific research to agriculture to healthcare are all applying a slight different lens in order to solve this challenge. For some, artificial intelligence is the only viable solution to handle volumes of data and make meaning from it in any sort of valuable way. For others like agriculture, the challenge is taking pockets of successful data analysis and merging them together into an ecosystem that helps the farmer on the ground. Investment in startups and innovation is taking off in an attempt to make this happen. And for healthcare, the solution is coming down to a rise in the art of human curation as a method to make meaning from hard to decipher visual data and data creators taking more responsibility to add context and meaning to this data before sharing it openly.

Who Should Use This Trend?

The potential and opportunity for data collection is blossoming in all types of industries, which means this trend is likely to affect almost anyone doing business in 2016. As it does, data overflow will challenge the potential value of collecting the data in the first place. The good news is that this is a highly visible problem and one that many different groups are trying to solve. Moving into 2016, industries are likely to develop their own individual solutions to this problem and the most savvy brands will be the ones keeping up to date with the latest solutions and investing time and effort to make them work for themselves.

How To Use This Trend

✓ **Learn data literacy** – The sad reality of business is that most of us lack basic data literacy skills. As a result, we misread statistics, misquote studies and draw incorrect or sometimes idiotic conclusions from data that is at best inconclusive. The only solution to this problem is to do something that most of us probably don't want to do … go back and improve our data literacy. This might involve taking an online class, or reading articles from those well versed in how to interpret data about a particular topic or from a particular industry.

✓ **Curate open data** – Central to this trend are the issues and challenges raised by a growing amount of open data being launched into the marketplace. One solution increasingly common within healthcare, but potentially useful for any industry, is to get better at curating this data and finding the valuable pockets of information yourself and using them to sharing them with others to generate more value back to your own efforts.

Chapter 15

HEROIC
DESIGN

What's the Trend?

Design takes a leading role in the introduction of new products, ideas, and inspiration to change the world in nuanced, audacious, irreverent, and sometimes unexpectedly heroic ways.

The largest oceanic cleanup effort in history is starting in 2016—thanks to a crazy idea from a 21-year-old Dutch entrepreneur named Boyan Slat. In three short years since founding, Slat's ambitious project, The Ocean Cleanup, has gone from a lofty concept of floating barriers designed to use the ocean's current to capture plastic waste (instead of the current standard of using boats and nets), to near reality.

At the Seoul Digital Forum, Asia's largest technology conference, Slat announced that the first array of floating barriers will be deployed in 2016 off the coast of Tsushima, an island between Japan and South Korea, to become the longest floating structure in world history.

The project is world changing, blatantly optimistic, and a perfect sign of the new role that design has taken in our culture as the solution to our biggest problems. Design was once considered just a step along the path to launching a project or effort. Designers were creative professionals who needed to be properly managed and art directed to achieve useful results.

Today, design is seen differently.

Thanks to the success of design-centric companies like Apple and Ikea, design has long been seen as the road to building a competitive advantage. The difference today is that this focus on design is continuing to evolve beyond offering a corporate differentiator. When I first wrote about this evolution back in 2014, I found countless examples where design itself was becoming world changing. In the two years since, this idea of *Heroic Design* has dramatically expanded.

In 2016, we will see more efforts like The Ocean Cleanup, where design is fundamentally driving a shift that changes how we deal with some of the biggest problems in the world. Even when it comes to problems on a smaller, local scale, design can be the ultimate weapon to convince governments, bureaucracies, industries, and conservative thinkers of the feasibility of new ideas.

As social media brings more attention to the needy and challenges become more public, global designers will continue to apply new thinking to develop solutions. As this happens, design will continue to take a leading role in the introduction of new products, ideas, and campaigns to impact the world.

Design Everywhere

In 2014 when Norway's Norges Bank held a design competition for the country's future currency, the results of the search attracted worldwide attention. When the final designs by graphic design studio The Metric System and Norwegian architecture and design firm Snøhetta Design were awarded (for the front and back, respectively), most of the coverage predicted the final combined design will be the world's best-looking currency when it launches in 2017.

From inspiring more beautiful currency to seeking "innovative technology-enabled design solutions for the aging population" (TechSAge Design Competition), there are now hundreds of design competitions for all types of categories. As more design competitions seek new solutions and outside thinking, design itself gains prestige and becomes more valued in the world of business.

Brands like Johnson & Johnson, 3M, and Pepsi all now have chief design officers overseeing the role of design in their day-to-day efforts. Philips, PepsiCo, and Hyundai have all added chief design officers as appointments to their boards.

In higher education, institutes like Stanford's d.school, University of Virginia's Darden School, and the University of Toronto's Rotman School of Management all have programs designed to teach students how to answer any type of challenge with design thinking, and how to collaborate effectively with other disciplines to add design process and methodology to the way they currently approach and solve problems.

Leading consulting and technology brands like Wipro, Google, Adobe, Accenture, and others have each been making major acquisitions of design firms for the past several years to inject more design thinking into their everyday services.

From education to design competitions, the role that design is taking as a discipline that offers a new way to imagine solutions to any type of problem is transformative. Increasingly, this is making design one of the most important capabilities of any effort in order to truly create impact or develop solutions that really work—even if they may not be technically possible, yet.

Imagined Futures

Public transportation is one of the biggest changes facing almost any city, and Austin, Texas, is one of the fastest growing cities in the United States. To reimagine a potential solution for their home city, a team of designers at interactive agency Frog Design created a solution based on high-wire, hanging gondola system. In addition to dreaming up the inventive solution, they created and designed a complete system, down to a full regional map and smart card. The project was introduced to local government officials and presented at urban planning and design events around the world.

Another design firm, Teague, created a new model for the "airline of the future," which it presented to executives in the airline industry at several events in 2015. The new design featured unique ideas such as doing away with cabin baggage (all luggage, apart from personal items, would be checked with RFID tags), offering certain seats up for corporate promotion (so the middle seat could be discounted/subsidized by a sponsor) and letting passengers easily swap seats or even resell them through a central marketplace if they have a change in travel plans. The vision is enough to actually offer hope that the airline experience of the future could one day offer pleasure instead of angst.

Yet together, these design-driven imagined futures do more than create dissatisfaction with what is available today. They also inspire entire industries to think bigger and consider different alternatives for the future, which is a heroic effect in itself.

Why It Matters

While the importance of design in business has certainly grown over the past several years, what makes design heroic are the myriad examples of how new solutions to the world's biggest problems are being imagined through great design. What we once might have described as a superficial outer layer aimed to make something look better goes much deeper today. Design is the solution itself, as well as the way we perceive it.

As a result, *Heroic Design* will continue to drive more organizations to instill design-centric thinking at the foundation of their business—and designers as well as design-minded engineers, scientists, and researchers will be the ones that bring this new vision into reality.

Who Should Use This Trend?

Governments, nonprofits, and organizations focused on bringing new, innovative products or services to market will all be affected by this trend. The idea of design thinking is one of the most impactful elements of this trend, which any company focused on differentiating and creating impact will be able to use.

How To Use This Trend

✓ **Adopt a design-focused mindset** - In IDEO leader Tim Brown's book Change By Design, he advocates taking a moment each day to deeply observe the ordinary. It is a simple suggestion, but one that illustrates the potential power of design thinking. The more you can encourage yourself and your organization to use this sort of thinking to spot the every day opportunities or inefficiencies in how you do business, the more you can encourage innovation from within.

✓ **Add design to your big ideas** - When Frog Design approached the impossible challenge of rethinking public transportation, they designed a solution on paper with illustrations. If you already have a big idea in your organization, but you struggle to convey it to others, design may offer the ultimate solution to help you take that idea from something that a small, core group of people are excited about to something that could actually have an impact on the world because others are able to understand it and share it.

Chapter 16

INSOURCED INCUBATION

What's the Trend?

Companies desperate to bring more innovation into the enterprise turn to a new model of intrapreneurship modeled after the best business incubators—bringing innovators in house, providing support and resources, and starting innovation labs.

Corporate entrepreneurship is the sort of term that has earned its status as an oxymoron. Talk to any business leader and you'll hear that innovation is a top priority, yet when it comes to actually thinking more entrepreneurially to do it, companies have failed for years.

The problem usually comes down to what a seminal 2006 article in the Harvard Business Review, by Harvard professor David A. Garvin and researcher Lynne C. Levesque, called the "two-cultures problem" where big company bureaucracy and traditional thinking usually manages to kill upstart initiatives long before they are able to make an impact. Citing the best known examples of companies meeting this challenge at the time, the article referenced P&G head A.G. Lafley's now-famous directive from the mid 2000s that brand managers needed to spend less time in focus groups and more time in consumer's homes. Starbucks, too, was using a similar outside-in approach of encouraging managers to take inspiration trips to better understand local cultures and trends.

The conclusion of the article was clear: if you were aiming to build a culture of innovation, the key was to get closer to your customers. This belief largely framed the next decade of managerial thinking around innovation. Over the past few years, this thinking has started to shift.

The new solutions for this two-culture problem focus squarely on the innovators themselves. Brands are investing in small innovation pilots and hosting startup competitions. They are following trends in entrepreneurship such as the rise of accelerators and incubators as regional groups that support innovation. They are using "acquihiring" to bring talented thinkers into a company by acquiring startup companies and integrating their talent.

In 2016, this critical ambition to build more entrepreneurial cultures will lead brands towards a new model of Insourced Incubators, where they build nimble, responsive teams designed to work and thrive within a company while still maintaining enough independence to work outside the usual innovation-killing constraints of large organizations.

The insourcing part of this trend is based on the growing idea that a skillset or team that was previously outside an organization could be brought in, more effectively managed and integrated, and run in a way that would generate better business results.

Incubators is a term chosen deliberately as well.

What are Incubators?

As a model, business incubators have been steadily growing as well. As opposed to business accelerators, which usually take startups through a predefined process aimed at launching quickly, incubators focus on providing the resources and support that startups need while allowing them to follow their own paths. The International Business Incubator Association (InBIA) estimates there are about 7,000 business incubators worldwide. Yet the vast majority, according to InBIA, are run by not-for-profit government entities.

Just a few years ago, only 4% of all incubators in the United States were run by for-profit companies, according to the 2012 State of the Business Incubation Industry from InBIA. There are signs that this is shifting and perhaps the most significant implication of this trend in the next year will be just how far reaching it is likely to be in terms of the various industries affected. Let's review a handful of the most exciting of these industries, which saw big changes in the past year.

Content Studio Explosion

The line between advertising and editorial used to be a clear boundary. An advertiser might create content for an advertorial or, more recently, pay for some type of brand integration, but the editorial team controlled the coverage and decided what stories to write, independently of the brands. This was (and still is) the foundation for producing quality, unbiased journalism.

In the past year, though, a new blended model has exploded among nearly every large media organization in response to advertiser demand for more native forms of advertising. The demand led to the creation of the past year of dozens of content studios.

Longstanding media brands like The New York Times, Wall Street Journal, Washingtonian, Forbes, New York Magazine, Crain Media, and Time Inc. are just a few of the larger groups who have invested in creating custom content studios to work with brands. The value proposition is appealing. Brands can now approach these studios and leverage the talents of top journalists, designers, researchers, and production talent in order to produce all kinds of branded content, from custom white papers to digital content hubs.

These new initiatives are examples of Insourced Incubators within the traditional media business, with big ambitions to explore a blended future for publishing brands, who are increasingly crossing over into the world of creative agencies. The custom studio group from Time Inc., for example, is described as an "innovative content and creative lab launched by the storytelling experts at Time Inc." The potential impact of this and other content studios is one that is far wider.

As more publishers experiment with a new form of content creation designed to serve promotional needs of brands (while leveraging the valuable assets of their top notch talent), they are testing another business model that has the potential to overtake (or at least to supplant) traditional advertising as the source of funding for the media itself.

In the coming year, these studios will continue to compete to win brand dollars on the production side instead of chasing media placement dollars alone. The winners will have the chance to pioneer a new future for the media industry, where publishers become adept at taking their storytelling heritage and putting it to work for a growing range of brands desperate to stand out through content but lacking the talent to do so.

There's an Incubator for That!

Though outsourcing content creation to a media studio may be en vogue right now, brands continue to struggle with the new realities of producing great internal content. The same trend driving publishing companies to develop their own studios is also driving brands to find new ways to bring more startup thinking into their organizations.

Coca-Cola has multiple programs serving this purpose, including The Bridge (a commercialization program for startups) and the Coca-Cola Founders platform (an incubator model for growing startups with Coca-Cola as the lead backer). A little over a year ago Marriott launched an incubator program designed to seek out culinary entrepreneurs.

The Unilever Foundry program is another example that drew a lot of attention near the end of 2015, when it introduced 50 top marketing-tech startups after a complex vetting process that allowed the brand to review hundreds of potential ideas and choose the best collaborators. Even efforts like these, though, which are designed to dip a corporate toe into the waters of working with startups, are steadily getting more immersive and truly insourced.

Brands today are seeking to showcase and connect with innovators while also assigning responsibility for developing and building innovation inside the enterprise. This is the innovation lab model, and it is taking off among large brands.

Here is a short list of some innovation lab initiatives that were launched or popularized in the past year alone:

- Ford launched its Research and Innovation Center, a lab in Silicon Valley focused on the intersection of cutting-edge technology and the driving experience.

- The Home Depot founded its innovation lab through the acquisition of an Austin, Texas, startup called BlackLocus, which now operates as a team within a team.

- CVS opened its Digital Innovation Lab to experiment with digital health initiatives and to further its vision of building a "personal integrated pharmacy."

- Despite the uncertainty of its recent merger with Marriott, Starwood Hotels & Resorts currently has an internal innovation lab called Starlab, which has already launched pilots of smart mirrors, digital chandeliers, keyless room entry via mobile device and a host of initiatives in smarter energy usage and efficiency.

- In the financial sector, Standard Bank, Capital One, Visa, Mastercard, Citi, Chase Bank, BBVA, Commonwealth Bank, and Wells Fargo all have dedicated innovation labs that are pioneering new models for digital payment and offering a sort of "show and tell" space for each bank's customers.

- Global alcohol brand Pernod Ricard created and launched a new network of semi-independent distilleries under the umbrella group Our/Vodka, designed to help them customize existing vodka brands with regional flavors for a more local feel. Early markets for testing include Berlin and Detroit, with plans to launch soon in Amsterdam, London, and New York.

- Worldwide shopping-center owner Westfield Group recently announced it would convert the fourth floor of its popular San Francisco shopping center into an incubation space for Westfield Labs, where brands can lease small spaces inside the mall to test pilot concepts.

- Trade groups like America's Health Insurance Plans (AHIP), the National Association of Home Builders (NAHB), and information technology consulting firm AEEC also announced new cutting-edge innovation labs to showcase how technology and new ideas may be changing entire industries.

- Fashion retailer Sephora opened a new innovation lab that is experimenting with augmented-reality storefront window displays and its own version of Amazon Prime, where customers can prepay for expedited shipping for an entire year.

- Fast food brand Wendy's is getting into the innovation lab game, launching its own idea incubator called 90° Labs to test mobile payment technologies and self-order kiosks.

With all the recent investment in these types of initiatives, it is reasonable to wonder how this trend may evolve once all these brands make it past the initial excitement of launching their labs. One answer to this question comes from the retailer Nordstrom, which was one of the earliest to pioneer this trend when they launched their own lab back in 2013.

In 2015, the brand announced that it was shrinking the lab and reassigning employees into other groups. When asked by online site Geekwire about the reasoning behind the move, a Nordstrom spokesperson explained it this way: "rather than just a team focused on innovation, it's now everyone's job." It is the natural evolution of any external skillset that starts with being insourced and eventually becomes integrated into the overall way business is done.

In 2016, these innovation labs and internal entrepreneurship (also commonly known as intrapreneurship) efforts will take an important step towards full integration by finally becoming insourced, and offer a vital chance for brands to benefit from new thinking and different ideas while keeping them separate enough to solve the two-culture problem and really have impact.

Why It Matters

For years brands looked at innovation as the responsibility of some type of research division within the group or something limited to developing new products or technology. In 2016, the popularity of building innovation labs and the necessity to experiment with new business models due to industry shifts will lead many companies to build some version of insourced incubators to inspire more innovation from within. These first efforts have already led to early positive results. Publishing companies are piloting content studios, which represent a fascinating experiment into the future of the media industry. Innovation groups at financial services firms are building and testing new models for payment. Retailers and hospitality brands are launching new self-service kiosks, smart mirrors, and digital displays to better engage consumers and make interactions faster and more personalized.

Ultimately, every new brand that makes this type of commitment to Insourced Incubators and launches some new innovation into the market will present a compelling case study on the value of this model to their industry. Competitors will be watching. Over the coming year, this collective innovation envy will lead even more brands to try this model and introduce the two-culture problem in yet another way. The losers will see these teams dissolve into bureaucracy, while the winners—like Nordstrom—will find new ways to take this commitment to innovation and integrate it even more fully into how they do business.

Who Should Use This Trend?

Any brand that is struggling to build a competitive edge will be able to benefit from the idea of bringing more innovation in house, but it is often not easy, as time has shown. In order to build this type of initiative to be successful, it is critical to find a way to keep this innovation team integrated yet separate. The value of this will be clear for brands in just about any industry—and particularly those who do not often think about their business or industries in terms of innovation.

How to Use This Trend

✓ **Invite innovators into the company** – Nearly every corporate-branded effort dedicated to innovation that works finds new ways to bring in entrepreneurs as a first step. Sometimes this takes the shape of startup competitions, or branded curation of the best or most promising startups to work with (as Unilever has done). In other cases, you might explore newer tactics like the "switch pitch" where established brands are invited to pitch to startups about the business challenges they face, then the startups can try to develop solutions that involve partnering with the brand.

✓ **Find and support internal innovators** – There are always employees or internal teams that are devoted to innovation—who are often overlooked. Insourced Incubators don't always need to start with creating expensive innovation labs with lots of technology and cool furniture. Instead, start by finding the pockets of innovation within your own organization—teams that may already be doing interesting things— and support those initiatives and use them as a starting point.

Chapter 17

AUTOMATED ADULTHOOD

What's the Trend?

As more people go through a prolonged period of emerging adulthood, where they focus on their career and life options through their twenties, and get married later and, a growing range of technology and services help to automate all aspects of their journey to adulthood.

Just over a decade ago a book called Emerging Adulthood by psychologist Jeffrey Jensen Arnett proposed a new period of life-span development, based on years of studying young people aged 18 to 29. While we have often been told that people become adults at 18 years old, Arnett argued that the widespread postponement of marriage, an increase in career and life options due to this delay, and, subsequently, having children later in life was leading to a major shift in our perceptions of what it truly means to be an adult.

Psychologist Jean Twenge also explored the attitudes and behaviors of young people in her latest book called Generation Me, which explores the entitlement, confidence, and optimism common among the younger generation. She writes specifically about the "relentless cultural message to young people: you can be anything you want to be, as long as you believe in yourself."

Rather than praising hard work and dedication, Twenge warns that this one-sided focus on instilling a superior self-belief may already be having some unintended consequences.

Sociologists Richard Arum and Josipa Roksa agree, and their book Academically Adrift argues that most college campuses across the United States had been so focused on the student experience that academics, true learning, and real-world skills were being left behind.

Exploring this cultural shift, New York Times columnist David Brooks summarized, "as emerging adults move from job to job, relationship to relationship and city to city, they have to figure out which of their meanderings are productive exploration and which parts are just wastes of time. This question is very confusing from the inside."

The struggle to answer these questions, though, is has become far more than a personal journey. It is now a business opportunity as well. In 2016, more services, products, and entire brands will evolve to help these emerging adults find their place in the world and live their lives in the process. Innovations are already adding an algorithmic layer to dating, helping manage the trickier parts of relationships, optimizing financial decisions, improving negotiation skills, and even automating cooking and home care.

This is the world of Automated Adulthood, where anyone on the emerging journey to independence and adulthood will find a host of new technology and services to augment their journey. Let's explore the impact of these technologies in four critical aspects of life and adulthood: work, relationships, finances, and the home.

Automated Relationships

Last year a controversial Vanity Fair story from journalist Nancy Jo Sales predicted a "dating apocalypse" coming at the hands of apps like Tinder, which allows anyone to swipe through photos with a hot-or-not" mentality, and quickly arrange casual hookups or sex partners via text.

Despite the criticism, everyone agrees that dating and how people form romantic relationships is fundamentally changing thanks to technology. What is even more interesting is that the daily intricacies of relationship management are changing as well.

One example is the often-ridiculed BroApp, an app designed to "outsource your relationship" by automating texts from men to their girlfriends, reminding them of how much they love them (or another similarly romantic message).

Less extreme versions of this type of relationship management app have popped up throughout the past year for everything from remembering birthdays and sending automated greetings to an inventive use of the IFTTT app which allows us to create "recipes" for a sequence of actions across multiple apps. One such recipe, for example, offers this sad-but-necessary functionality for hapless partners of the social media addicted: "Get a notification when your girlfriend posts a new picture so that you can like before she gets mad."

Dating, romance, and sex are some of the biggest parts of life for emerging adults, and in 2016, this automation of the intricate details of not only dating but also maintaining relationships will lead to continued exploration of how relationships could be improved. The automation goes beyond relationships as well.

Automated Home

Cooking is hard if you aren't used to doing it for yourself.

On the journey to adulthood, learning to cook for oneself is typically a major bump in the road for many. Of course, the easy solution would be to eat out more often, and according to a 2015 study from the Food Institute, Millennials are doing exactly that by spend an average of $50.75 per week out of the home.

To encourage more home cooking (which is generally cheaper and healthier), several successful startups are aiming at curing the motivation challenge and adding a boost of confidence and guidance through a combination of pre-prepared ingredients and detailed instructions shipped to your door. This new category of boxed meal services is exploding and the two biggest leaders are Blue Apron (delivering about 3 million meals per month) and Plated (delivering about 2 million per month). Industry estimates predict that this meal-kit segment of the market could grow to between $3 billion and $5 billion in sales over the next 10 years at current adoption rates.

In addition to this type of technique automation in cooking, other parts the home and home ownership itself are starting to see more automation through technology as well. A Netherlands-based design studio, for example, created a countertop projection screen called the Vegetable Recognizer that can automatically recognize vegetables placed on the counter and suggest a recipe based on what you have available. Two former Apple employees built a smart oven called June, scheduled to ship in mid 2016, which features an integrated app that can adjust temperature or cook time remotely.

Innovation is coming outside the kitchen for the rest of the home as well. Roomba has provided robot vacuum cleaner products for years, and this coming year promises innovations in everything from smart toilets to self-cleaning glass to automated door locks and lights. In the automated home of the future, you won't have to remember to dust or clean or lock the doors or turn off the lights—not to mention never having to cook a meal from scratch without detailed instructions or items prechopped for you.

These are not just conveniences for the modern busy professional. If you're an emerging adult, you may not ever need to learn how to do these things in the first place.

Automated Work

Most professionals receive an estimated 100 to 150 emails a day, and the resulting stress and loss of productivity is well documented. Email is a time waster, yet at most organizations it is categorized as a necessary evil.

Over the past year, the latest darling of the San Francisco tech community is a tool that many have called an "e-mail killer," built specifically to help teams at organizations to reclaim some of that wasted time. Slack is a lean app-based tool that is part chat software and part message board. Growth of the tool has been exponential since its launch in February of 2014, prompting this doting description from a journalist for

Time magazine (and Slack user): "not in a generation has a new tool been adopted more quickly by a wider variety of businesses or with such joy."

Automating the most reviled of communications forms is certainly a cause for joy—but it is only one symbol of how technology is making previously painful work evils easier to handle. There are dozens of apps to teach any worker how to negotiate a better salary or deal with communications issues in the workplace. Dictation software is getting better and better, enabling entire documents to be "typed" virtually without the author ever sitting down in front of a computer. Meanwhile autocorrect and real-time suggestion tools make the process of writing anything less of a challenge.

What is the effect of all this automation? Increasingly, we will see communications, organization, negotiation, conflict resolution, and many other critical, longtime workplace skills become augmented by automation—helping young adults and older people alike automate more of the things that once were learned behaviors and skills to be built and honed over time.

Automated Finances

For the past several years author and entrepreneur Ramit Sethi has been teaching people how to manage their finances in a way that no one else does. His website I Will Teach You To Be Rich (and his best-selling companion book of the same title) focuses on sharing a process that anyone can use to reclaim their financial independence and avoid sinking (or sinking further) into debt. His techniques range from tested scripts for how to negotiate with credit card companies to have them drop fees and an entire module on how to automate your finances.

This automation of finances is a big deal. A large portion of the fees built into the financial system for most consumers come down to organization. If you keep track of how much money is in your accounts, when your bills are due, and who is charging you convenience fees, and who isn't, you can save hundreds or sometimes even thousands of dollars a year in unnecessary fees. Of course that is easier said than done—and normal human behavior is to forget to pay.

Automation is the clear answer. Credit cards can be set up for automatic payment. A recently launched app called Acorn automates saving by rounding up everyday purchases and putting extra money into investments based on predefined savings goals. Payment between people is transforming, thanks to services like Venmo and Paypal, which make it easy to send payments back and forth, and dozens of apps for everything from splitting the check at a restaurant to sharing a cab fare home.

Even the universally dreaded adulthood rite of passage of doing taxes has become more automated, thanks to rapidly evolving and predictive interfaces built into popular self-service online tax preparation tools like TurboTax and H&R Block's online services.

What all of this automation in finances also offers to emerging adults is the chance to feel in control of their finances and to feel more confident about making complex financial choices for the short and long term—even though the bulk of it may be fully managed by algorithms that are set up once and then forgotten.

Why It Matters

As research of the past 10, years has become stronger about uncovering and understanding this new phase of life that is called emerging adulthood, the new slate of companies and technologies that cater to this age group of twentysomethings will continue to grow. As young people grow to count on this technology to teach them new skills, manage the parts of their life that they want to outsource for the sake of productivity, and even help them to optimize their relationships and work lives, adulthood will truly be automated in the future.

Who Should Use This Trend?

Any brand seeking to make a lasting connection or to drive brand loyalty with the highly alluring Millennial demographic should consider the impact of Automated Adulthood. The next generation of young consumers expect technology to help them automate all parts of their lives and to help them make better use of their time. They demand work-life balance and expect those who serve products to them or employ them to be focused on delivering this level of care through technology and processes.

How to Use This Trend

✓ **Appreciate emerging adulthood as a phase** – One of the newest ideas that may have come from this phase for some businesses is the idea that there is even a phase of development that sits between adolescence and adulthood. Whether you choose to go with the term emerging adulthood or not, the implications of understanding this as a phase of development can change how you think about reaching them. Emerging adults are hungry for information, need support and automation, and expect that the companies who appreciate and respect them through this growth period will be the ones they stick with later in life. Your aim should be to become one of those companies.

✓ **Automate complexity** – If there is one thing that emerging adults have little patience for, it is needless complexity. When reaching this group, it is critical that you focus your experience on trimming any unnecessary steps or complex requirements in order to better cater to this group. Are you asking for too much information up front? Do they need to use paper forms instead of electronic forms? These are the small sorts of details that make a big difference in keeping the Millennial customer happy in the near and longer term.

ECONOMICS & ENTREPRENEURSHIP

Chapter 18

OBSESSIVE PRODUCTIVITY
(ORIGINALLY CURATED 2014)

What's the Trend?

Thanks to our reduced attention spans and always-on technology, many people are developing a built-in necessity to be productive in every moment, a tendency that is rapidly evolving into an obsession that underpins every brand interaction or other experience they have.

Several years ago an anthropologist named Wednesday Martin stumbled across a secret only rich Manhattan-based moms were supposed to know. In researching her book Primates of Park Avenue, she learned of an inside trick these moms were passing along to each other to optimize their upcoming trips with kids to Walt Disney World.

These moms were all raving about a service that would pair rich families with a disabled tour guide, who could pose as a member of their family to help them cut lines and avoid waiting. These "black-market tour guides" as one article called them, were the ultimate status symbol. As Martin shared in an interview, "when you're doing it, you're affirming that you are one of the privileged insiders who has and shared this information."

It was a perfect example of a trend I first noticed and wrote about in 2014—our growing obsession with constantly being productive. At any given time, a quick search of top trending articles on any online business publication will typically include at least one article on how to get more done by learning from the productivity secrets of the world's most creative/successful/rich/busy people. The tips range from the obvious (spend less time on Facebook!) to the difficult-but-aspirational (Inbox Zero!).

The more we see and hear about this combination of emerging tools and expert techniques, the more urgency there is to make sure we don't accidentally waste a single moment. The new heroes of the business world have become those entrepreneurs who have embraced the outsourced lifestyle, reclaimed their time, and now live on an island, implementing their four-hour workweeks.

For the rest of the world, this ambition translates into smaller but equally important lifestyle choices. This chapter focuses on several of them, starting with a new breed of devoted curators who are bringing back our allegiances to the individual who delivers our news—a loyalty that seemed dead after the decline of the evening new broadcasters.

Let's focus on two of the most popular of these curators.

Curators of the Mind

Dave Pell has been called the "Internet's managing editor" and has built a loyal subscriber base for his daily email, curating the 10 most fascinating items of the day from the "swirling nightmare of information quicksand" that is the web. Praised for his wit and originality, author and writer Maria Konnikova endorses his site as a "consistently informative and entertaining guide to some of the best stories on the web, with a healthy mix of news you should know, want to know, and prefer to pretend you didn't read."

Another site with a similarly loyal fan base is Brain Pickings by Maria Popova. Her site promises to offer an "inventory of cross-disciplinary interestingness, spanning art, science, design, history, philosophy, and more." The weekly updates she writes are meaningful, multifaceted—and long. Both she and Dave Pell are curating and commenting on media in a form that is intentionally different than a hastily posted tweet.

Great curation takes time—and when you build trust from an audience in the hours you take to create value from a curation, then you can offer value while saving people time in the process. It is this combination that fits perfectly into a world of media consumers who are obsessive about their productivity.

On the surface, it may seem like a contradiction that people with this obsession would spend time reading a lengthy piece of content (as most of these curated updates tend to be). Yet the truth is, productivity is not about reading as little as possible. There is far more value in spending a good 20 minutes reading something which has been specifically curated to cut out all the noise—so your time spent reading isn't wasted.

App-timizing Your Time

It is this desire to avoid having any time wasted that lies at the heart of this trend. As a result, it's not surprising to see rapid growth in all kinds of innovative new apps, services, and startups focused on finding new ways to help us value our time by automating things we used to waste time doing ourselves.

Dozens of food services brands from Starbucks to Domino's Pizza let customers use apps to order meals on their mobile devices and either pick up food or have it delivered. Grocery brands from Fresh Direct in the United States to Sainsbury in the United Kingdom offer online grocery shopping with either home delivery or "click and collect," where customers can simply pick up groceries from the curb, never setting foot outside their cars.

Plenty of startups outside the world of food are also offering new ways for us to optimize our time by taking on tasks that most of us hate doing ourselves.

WinIt, for example, allows you to more quickly and easily dispute and potentially win dismissal of your New York City parking tickets via a smart mobile app. The LucyPhone app offers a service that takes over once you connect to a company's call center, and then provides an automated call back when it's your turn to speak with an agent. The site boasts that it has cumulatively saved its users over 80 years of time so far.

In financial services, this trend towards apps saving customers time while banking has become so common that apps for banks are taken for granted today, considered as commonplace and expected as ATMs. The most popular non-gaming apps today are almost exclusively focused on productivity, and almost all the innovation in banking and financial services apps is entirely aimed at the same thing.

Internet of (Productive) Things

Back in 2014, I also wrote about a product called the Narrative camera, which was designed for "life logging," the idea of having a camera on for an entire day to capture all of your daily activities and actually realize the long-standing human desire for a photographic memory.

For some people, that product may have seemed like the ultimate digital life invasion gone too far, but in the past year plenty of other products tailored for a more mainstream audience were introduced – all promising to optimize your time by automating the mundane.

Digital life optimizer products were introduced to allow everything from automatically scanning barcodes in the kitchen to add to a shopping list (Hiku) to an industry-redefining smart bottle that uses a unique system of pods to deliver vitamins and flavors to water (Lifefuels). Dozens of styles of noise-canceling headphones come into the market each season, all promising to offer a respite from the noisy distracting world and aid productivity. In the health and wellness space, hundreds of sensors and wearables are now on the market to track everything from our quality and quantity of sleep to the optimal posture when sitting in a chair at the office—all to help us be more productive.

As this intersection of wearable devices and smart products continues to grow, the range of products will allow anyone to further explore and feed their obsession with productivity in an even more automated way.

Zero UI

One consistent priority for any design team is to reduce the amount of friction involved in using any interface. Usually, this involves trying hard to achieve a Zen simplicity that balances utility with intuitive design. In 2015, a new movement, ambitiously known as Zero UI, started to take shape. Zero UI is a philosophy of design that is based on the prediction that artificial intelligence (AI), smart bots, and voice commands will soon make the idea of what we typically think of as an interface irrelevant.

When you can talk to a computer as easily as to a person, who needs an interface anyway?

Some of the biggest brands in technology, including Amazon, Microsoft, Google, and Apple all have large investments in trying to realize the real potential of AI and Zero UI first. Microsoft's version is called Cortana, Apple has Siri, and Amazon has Alexa, the voice behind the company's newly launched, always-listening device the Echo. Even Facebook launched early tests in 2015 with M, a digital personal assistant built into its messaging app.

Microsoft Research NExT general manager Lily Cheng describes the potential for all this innovation with an interesting prediction: "Our online conversations will increasingly be mediated by conversation assistants who will help us laugh and be more productive. This will lead us to question and blur the way we think about our computers, phones, and our memories and relationships."

The idea of Zero UI is also impacting designs from those with smaller ambitions than bringing AI to the world. Digit, for example, is an app that you can connect to your bank account to transfer money quickly and in a more automated way. ClassDojo is an app that allows teachers to easily send instant messages to parents. Peter is an "AI-based business lawyer" that offers simple legal tasks through automated messages (like reminders of tax numbers and managing signoffs).

Each of these tools are experimenting with the idea of integrating into the tools you use every day (like email) instead of giving you yet another app to download. It's a sign of the post-app world, where interfaces are a thing of the past, and the mission is to make us more productive than ever.

Why It Matters

As technology gets smarter at predicting exactly what we need and startups focus their innovations on saving us time and energy, more consumers expect this type of productivity and look for it everywhere. This desire has transformed productivity from a nice-to-have aspiration to a full-blown obsession.

In 2016, we will see more technology catering to this obsession and brands updating or changing the way that they interact and engage with consumers to find more ways to optimize their experiences and respect consumers' need for productivity. Speed itself will also become a serious competitive advantage for some brands, making them worthy of charging a premium for consumers whose number-one concern is exactly how much time they will be able to save in any moment, or how useful they can make that time by taking care of multiple things at once.

Who Should Use This Trend?

If you can consider the processes that are inherent parts of your business, you can start to realize which brands are ripe for utilizing this trend as well. Ecommerce brands that drive people through an online experience in order to buy can use this trend to optimize their process. Teams working to develop products or packaging can consider how every step of the consumer experience is impacted by time and what they can do to optimize that.

How to Use This Trend

✓ **Fix your inefficiencies** - As consumers become more conscious of every aspect of their interactions with brands, their patience for any sort of delay or inefficient interface gets lower and lower. The result is that customers can be won or lost in microseconds, as they sometimes make decisions, based on the smallest of details, to abandon interactions or not to reward businesses with their time or money.

✓ **Promise and deliver speed** - When productivity is the ultimate goal for consumers, speed becomes the ultimate competitive advantage. What this means is that the brands who will find new ways to save their customers time will be the preferred choices for all kinds of products and services. The Amazon Prime standard of one-click service is now the standard by which other brands are measured, which means you either need to deliver on this extreme expectation for productivity, or offer a compelling reason why slowing down may be necessary or desirable.

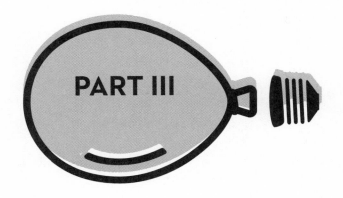

THE 2015 NON-OBVIOUS TREND REPORT

2015 NON-OBVIOUS TRENDS OVERVIEW – SUMMARY

WHAT IS A TREND?
A trend is a unique curated observation about the accelerating present

CULTURE & CONSUMER BEHAVIOR - Trends in how we see ourselves and patterns in popular culture

Everyday Stardom

Selfie Confidence

Mainstream Mindfulness

MARKETING & SOCIAL MEDIA - Trends in how brands are trying to influence and engage consumers

Branded Benevolence

Reverse Retail

The Reluctant Marketer

MEDIA & EDUCATION - Trends in content and information impacting how we learn or are entertained

Glanceable Content

Mood Matching

Experimedia

TECHNOLOGY & DESIGN - Trends in technology innovation and product design impacting our behavior

Unperfection

Predictive Protection

Engineered Addiction

ECONOMICS & ENTREPRENEURSHIP - Trends in business models, startups and careers affecting the future of work or money

Small Data

Disruptive Distribution

Microconsumption

Chapter 19

EVERYDAY STARDOM

What's the Trend?

The growth of personalization leads more consumers to expect everyday interactions to be transformed into celebrity experiences with them as the stars of the show.

The 2016 Perspective

Fame has always been an elusive ambition, but in the coming year it may become increasingly easy to obtain at least for a fleeting moment – and therefore more of an expectation from consumers used to being pampered through personalization.

One example from early last year was the Nike+ team's creative method for celebrating the cumulated annual fitness achievements of their members. Rather than send an email destined to be deleted, they created something more personal. The team combined location and weather information along with fitness data to create more than 100,000 algorithmically generated animations commissioned from a well known French illustrator. These animations were then stitched together into highly personalized videos for each Nike+ user that challenged them to reach a new milestone in 2015. The consumer, in effect, was the star of her own show ... courtesy of Nike+.

This example was just one of dozens of personalized initiatives from companies in 2015 that continued to celebrate individual consumers as superstars. Coca-Cola created bottles with individual names on them – and then let consumers buy them playfully for one another. YouTube personalities like video blogger Marques Brownlee (who former Google Exec Vic Gundotra called "the best technology reviewer on the planet") are having big impacts on how consumers select products.

In the next year, treating individuals like superstars and seeing media personalities emerge through social platforms is likely to grow exponentially – and consumer expectations are likely to do the same, leading to even more pressure on brands of all sizes to create personal experiences and make every customer feel like a VIP no matter how much they spend.

Who Should Use This Trend?

The most powerful element of this trend is how it crosses between leadership and business. Retailers and those who offer a physical experience will find this trend particularly valuable, however they should also consider the implications when it comes to leading a team and inspiring them to believe in a mission. This trend is equally applicable whether you happen to be trying to integrate more personalization to improve a customer experience, or trying to inspire more loyalty from a group of people you are trying to lead or influence.

How to Use This Trend

✓ **Ask personal questions** – Most of us have been taught that it is impolite to ask questions that are too personal. The problem with censoring ourselves against getting personal is that you may lack the information you need in order to really treat someone else like a star. Disney's MagicBand asks for an extraordinary amount of personal data, but they reflect it back to their customers in an obvious way that makes it useful. When you ask customers to share more, it can lead you to a valuable insight to help personalize an experience in a way they may remember for a lifetime.

✓ **Use data you already have** – One of the biggest missed opportunities of many organizations is the store of data that has been collected but never used. Do you have your customers' physical addresses? If so, do you ever send them something proactively that isn't a marketing offer? The point is not to collect data simply to fill a hole in a spreadsheet. If you ask for a piece of information, be sure you're going to use it—or don't ask for it in the first place.

✓ **Focus on memories people can share** – One of the most frequently shared pieces of advice in business today is about creating experiences instead of selling products. It is good advice, most of the time. To effectively use the trend of *Everyday Stardom*, though, may require more effort not only on creating a memorable experience, but also on helping people to actually remember it by helping them share it as it happens.

Chapter 20

SELFIE CONFIDENCE

What's the Trend?

The growing ability to share a carefully created online persona allows more people to use social content such as selfies as a way to build their own self confidence.

The 2016 Perspective

As our online identities continue to reflect our "digital faces" to friends and family, it will continue to impact how we each feel about our true selves in real life.

Late last year, for example, the story of Lexxie Harford went viral after haters online called her "too ugly to love." A British woman who was born with a large birthmark on her face, Harford responded by sharing beautiful selfies online which featured her looking directly at the camera confidently and without makeup. Her photos were shared by thousands and she instantly became a hero for standing up to cyberbullying.

The past year saw several feel good stories like this all illustrating the same basic premise – that confidence can be built through managing the way you portray yourself online.

Advertising campaigns over the past year also illustrated a growth in this trend with several hashtag driven "body positive photo shoots" where brands like Lane Bryant (#ImNoAngel") and Dove (#NoLikesNeeded) promoted the message of being comfortable with yourself. The latter campaign encouraged girls to share their selfies and their best vision of themselves while also encouraging their friends and the online community *NOT* to press the like button. In other words, those selfies and the rise in confidence that results is starting to be separated from the quest for outside validation. Selfies have become a statement rather than an insecure cry for approval.

Beyond selfies, this trend also expanded into other interesting ways for individuals to grow their confidence. In one unique example, *Fast Company* named tattoo artist Vinnie Meyers to its 2015 list of Most Creative People for his work with the The Center for Restorative Breast Surgey in New Orleans to create realistic looking nipple tattoos for breast reconstruction patients to help them feel more confident.

Moving into the coming year, this link between the identity we share through images online and the impact it has on how we build or evolve our own self confidence will continue to drive the way we perceive themselves and how we expect to be treated by the people (and brands) around us as well.

Who Should Use This Trend?

If you have an experience that you offer for people in real life, this trend will clearly be valuable to think about in terms of how people can share that moment in a way that is likely to help them tell a story about themselves that has personal value. In addition, brands that are celebrated by their most passionate customers by appearing frequently as props or backdrops in selfies will have a huge opportunity to find and support their greatest evangelists through social content—if they know how to look for it.

How to Use This Trend

✓ **Overcome the Narcissism Bias** – The common criticism of selfies is that this newfound ability to be both the photographer and subject of the photograph is creating a generation of me-first divas unable to empathize with others. If you don't fit into what some have called the "selfie generation", it is tempting to condemn all those selfie sharers as shallow and narcissistic. To benefit from this trend, the first thing you must do is force yourself to avoid being closed minded about the potential value of selfies.

✓ **Leverage Photo Analytics** – If you are going to connect with customers who are featuring your brand in selfies, you'll need to find them first. Unfortunately, without text these images can be impossible to find. Thankfully, more software innovators like Ditto Labs are pioneering solutions to help scan photos posted online for everything from brand logos or fabric patterns to celebrity faces.

✓ **Make Experiences Easy to Share** – When food research firm Technomic published 10 restaurant trends that would take off in 2015, near the top of the list was the belief that a meal would become a "staged event that imparts bragging rights." This idea of staging real life experiences to share them is increasingly central to the experiences themselves. As a result, providing great Wi-Fi or interesting backdrops can help insert your brand or experience into content and selfies being posted by social media–savvy consumers.

Chapter 21

MAINSTREAM MINDFULNESS

What's the Trend?

*Meditation, yoga and quiet contemplation overcome
their incense-burning reputations to become
powerful tools for individuals and organizations
to improve performance, health and motivation.*

The 2016 Perspective

One of the most popular ideas of the past year was inspired by Japanese organizational consultant Marie Kondo's translated book *The Life Changing Magic Of Tidying Up*. The short book sold more than 2 million copies worldwide and inspired thousands of "Kondos" to share their own photos of themselves using her principles to clean their houses and rooms. Her method, inspired by Eastern philosophy, was seen as a remedy for the chaos that results from accumulating too much "stuff." It was also yet another example of the sort of mindfulness that was once considered the foreign but has rapidly become commonplace.

The past year brought continued signs that this mindset is changing the way high profile business leaders think as well. Another story from Japan gaining international recognition was the unique management principles of 83 year old billionaire, Buddhist priest and entrepreneur Kazuo Inamori. After having built $64 billion Japanese electronics giant

Kyocera Corp (now known as KDDI Corp), he took over the reigns at struggling Japan Airlines in 2010. The next year, he lifted it out of bankruptcy, turned its fortunes around and relisted it on the Tokyo stock exchange. What was his secret?

"Company leaders should seek to make all their employees happy, both materially and intellectually," he told Bloomberg News in a recent interview. "If you want eggs, take care of the hen. If you bully or kill the hen, it's not going to work."

In another example of this growing focus on Mainstream Mindfulness, the high profile 2015 TED conference incorporated a branded experience from Delta Air Lines which aimed to bring mindfulness to life through an experience it called "Stillness In Motion." The interactive exhibit allowed participants to enter a room where biometric sensors measured your heartbeat and created a calmer or clearer experience the more you relaxed. Ultimately, you were presented with a glowing orb with data on your lowest recorded heartbeat. Nearly half the Ted attendees visited the experience and shared it online.

The idea of mindfulness also inspired several emerging successes in the world of business, including luxury cosmetics brand Tatcha, a company founded by a Harvard MBA named Vicky Tsai after she encountered and had her skin transformed by the traditional beauty secrets of Geishas from Japan. Those insights led her to create a range of products that offered the same inspired treatments for women on the other side of the world.

Probably the quirkiest example from the past year that *Mainstream Mindfulness* has really taken off was the astronomical rise of adult coloring books as a way for those with overly stressed lives to enjoy a moment of quiet reflection and satisfaction filling in a sketched, often mandala shaped page with color. The craze even inspired Crayola to launch its own line of adult coloring books in late 2015 – along with crayons and colored pencils, of course.

Each of these examples inspired by traditions of mindfulness illustrate that the trend of merging Eastern philosophy with the Western lifestyle is continuing to drive new thinking and inspire unexpected new businesses – and this trend shows no signs of slowing down in 2016.

Who Should Use This Trend?

As mindfulness shifts from an individual aspiration to an institution-based philosophy, anyone responsible for training or learning programs in an organization or company should watch this trend with interest. It has the potential to impact consumer behavior in terms of how we shop and which companies we align ourselves with. It also will impact leadership and team management as the "softer side" of business becomes a focus area. A final audience that may see great value from this trend is anyone in an overworked position or seeking more balance from the things they do for work and their own ability to relax and enjoy their down time with family or alone.

How to Use This Trend

✓ **Start with short bursts of mindfulness** – Meditation and yoga can seem intimidating to start. It is not always clear what to do and we can't all hire private instructors or visit yoga studios consistently. The good news is there are more apps and tools like Headspace that can help you start slowly. Another technique gaining popularity is to intentionally take a pause between meetings or activities for a set period of time in silence to reset for the coming activities of the day.

✓ **Seek out mindful moments for bonding** – In every team there are activities that relate to your daily work and those that can build a team. Most everyone wants to be part of a great culture, but fostering that type of culture means offering teammates a chance to bond over something other than the work. Conferences or live events can be great ways to inspire this to happen. If members of a team can experience significant mindful or meditative moments together, they are far more likely to connect on a deeper level and build trust in one another.

Chapter 22

BRANDED BENEVOLENCE

What's the Trend?

Companies increasingly put brand purpose at the center of their businesses to show a deeper commitment to doing good beyond just donating money or getting positive PR.

The 2016 Perspective

If there is one sign of hope for the role of companies in our culture, it is that kindness continues to be a priority for an increasing number of companies year after year. In fact this kindness, whether to the environment or customers or society as a whole, is rapidly becoming the ultimate competitive advantage in a world where consumers are increasingly making purchase decisions based on an on demand real time knowledge of a company's ethics and business practices.

In one of the highest profile marketing campaigns of the past year from the travel industry, Southwest Airlines' launched a new campaign called "Transfarency" to spotlight their fair and transparent model for charging travelers for everything from seats to amenities. As Chief Marketing Officer Kevin Krone described it, "we don't hide fees … [and] disagee with the concept of charging fees for things that used to be considered a normal part of flying. What you see is what you get." The move continues to be unique among US based airlines and helps Southwest enjoy loyalty and customer satisfaction scores that eclipse those of their competitors.

Across the year, other brands also made big purpose driven statements around a variety of issues that matter for their businesses and their customers. Salesforce CEO Marc Benioff, for example, committed to making gender equality real by methodically going through all the company's salaries to ensure women's salaries were on par with men's for the same work.

Moving into 2016, the idea of brand purpose is commonly discussed in business strategy meetings, and has become a critical part of how leaders think about the value their companies offer to the world. Purpose matters deeply to consumers, potential employees and current employees alike – which means Branded Benevolence will continue to be a major trend shaping how businesses inspire brand loyalty and attract the best talent over the next year and beyond.

Who Should Use This Trend?

The idea of injecting more kindness into how an organization interacts with customers or does business is almost universally applicable for companies in any industry. In particular, this trend can make a big difference for brands that have existing social-good programs but are struggling to make them more strategic and integrated into something bigger.

How Can You Use This Trend?

✓ **Give time alongside money** – Nothing can doom a well-intentioned effort more quickly than only offering money without any other commitment. As consumers get savvier about tax-deductible promises, it is important to think outside the donation. How could your employees get involved with the cause? What else can you offer beside money? Answering these questions can help you add more significance and make your efforts more human in the process.

✓ **Make kindness a goal** – An important element to remember about *Branded Benevolence* is that the trend also goes far beyond social good. Sometimes adding value to culture means sharing an important message in an entertaining and shareable way.

✓ **Offer unexpected sacrifices** – Tesla opened their patents to the automotive industry. CVS stopped selling cigarettes, despite a full-year loss of revenue estimated at nearly $2 billion. These brands illustrate that sacrifice can be a powerful way to demonstrate *Branded Benevolence*; you are choosing to give something up because you believe in something bigger.

Chapter 23

REVERSE RETAIL

What's the Trend?

Brands increasingly invest in high-touch in-store experiences as a way to build brand affinity and educate customers, while seamlessly integrating with online channels to complete actual purchases and fulfill orders.

The 2016 Perspective

When this trend was first introduced, the idea of Reverse Retail was heavily driven by traditional retail brands in industries like fashion and electronics struggling to find the balance between maximizing in store revenue and creating a truly "omnichannel" retail experience where consumers could interact with a brand in any way they chose.

In the past year, the trend came to life through initiatives like a push by The SPC Mall in Singapore to integrate online and offline shopping. A new mall development introduced by the Singpost (Singapore's postal service) aims to merge the logistics of home delivery (potentially even using drones) with in store shopping and online ordering. The new mall concept is due for completion in mid-2017 and is already being promoted as the "mall of the future."

Adding an interesting dimension to the trend, over the past year there was growing discussion of the emerging potential for "nearables"

– a term used to describe smart connected objects that leverage data about proximity (usually from your mobile phone) in order to improve a consumer experience or better personalize offers.

In 2016, these nearables will create a new battleground for companies who want to leverage real time location data from your mobile device to share relevant messages with those who opt in to receive them. Early tests focused on delivering simple promotional offers, but future applications could range from collecting browsing data from consumers (ie – how long they pause to look at a particular shelf) to providing instant assistance to consumers via roaming sales assistants.

Outside of location based opportunities in retail stores, the other interesting development in Reverse Retail was how the idea has spread to unexpected industries like healthcare. Pharmacy brands like Walmart and CVS are each investing in creating more of a retail experience with mobile apps, location data and on-site clinics staffed by doctors. Online and telemedicine providers are getting better at providing virtual advice and treatment. As we move into 2016, this expansion of the Reverse Retail trend with better technology and adoption from new surprising industries will continue to grow consistently.

Who Should Use This Trend?

Clearly the biggest users of this trend will be retailers or brands that make a product sold through some type of retail channel who must think about how to create an engaging live experience. The real life theater of retail has become the sales engine for later conversion online. This is also a clear win for any company that helps retailers to create these real life experiences or offers some type of event based service or platform to help make the retail experience more interactive.

Beyond retail or products, there is also an implication to reverse the sales process for many other activities, such as getting hired for a job or even teaching a group of people a new skill. No matter what you sell, this trend should inspire you to flip the model for selling it to use real life experiences as a way to entice an online engagement and purchase.

How to Use This Trend:

✓ **Create your own Genius Bars** – The most visible inspiration of the *Reverse Retail* trend is certainly Apple's long-standing Genius Bar method of putting experts in the store to offer customers help with their products (which have been mostly purchased online). The reason this works is because people often want personalized help with technology—and love the experience when they are able to get it.

✓ **Pilot new technology** – One of the ways that fashion retailers in particular are trying to stay ahead of this trend is to find new pioneering technology to test in stores, using everything from "magic mirrors" to interactive touch screens with automated product ordering. Regardless of the technology, working with partners and experimenting with existing technology allows you to be innovative without the burden of building it yourself.

✓ **Embrace spectacle for marketing** – BMW Performance Driving School teaches driving and offers factory tours without ever selling any cars. Microsoft puts motion-controlled Xboxes in the middle of shopping malls to let passersby play or watch motion-activated games. Both tactics work because they offer a highly engaging spectacle that encourages consumers to consider a later purchase of a larger and more expensive product or experience.

Chapter 24

THE RELUCTANT MARKETER

What's the Trend?

As marketing becomes broader than just promotion, leaders and organizations abandon traditional silos, embrace content marketing and invest in the customer experience.

The 2016 Perspective

The marketing industry shift introduced in this trend certainly continued to escalate over the past year as agencies of all types struggled with an identity crisis stemming from industry pressure to abandon the idea of being called agencies at all. Partly fueled by an irreverent and frequently shared conference presentation from Pepsico marketing executive Brad Jakeman where he suggested leaving behind "dated" terms like "digital marketing" or "advertising agency" – marketing shops throughout the past year experimented with a variety of stand-in descriptions for their services.

One agency, for example, described themselves as a "digitally informed marketing lab." Another settled for being a "reformed ad agency." Ultimately, all the angst was about more than a name. The fundamental challenge came down to a shift in the industry from niche services to a single integrated agency that could do it all … and many agencies being unprepared to make the leap.

Outside of the practitioners, the focus on content marketing and saying something valuable instead of interruptive promotional messages continued. Johnnie Walker came back this year with a second edition of its special film called *The Gentleman's Wager II* starring Jude Law. Marriott International invested to build its own in house content studio. Content centric integrated campaigns like Always' #likeagirl campaign took top honors at the Cannes Lions International Festival of Creativity. As this blending of marketing, journalism and art continues – the trend of the Reluctant Marketer is likely to impact even more brand communications across 2016.

Who Should Use This Trend?

This trend most readily affects anyone who is currently working in a marketing position or navigating their path as a leader or CMO of an organization. The world of marketing has always changed rapidly, but 2016 will be a defining year for the CMO within an organization and a moment in time for leaders to carve their own path for how they will evolve the role of CMO to suit their own skills and the companies they work in. A secondary audience for this trend is anyone who creates various forms of media and may never have considered the role in the context of marketing, but who may now increasingly be working with organizations to put their skills to work building compelling stories on behalf of companies.

How to Use This Trend

✓ **Focus on experiences instead of promotion** – For anyone who has been trained in marketing, other customer experience elements like delivery to service to sales may seem as though they belong outside of marketing. That is increasingly no longer true. Are you building content to help your customers use your products *after* they have already purchased them? The key is using these moments to focus on improving experiences which generate more positive marketing and word of mouth, instead of just trying to upsell more stuff.

✓ **Support broader team integration** – Many reluctant marketers will have a background in other disciplines, from operations to finance to documentary storytelling. These outside skill sets can add big value, so a key priority of marketing leaders is to create a workplace where these sorts of intersections and integrations become commonplace and allow an entire team to escape the traditional confines of their own roles and broaden their collective vision.

Chapter 25

GLANCEABLE CONTENT

What's the Trend?

Our shrinking attention spans and the explosion of all forms of content online lead creators to optimize content for rapid consumption at a glance.

The 2016 Perspective

In the past year, online video ruled the Internet, got even more viral, and even got shorter. One of the most popular new social networks of the year was called BeMe and allowed users to record and share videos in four second bursts. The annual celebration of online video creators and fans took place once again in the sixth annual VidCon event in Anaheim. The three day gathering brought together some of the most well known online video personalities and inspired wide ranging discussions on the astronomical rise and popularity of short form content.

Panels and presentations at the event spanned from discussing vertical ads for vertical screens, to new "glanceable" platforms like BeMe, to the evolution of YouTube itself. In total the event attracted more than 20,000 attendees and described itself with this telling vision statement:

One year's VidCon attendee is the next year's superstar. Entire genres are created in the time it takes a full season of TV to meander its way to conclusion ... we believe that online video is the most important cultural force since the motion picture.

Seeing the central role video online has taken in the entertainment of the future, how we learn to do anything and the new gatekeeper-free path to celebrity it is offering to just about anyone ... it is hard to disagree with that vision.

Beyond online video, Glanceable Content was a force that also affected design of the world around us in intricate and unexpected ways offline. Last year, for example, Los Angeles councilman Paul Krekorian piloted a program to install over 100 new parking signs inspired by an easier-to-read grid style sign design created by interactive designer (and frustrated parker) Nikki Sylianteng. The idea, playfully called "To Park Or Not To Park," inspired inquiries from other regions around the world to explore using the idea in their own municipalities as well.

This intersection of design, content creation, and human desire for faster and easier consumption of all types of content (from entertainment to parking signs) is likely keep driving this trend of Glanceable Content to affect content, design and communications in multiple forms in 2016.

Who Should Use This Trend?

The industries most readily affected by this trend are media and entertainment brands that rely on capturing our attention to offer knowledge or pleasure. This trend also expands widely beyond the media industries to any brand trying use content to gain visibility or sell a product. As content marketing continues to become a key tactic for all types of brands, the challenge to create *Glanceable Content* should be one that is used by all types of marketing and communications teams who are actively using content as a part of their sales process. In particular, it has implications for more complex or B2B brands who are used to creating in-depth content that may not be as easily consumed in a glance or be optimized enough to connect with this new consumer mentality.

How to Use This Trend

✓ **Create valuable curations** – In a little over three and a half years, an email summarizing the day's news for professional women called theSkimm has gained more than 1.5 million subscribers. Founded by two 28-year-old entrepreneurs, the daily email offers a fresh take on the news with irreverent views, and boasts an impressive average open rate of 45% (compared with the industry average of 18%). It is a powerful example of how curating content can add big value.

✓ **Focus on headlines** – The trick that many of the more popular and sensationalized media sources today have mastered is the art of writing compelling headlines. While I rarely advocate following the same "you won't believe what happened next" style of *Curated Sensationalism* (one of my 2014 trends), it is critical to spend enough time to craft interesting headlines in order to entice people to engage further.

✓ **Reverse engineer content topics** – A key component of creating *Glanceable Content* is knowing what your audience cares about most. Using Google's keyword analysis tools or "most popular article" lists are great ways to uncover content ideas that may be valuable for your audience. Once you know that, you can create the most valuable content possible.

Chapter 26

MOOD MATCHING

＿＿

What's the Trend?

As tracking technology becomes more sophisticated, media, advertising and immersive experiences like gaming or learning are increasingly tailored to match consumer moods.

The 2016 Perspective

Last year a smart ring launched with the bold claim of being the "world's smallest wearable to contain a biometric sensor." The product is the Moodmetric smart ring, and it promises to measure the "emotional voltage" of the wearer and change color based on levels of stress or anxiety. It is just one of a growing number of innovative products that promise to bring our constantly changing moods to the surface and better use them to tailor experiences for us, or improve our interactions with others.

Apple made waves in October of 2015 when the company filed a patent application for a "smart ring." At the same time both Moodmetric and a Finnish startup called Oulu (maker of the Oura smart ring) featured wearable devices at that renowned Scandanavian startup technology conference called Slush in front of over 15,000 international forward thinking attendees.

The promise of this mood measuring technology, according to Moodmetric COO Niina Venho, is "to [make] it possible for people to analyse their emotional levels throughout the day and learn when they're the most stressed, what makes them calm down... by naming those feelings Moodmetric allows people to get to know themselves better."

This mission of amplifying emotional self-awareness is also driving new innovation designed to improve our emotional well-being at work. For example, Niko Niko is one of the most popular in a range of apps focused on workplace happiness of employees. With a simple swipe right or left, employees can share their level of satisfaction (or dissatisfaction) on all kinds of topics, from the level of supervision they are receiving to the quality of food in the cafeteria.

The data generated by these real time daily surveys is meant to allow instant mood checks among employees, and give managers the data to correct problems long before they may be voiced or reach a tipping point. As mood tracking devices and tools become more commonplace, this idea of how mood affects our behavior and the promise of being able to impact and improve that in real time will continue to direct attention to the trend of Mood Matching, through wearables as well as new tools to help us assess, share, understand and quantify our moods in every moment.

Who Is Using This Trend?

Right now this trend is affecting industries as varied as media and publishers to big brand advertisers. Rather than being only valuable for a certain industry, though, this trend offers an underlying lesson that is likely to be useful for anyone faced with influencing anyone else to buy, sell or believe anything. Moods cannot be ignored and the better you get at tracking them and tailoring your experience, the more likely it is you will be able to make an impact or keep people happy.

How to Use This Trend

✓ **Focus on mood priming** – A big conclusion from the research around how moods affect the way we think and behave is that the mood a consumer has coming into an interaction will likely affect their perception dramatically. As a result, priming your customers by focusing on the mood they first acquire when interacting with you is critical. In the real world, this is yet another piece of evidence that first impressions matter. In the digital world, you can also lose customers right away by not welcoming them in the right way or having a bad initial user experience.

✓ **Build content for moods** – When people consume content based on their moods, it should affect how you create that content in the first place. What this means for any brand looking to use content marketing is that it's worth considering not only the usefulness of the content, in terms of whether it answers a valuable question, but also whether it is tailored to the right mood. If a consumer is likely to be frantic when seeking the content, it needs to be calming. If a consumer is frustrated, then simplicity and humanity is key. Content can and should be tailored by mood.

Chapter 27

EXPERIMEDIA

⊷

What's the Trend?

Content creators use social experiments and real life interactions to study human behavior in unique new ways and build more realistic and entertaining narratives.

The 2016 Perspective

Over time, some trends evolve to become deeper more incisive commentaries on our social behaviour or expand into adoption from new industries or unexpected brands. Then there are trends like Experimedia which remain exactly as they were originally described – and just bring plenty more of the same types of examples a year later.

In the past 12 months since this trend was first introduced, dozens more examples from the world of media, brand marketing and consumer behavior appeared to illustrate that this trend has no signs of fading in the near future. Honest Tea, for example, created a series of 27 pop-up stores in major U.S. cities all designed to test the honesty of the city's residents by giving them to opportunity to pay for their beverages on the honor system if no one appeared to be watching. The winner of this "National Honesty Index" by thin margin: Honolulu, Hawaii.

Longtime social good pioneer Toms Shoes invited people around the world to enjoy a day #withoutshoes on May 21 for the eight straight year in order to support their mission to provide shoes for the poor and gave more than 265,000 pairs of shoes to kids in need.

Greeting Card brand Hallmark followed its highly successful Valentine's Day involving hidden cameras with a Mother's Day campaign using the same method to challenge adult children to show their love without using the usual greeting card platitudes.

Even Dove, the brand that started using social experiments back in 2004 when it first launched the *Dove Campaign For Real Beauty,* continued to evolve its insight that only 2% of women consider themselves beautiful. In 2015, the latest effort from the brand involved creating signs above two doorways into buildings – one labeled beautiful and the other labeled average. Women were encouraged, via a campaign hashtag, to #choosebeautiful – yet another social experiment designed to remind women that they are more beautiful than they think.

All these examples from brands seeking to create more moments to engage consumers to charitable brands aiming to bring the urgency of their causes to life led to plenty of examples of *Experimedia* – and 2016 is likely to bring more of the same.

Who Should Use This Trend?

This trend has been used quite frequently by brands targeting beauty and health products, thanks to the highly visible efforts of Dove over the past decade. Outside of beauty and fashion, though, plenty of consumer packaged goods, alcohol and even financial services brands can realize value from trying to use this technique of *Experimedia* to create interesting and engaging content that people want to share. It is also increasingly used by independent content creators who are trying to build their own audiences to start careers in media and entertainment, or to build enough of an audience individually to get discovered by larger platforms.

How to Use This Trend

✓ **Visualize complex topics** – One of the most successful recent efforts using this trend was a series of ads from Prudential Financial produced in partnership with Harvard professor Dan Gilbert. The ads depict real-life visual experiments designed to motivate Americans to better understand and prepare for retirement. The brand's latest ad in the series involved toppling the world's tallest domino and setting a world record in the process. What it illustrates is that using visual experiments can simplify a complex topic and capture attention in the process.

✓ **Tell an emotional story** – In 2013, Dove crossed the 50 million-view mark on YouTube with its latest video in the "Campaign for Real Beauty." Like its previous efforts, Dove used a social experiment—this time a former FBI sketch artist drawing women's faces—in order to underscore the brand's message: "you are more beautiful than you think." The real life social experiment was so compelling, that delivered the brand message far more powerfully than a traditional ad.

✓ **Recreate experiments** – One of the nicest things about the rise of social experiments covered in the media is that you have plenty of ideas to pull from for when it comes to building your own experiments. While doing this well may seem like it requires an entire video team and a vast experience you may not have internally, launching your own experiments only takes curiosity and a willingness to engage people and freelance resources online who may be able to help with the details.

Chapter 28

UNPERFECTION

What's the Trend?

As people seek out more personal and human experiences, brands and creators intentionally focus on using personality, quirkiness and intentional imperfections to be more human and desirable.

The 2016 Perspective

One of the biggest viral social media stories of the past year involved 18 year old Australian Instagram model Essena O'neill making waves by deleting 2000 pictures "that served no purpose other than self promotion" on her popular Instagram account and renaming her account "Social Media Is Not Real Life." Over the following weeks, she captivated her half million followers by changing the captions on remaining photos to share truthful stories behind their creation, such as the following caption on a photo of her lying sideways on a beach towel in a bikini:

NOT REAL LIFE – took over 100 in similar poses trying to make my stomach look good. Would have hardly eaten that day. Would have yelled at my little sister to keep taking them until I was somewhat proud of this Yep so totally #gross

In another challenge to the status quo of the world of fashion and beauty, comedienne Amy Schumer posed partially nude in a calendar photo shoot for tire maker Pirelli. Already a rising star for her frequent mocking of cultural expectations of women (the poster of her solo standup comedy tour features her dressed in a men's suit holding a cigar and a whiskey), Schumer posted the following message about the photoshoot on Twitter: "Beautiful, gross, strong, thin, fat, pretty, ugly, sexy, disgusting, flawless, woman. Thank you @annieleibovitz." Her experience was part of a larger trend towards makeup-free and unretouched images of women and men being shared as part of fashion and entertainment campaigns across the globe.

Even the "Ugly Sweater Party" craze spotlighted in the original trend chapter reached an unexpected milestone late in 2015 when the champion brand of ugly knitwear (Tipsy Elves) passed the $6 million revenue mark and landed on the Inc list of the top 500 fastest growing brands in America at number 258.

As the year went on, a broader embrace of online vulnerability also became commonplace as sharing on social media took a more imperfect turn and many people stopped shying away from sharing the sad, insecure or turbulent times on their lives with friends and family. Rather than being ridiculed, many started to find solace in the virtual sympathy and encouragement of their extended social media network. Seeing more of one another's flaws, in other words, brought out more empathy and understanding for one another.

In 2016, this macro trend toward people and businesses embracing their Unperfection is likely to continue on many levels and create more opportunities for the boldest companies and people who are able to conquer their fears and share something real, different, and bravely honest.

Who Should Use This Trend?

This trend is important for anyone selling a product or service that has many competitors with similar offerings. The challenge in any crowded marketplace is finding new ways to be unique and stand out. Focusing on *Unperfection* can help you to add more humanity to your products and services and help them to stand out for what they are or for how you describe them.

How to Use This Trend

✓ **Remember, imperfect is different than broken** – Following the news that we throw 300 million tons of food away each year, French supermarket Intermarché created a series of posters featuring "the grotesque apple, the ridiculous potato, the hideous orange, the failed lemon, the disfigured eggplant, the ugly carrot, and the unfortunate clementine." The posters were a viral success and managed to encourage hundreds of consumers in several pilot locations to purchase this "disfigured" produce at a discount. The point is, sometimes we equate imperfect as being the same thing as broken or unusable, but as Intermarché illustrated, these perceptions can be changed.

✓ **Make it purposefully flawed** – When describing his insight for Wrong Theory, *Wired* editor Scott Dadich was sharing the idea that sometimes it may be perfectly acceptable to create something that is purposefully flawed. It is a sentiment that many food manufacturers certainly agree with; consider the rise in so-called artisanal foods, or McDonald's imperfect new Egg White McMuffin (versus the perfect "hockey puck" regular McMuffin). If you can add the flaws on purpose it becomes more distinctive and desirable.

✓ **Embrace your "flaws"** – For NPR listeners, radio personality Diane Rehm has one of the most easily recognizable voices on the air. Yet for many years she has suffered from a neurological condition known as spasmodic dysphonia, which affects the quality of her voice. Rehm's "unperfect" voice is part of her personality and charm, and it helps her stand out. Amongst a sea of perfect altos reading the news, her voice offers something different, and millions of loyal listeners reward her for it with their attention.

Chapter 29

PREDICTIVE PROTECTION

What's the Trend?

*The combination of high privacy concerns with elevated
expectations about the role of technology in our lives leads
to more intuitive products, services and features
to help us live our lives better, safer or more efficiently.*

The 2016 Perspective

In the past year, this trend continued to grow thanks to a slate of smart design initiatives that are building protection into many more aspects of our daily life. In apparel, for example, athletics brand Under Armour introduced a new protective base layer for athletes to absorb impact and provide better overall protection in high contact sports such as American football.

Thanks to growing privacy concerns and high profile data breaches, mobile chip maker Qualcomm also announced new safeguarding technology designed to protect chipsets from various forms of mobile malware.

Perhaps most significantly, conceptual designs from architects moved into reality as pioneering new "smart buildings" served as showcases for a new fully integrated building design that could predict human needs, offer proactive protection from dangers and offer a new kind of personalization straight from the pages of science fiction.

One such structure, sometimes described as the "building of the future" in Amsterdam anticipates its residents' needs. Consulting firm Deloitte's Amsterdam headquarters (known as the Edge) lives up to its reputation as the world's most intelligent building. The building syncs with your phone, knows when you arrive into the parking garage, can suggest a desk for you based on the temperature you like to work in, and even features an open atrium design with slight heat variations and air currents to make it feel like the outdoors – even when it is raining outside.

Slowly as technology improves and more products, buildings and wearables are called "smart" – we will assume this also includes features to offer us predictive protection from the severe (like viruses or injury) to the inconvenient (like wasted time searching for a parking spot). What this means for 2016 is that many new innovative forms of protection, both virtual and physical, will soon be baked into the products that we buy as well as the environments we inhabit. Each will be designed to protect us from harm of any severity, and usually before we recognize it ourselves.

Who Is Using This Trend?

The industries using this trend tend to overlap with the ones who are collecting the most ongoing data, and that fact has value. After all, offering *Predictive Protection* comes down to having the right data and then creating a way to consistently use it in a way that adds value for your customers or users. This data does not need to be proprietary, however. Other industries like athletics and retail also have many customer situations where there could be a benefit to creating *Predictive Protection* for customers through anticipating the likely hurdles in their customer journey and solving them proactively.

How to Use This Trend

✓ **Reprioritize Your Features** – When you think about the different features or benefits of your product or service, it seems logical to list the most significant elements first. Yet as my story of using a fitness tracker illustrated, sometimes the feature you think is the most useful isn't most valuable to your customer. Instead of listing and promoting your features in terms of significance, what if you listed them in order of *proactiveness*? In other words, the features that make your customers' lives easiest and require them to do nothing would be the most important and everything else would be secondary. Considering that might change how you promote your products and services, and understanding how can help you offer exactly the type of protection your customers are looking for.

✓ **Let Them Set It and Forget It** – One of the reasons that subscription commerce models work so well is because they allow consumers to "set it and forget it"—which essentially means that once they are subscribed, many of them won't remember or take the trouble to unsubscribe at a later time. Though this can be somewhat sneaky as a marketing strategy, the point is people want ease of use without the need to continually come back and modify it. Let them do this, and they are more likely to stay loyal.

Chapter 30

ENGINEERED ADDICTION

What's the Trend?

Greater understanding of the behavioral science behind habit formation leads to more designers and engineers intentionally creating addictive experiences that capture consumers' time, money and loyalty.

The 2016 Perspective

Addiction in the context of new forms of technology itself continued to be a big trend across the past year. A story from a recent issue of *The Atlantic* magazine, for example, focused on the rise of an entire industry of treatment centers opening across the US designed to treat Internet Addiction.

One such program, designed for phone dependent adolescents is called Outback Therapeutic Expeditions and takes "patients" out into the western Utah desert for some good old fashioned outdoor activities like building a shelter and learning to tie knots – all while their devices and technology is confiscated. The point, as it often is with any sorts of addicts, is to cure the dependency by showing the kids it's possible to live without their phones.

Another field of research related to addiction was the emerging science of neurogastronomy – the study of how our five senses all contribute to how we each perceive flavors. At the International Society of Neurogastronomy's annual conference, new research and much of the discussion focused on whether it might be possible to manipulate our flavor experiences or even for science to change the way that food tastes for certain people. The implications for positive (helping patients struggling with obesity or compulsive eating to adopt healthier habits) or negative (selling addictive and highly profitable junk food) uses are wide open.

The third booming industry that shined a light on the trend of Engineered Addiction was the rise and incessant promotion of daily fantasy football gaming platforms like FanDuel and DraftKings in the US. Thanks to million dollar advertising budgets, the high visibility and popularity of the NFL and the gray areas of online gambling platforms dedicated to betting on sports – the issue came front and center for litigation and consumer attention in 2015.

As the storm clears and legislation gets signed – these sites are becoming more regulated and attention has started to turn to the people affected by these sites and those who have become all too easily addicted to the underlying ability to easily gamble online.

In the coming year, stories of how these new platforms are leading to more addictive behavior and how they are engineered to do it on purpose will lead to a new focus on the idea of how these addictions start (particularly for technology with high potential for addiction - like virtual reality), who is behind them, what role they play in all types of interfaces which we typically use and what exactly normal consumers can do to fight back.

Who Should Use This Trend?

Game designers have plenty of advice on how to leverage this trend, but any product design team or group responsible for creating a user interface will find the principles of this trend very useful. Information, education and learning organizations should also consider the lessons of this trend, in particular how to leverage some of the techniques that other industries such as gambling or software are actively using already.

How to Use This Trend

✓ **Reward engagement** – Loyalty programs reward engagement, and that same framework may be useful for building an addictive experience as well. Whether you use points, badges or some other type of incentive—the key is making these rewards visible and emotional enough that people will continually keep coming back for them.

✓ **Cater to a common human emotion** – Online learning website Curious.com features compilations of short videos on subjects like how to curl your hair and how to play the ukulele. The site is filled with snack-sized content, with high-quality videos and the promise of quick learning that happens so fast you are tempted to try another and another. The temptation and motivation is inferred perfectly by the URL of the site: curiosity.com.

Chapter 31

SMALL DATA

What's the Trend?

As consumers increasingly collect their own data from online
activities and the Internet of Things, brand-owned big data
becomes less valuable than immediately actionable
small data collected and owned by consumers themselves.

The 2016 Perspective

This chapter spotlighted the potential for small data to change the way consumers used their own data as leverage to entice brands to offer better experiences for them – and opportunities for brands to take advantage of new data sets that were previously either non-existent or at least not available. In late 2015, a small group of managers running digital commerce and contact centers for a range of brands came together for the second annual *Intelligent Assistants Conference*.

The event featured presentations from founders of technologies that focused on the intersection of artificial intelligence, machine learning, natural language processing and the customer experience. At the event, a small New Zealand based company called MyWave introduced their already popular Intelligent Assistant app to the US market with a bold prediction: "Ultimately, consumers will decide how and when to share their personal data with brands."

This future, which MyWave Founder and CEO Geraldine McBride termed "Customer Managed Relationship" (CMR) had the potential to change the way that the entire field of Customer Relationship Management (CRM) is practiced.

Leveraging the power of this trend of Small Data, Intelligent Assistants like the one created by MyWave are already predictively help users to shop for the best price, navigate traffic situations, automatically handle mudane tasks like filling out the warranty form for new purchases, and even selectively share a user's data (with permission) with retailers in order to get more personalized offers and savings.

Examples like this are taking the promise of "Small Data" that was introduced in this trend more than a year ago and making it into reality for everyday consumers. Yet this is only one sign of the growing focus on the idea of leveraging smaller and more personal consumer created data versus sifting through bigger impersonal data collected en masse.

A slightly different definition of Small Data will emerge in February of 2016 when best selling business author and consumer researcher Martin Lindstrom releases a book called *Small Data* all about his insights gathered through direct observation and conversations with consumers gleaned from years of direct research with consumers. According to Lindstrom, the term "small data" is the perfect way to describe these clues and insights into people's lives that he gathers through direct observation.

"No matter how insignificant consumer observations may appear to be," he says "I've learned the every single thing we do in life consciously or unconsciously reveals incredible insights about who we really are. While big data spews out constant terabytes of impersonal data in an attempt to predict future directions of businesses that brands it is the uniquely human small data right in front of us that reveals all the real truths and insights."

In the coming year this "uniquely human" *Small Data*, whether collected by popular consumer researchers or by consumers themselves, will continue to shift how personalization works and the opportunities any brand will have to better tailor their products and services to empowered consumers.

Who Should Use This Trend?

Though big data sometimes seems like the domain of large brands and governments, small data is accessible to any of us, whether you happen to be a blogger trying to optimize your own website, or a small business collecting customer feedback through surveys. The key will be to combine a smart approach to capturing and reviewing only the data that matters, then with finding new ways to act upon your customer's personal data if they choose to share it with you.

How to Use This Trend

✓ **Offer to use consumer-owned data** – Just because a consumer may be collecting their own data and you don't have an easy technological method to download it doesn't mean you can't benefit from it. For example, if you own a sports and fitness store, you could ask consumers to bring in a printout of some of their self-collected wellness data in order to help them select better products. The point is, there are many ways to use customer data, whether you can download it or not.

✓ **Watch for new popular products** – One of the lessons from the Consumer Electronics Show that may offer interesting opportunities for you is to track what products are starting to take off and gain widespread adoption. As more people put a smart thermostat like Nest in their homes, it may open more opportunities to speak with them about energy conservation. If your business is in this space, the adoption of this type of product can open new doors. Similarly, there may be other products coming that could affect your industry, if you can make sure you are watching for them.

Chapter 32

DISRUPTIVE DISTRIBUTION

What's the Trend?

Creators and makers use new models for distribution
to disrupt the usual channels, cut out middlemen
and build more direct connections with fans and buyers.

The 2016 Perspective

Near the end of 2015, Fortune magazine released its "Unicorn List" featuring more than 100 companies that had reached a $1 billion or more valuation based primarily on fundraising. Many of these companies are recognizable mainly for the industry disruption they have caused. Uber, AirBNB, and Facebook are all household brands that have changed the way that their previous industries handled distribution of services or products.

In the coming year, the emerging category of Financial Technology startups (often referred to as "FinTech") is also a space that will see continued growth and opportunity. Hotly debated virtual currency Bitcoin, for example, saw plenty of investment and attention across the year as leading startup Coinbase managed to collect support from both venture capital firms and banks themselves.

In the middle of the year, crowdsourcing advisory firm Massolution released a research report predicting that by 2016 crowdfunding would account for more startup investment that traditional venture capital. Despite its industry bias, the report does spotlight an interesting development in the world of financial investment which continues to rise – the widespread acceptance of nontraditional sources of funding.

As the collaborative economy continues to force more disruption among financial services firms, thanks in part to a growing surge in equity based crowdfunding, a recent *Venture Beat* report led by analyst Jeremiah Owyang estimates the sharing economy has created 17 billion dollar companies so far and 10 "unicorns."

Disruptive Distribution is also fueled by smaller but no less significant experimental initiatives from entrepreneurs hungry to experiment with new models. In another example, the world of wine and spirits saw entrepreneurs experiment with distribution thanks to a recent law passed in Alaska that allowed independent distilleries to open tasting rooms. Across the past year, a range of popular new distilleries including Port Chilkoot Distillery, High Mark Distillery and Anchorage Distillery are making the remotest of US states a tourist destination for an all new reason.

In May of 2015, a Japanese bookstore clerk named Yoshiyuki Morioka launched a bold experiment with his Morioka Shoten bookstore in the upmarket shopping district of Ginza in Tokyo. The store captured the attention of the world for its radical idea – it would only sell one book at a time and devote an entire week to author events, community discussions and engagement around that book.

Whether or not the bookstore lasts and the concept catches on – it is a perfect example of the logical extremes that this trend of *Disruptive Distribution* has been driving entrepreneurs to explore across the past year. As time moves on and new startups enter unexpected markets and innovate faster than the incumbents are able to match – disruption in the fundamental distribution of how goods and services are sold and delivered will continue to escalate.

Who Should Use This Trend?

Any business that sells products or services in a marketplace or through channels controlled by a central distributor will see some impact of this trend. The opportunity exists then, to find ways to leverage the audience you already have and deliver directly to those who want to buy from you.

In a world where the method for how you have sold your products or services and distributed them is undergoing seismic changes, how can you make sure your business is ready to survive? That is the ultimate question that this trend will force many businesses to confront in 2016.

How to Use This Trend

✓ **Make a big statement** – When a group of North Dakota farmers decided to create a restaurant on the East Coast called Founding Farmers, part of the idea was to bring the direct model of farm-to-table restaurants to Washington, DC. The aim, aside from reconnecting people to the growers and sources of their food, was to put a themed restaurant in a high-profile location filled with foodies and influential politicians. The lesson is an important one for leveraging the value of *Disruptive Distribution*: sometimes the ideal way to start is by creating a small pilot and building from that.

✓ **Take the better deal (even if it's not perfect)** – Russian eretailer Lamoda solved its distribution problem by building a fleet of delivery vehicles and its own transportation network. While the model of Lamoda is tempting, it is also hugely expensive and complex. The far easier path is to find a distribution model that is disruptive enough to offer *more* control. Amazon's model for book selling is a perfect example. It offers higher margins back to authors and publishers, yet it is still far from perfect because it also separates authors from readers while Amazon retains ownership of customer data. The point is, sometimes using *Disruptive Distribution* means taking the best available option and getting as *close* to direct distribution as possible.

Chapter 33

MICROCONSUMPTION

What's the Trend?

As new payment models and products and experiences become available in bite-sized portions, multiple industries will experiment with micro-sized new forms of pricing and payments.

The 2016 Perspective

As attention continues to shrink and new technology empowers consumers to skip, filter or block out marketing messages – the necessity for advertising to evolve has become urgent. In the past year, this urgency led to plenty of angst in the world of marketing as cover stories in multiple publications focused on the "death" of advertising –challenged in all directions by online click fraud, indifferent consumers, stodgy creativity and a lack of relevance to the modern world.

The common platitude for struggling marketers is to advise creativity as the solution. In the past year, there were multiple signs that this creativity may be best directed towards the platforms themselves rather than the stories told upon them. Microadvertising, for example, is a new short form of promotional message designed to be digested in quick bursts, on mobile devices, and adept at creating engagement in a branded message through an entertaining piece of content.

One leader that emerged in the past year around this growing shift was a mobile app called MikMak which features short stoppable infor-mercials which they dub "minimercials." The aim for these is ambitious – to get millennials to binge watch them the same way they might watch other programming. Engagement, not promotion, is the priority here. According to MikMak founder and CEO Rachel Tipograph, "we're an entertainment company first that happens to sell things."

This is a model designed to use tiny bite sized messages to drive engagement versus longer irrelevant commercial messages created for mass audiences and distributed as tone-deaf 30 second spots to be suf-fered through as payment for watching entertainment provided for "free".

Another innovator in the space of Microconsumption was popular morning email service The Skimm which reports over 1.5 million active users of their daily news email service and an enviable 45% open rate. "We are deconstructing morning behavior," say founders Danielle Weis-berg and Carly Zakin as they talk about their ambitions fueled by the new morning ritual of checking our phones from bed.

As more marketers and providers of media continue to cater to his shifting attention span – the coming year will likely see more efforts to create smaller pockets of engagement through short form content.

Who Should Be Using This Trend?

The first to utilize this trend will be those in the content and media industries as they work to build new models for allowing people to pay for access, or to charge advertisers to reach those users. Outside of pub-lishers of content, this trend will also be very important to watch for any organization that can find unique ways to break up its products or expe-riences into smaller pieces to enable more turnkey payments, particularly in a recurring fashion. Automotive manufacturers and car rental agencies will allow consumers to rent by the minute. Media sites will charge by the story. Any industry that can rethink how their current products and ser-vices are packaged and paid for can start to utilize this trend to prepare their own models for new opportunities in 2016.

How to Use This Trend

✓ **Be first to accept different payments** – The past year was filled with announcements from a number of companies wanting to become the "first to accept bitcoin" in their industries. Air Baltic was the first airline. Meltdown Comics was the first comic book store. Time Inc. was the first major magazine publisher. In 2016, more brands will aim to be first at accepting new forms of payment. As they become easier to implement without big technology investments, this opportunity to be first will continue.

✓ **Produce more bite-sized content** – Related to the idea of making your content instantly glanceable, there is also a corresponding value to keep it short and consumable. When Netflix analyzed customer sessions, they realized that 87 percent of all mobile sessions lasted less than ten minutes. The only problem was, Netflix didn't have any content shorter than ten minutes long. As a result, the brand announced its intentions to create 2–5 minute clips designed for mobile users. This same technique can help you target consumers' desire for *Microconsumption* as well, by giving them value in short, digestible bursts.

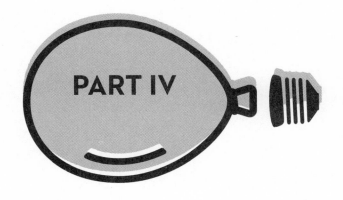

PART IV

THE TREND
ACTION GUIDE

INTERSECTION THINKING:
How to Apply Trends to Your Business

In 2009 Tom Maas, a former marketing executive for distiller Jim Beam, finally created his perfect drink. For years he had been working on developing and promoting a new cream liquor based on the popular traditional milky cinnamon and almond drink from Latin America known as *horchata*.

This new drink, RumChata (a mashup of its primary liquor and the drink that inspired its flavors), was a mixture of light rum, dairy cream and spices like cinnamon and vanilla.

It was not an instant hit.

The drink took some inventive selling, and it was only when bartenders started comparing its taste to the milk at the bottom of a bowl of Cinnamon Toast Crunch cereal that it started to take off.

Bartenders started using the liquor to create more inspired blends, which quickly led to more liquor distributors and retailers ordering it. Meanwhile the brand ran inventive promotions like "cereal shooter bowls" designed for bars to serve RumChata based drinks and to further build the brand.

Eventually the creativity finally started working.

A recent *BusinessWeek* article noted that the drink has taken one-fifth of the market share in the $1 billion U.S. market for cream-based liquors, and even started outselling Diageo's Baileys Irish Cream (the longstanding leader) in certain regions.

More importantly, experts described the drink as a crossover game changer, due to its popularity as a mixer and its popularity as an ingredient for food and baking recipes.

How to Create a Game-Changing Product

RumChata is a perfect example of the type of result that can ultimately come from putting the power of observation together with an understanding for the intersection of consumer behavior and the open space in a market.

While Maas may not have used this same trend curation approach in order to come up with his product idea, we can still reverse engineer its success in order to find some lessons in the example.

When you do that, it becomes easy to spot a few of the big trends over the past several years that clearly support the concept of RumChata and perhaps explain some of its success:

- A growing consumer desire for authentic products with interesting backstories
- The rising prevalence of food entertainment programming on television inspiring more creativity in home cooking
- The increased interest across the United States in Hispanic culture and heritage

In retrospect, these observations clearly seem to support the arrival of a product like RumChata. Of course, putting the dots together looking backwards is easy.

The real question is: how can you do it predictably in a way that can help you to create your *own* success in the near future?

An Introduction to Intersection Thinking

Trends are typically big ideas describing the accelerating world around us. Unfortunately, the value of big ideas are not always easily understood when it comes to applying them to real life situations.

Trend forecaster Chris Sanderson from *The Future Laboratory* describes trends as "profits waiting to happen." As tempting as that sounds, realizing those profits takes more than skill at uncovering, curating and describing a trend.

Trends only have value if you can learn to act on them.

Is a trend telling you to abandon an existing product line? Or to pivot the focus of your business? Or to stay the course in a direction that hasn't yet paid off? These are the sorts of big questions that leaders are likely to contend with in our business ventures, and they are not easy to answer.

The good news is that we can usually find the answers if we apply the right model of thinking. The rest of this section is dedicated to giving you the tools, processes and knowledge to be able to apply trends in your own business and career.

Over the past several years of helping dozens organizations and thousands of people learn to apply trends, my approach always starts with the single simple concept of intersection thinking.

Intersection thinking is a method for creating overlap between seemingly disconnected ideas in order to generate new ideas, directions and strategies for powering your own success.

Most of the time, I have used a workshop model to help teams and brands apply intersection thinking to their challenges in order to create new approaches based on trends in the marketplace. The chapters following this one offer a step-by-step approach to take you through four of the most popular workshop models I typically use. Before engaging in these workshops, it is useful to share three basic principles behind applying intersection thinking in real life.

PRINCIPLE #1: SEE THE SIMILARITIES INSTEAD OF THE DIFFERENCES.

My friend Paolo Nagari is an intercultural intelligence expert who teaches executives the skills they need to succeed while living overseas.

Unlike many other experts, however, his model doesn't rely on teaching the "dos and don'ts" of a particular culture. Succeeding in a culture other than your own takes more than memorizing checklists.

Nagari's first rule for executives is all about learning to focus on the many similarities in cultures instead of the differences. It is a valuable lesson when considering how to embrace unfamiliar ideas as well.

Though the stories or industry behind a certain trend may seem disconnected from your own, there are always more similarities than you think. When former Coca-Cola executive Jeff Dunn became president of Bolthouse Farms in 2008, for example, he walked into a billion-dollar agricultural company that had literally reinvented the carrot industry by creating "baby carrots."

By the time Dunn took over, sales of carrots (and baby carrots) were experiencing a slump and he needed a solution, so he turned to advertising agency Crispin Porter + Bogusky (CP+B).

It wasn't the usual challenge for the agency, but they were inspired by a unique idea based on a simple consumer insight: people love snacking on junk food and hate being told to eat healthier.

As CP+B creative director Omid Farhang later said in an interview "the truth about baby carrots is they possess many of the defining characteristics of our favorite junk food. They're neon orange, they're crunchy, they're dippable, they're kind of addictive."

Using this insight, CP+B built a new campaign that enticed consumers to "Eat 'Em Like Junk Food," inspired by the marketing tactics of other consumer packaged goods companies (like Coca-Cola). In campaign test markets, sales immediately went up between 10% and 12%, all thanks to a campaign built from seeing the similarities between the wildly divergent products of junk food and vegetables.

PRINCIPLE #2: PURPOSELY LOOK AWAY FROM YOUR GOAL.

Frans Johansson is a keen observer of people and companies. His first book, *The Medici Effect*, talked beautifully about the power of intersections between diverse industries and people as a way of generating game-changing ideas, products and organizations.

In his second book, *The Click Moment*, he focused on the related idea of serendipity in our lives and what any of us might do in order to increase the chances of having our own serendipitous meetings or interactions with others.

In this second book he also retells the well-known origin story of the inspiration behind Starbucks, inspired by a trip Howard Schultz took to Milan, where he saw the dominance of the Italian espresso coffee shops on every street corner and imagined that a similar type of establishment might work in America as well.

Schultz's insight led to a pivot for Starbucks from a supplier of high-end home brewing equipment at the time to a retail coffee establishment. Interestingly, the original purpose of his trip to Milan was only to attend a trade show.

It was on a chance walk from his hotel to the convention center that he noticed and became inspired by these espresso bars. His story is a perfect illustration that sometimes it is better to explore ideas outside your main goal so you can see even bigger ideas waiting to be discovered.

PRINCIPLE 3: WANDER INTO THE UNFAMILIAR.

If you happen to be walking the streets of Bangkok around 6pm on any particular day, you will see people stop in their tracks for seemingly inexplicable reasons. Ask anyone afterwards and you will quickly learn that there are two times every day when the Thai national anthem is played (8am and 6pm) and all citizens stop what they are doing and observe a moment of silence out of respect.

Once you see this cultural practice in action, it is impossible to forget.

Travel experiences are like this—whether they happen across the world from your home, or simply during a visit to an unfamiliar place. Wandering is a form of exploration that we often think to embrace only when traveling, but it has great value on a more daily basis.

In a world where we have a mobile map in our pocket, ready to assist us with turn-by-turn directions to anywhere, wandering must be a choice. It is the perfect metaphor for why intersection thinking matters, and why it can be difficult as well.

Sometimes we must choose to leave our maps behind. Workshops can help you do that – so let's explore further exactly how and why they can be so effective.

Why Workshops Work

A workshop is a gathering or meeting where an individual or a group of people focus their conversation and ideation on solving a challenge or thinking in new innovative ways.

While it may seem like a complicated endeavor (particularly if you are looking to apply trends more individually for yourself and your own career), there are several reasons to consider taking a workshop-driven approach to applying trends.

1. **Focus your attention.** We are all busy and usually don't have the time to be sitting around thinking about trends all day. To ensure you can have the right focused attention, it is most valuable to block out a set period of time for a workshop, even if it happens to be minimal. Just the act of making sure this time is scheduled and separate from your usual daily activities will help ensure that it feels and actually becomes significant.

2. **Follow a defined process.** While you don't need a step-by-step map, it is always useful to have a purpose or destination defined. There are many ways to engineer the structure of what you do in a workshop. The important thing is that, like any good meeting, your workshop has a purpose so participants know what you aim to accomplish and make a commitment to the same shared goals.

3. **Establish accountability.** Another critical reason that workshops can be so effective is that they help bring the right people together in a single moment so they can make commitments about action steps and what to do next.

Accountability, of course, is equally important if you happen to be working alone to decide how to apply these trends.

Almost every one of the dozens of workshops I have given on marketing and business trends and the future starts the same way, with a presentation of trends and the situation as it is today. Yet it is important to remember that most of the time, *the ultimate goal in a workshop is not to uncover new trends.*

A workshop is most useful after you have *already* used the process in the first part of the book to curate your own trends, or selected trends produced by others (such as those featured in Part II of this book) or trends from other reputable sources (see Chapter 35). The goal of any trend workshop is to take those trends and discuss how to put them into action to solve your business challenges.

Five Keys to Running a Great Trend Workshop

When considering using a workshop, there are a few basic ground rules to keep in mind to help you get the best result:

1. **Always have an unbiased facilitator** – It is easy to assume that the person closest to the issue will be the right person to lead a workshop, but this is often not true. Instead, the best workshop facilitators are individuals who can lead a discussion, keep a conversation on track and ask bold questions without being biased or intentionally leading a group toward a particular answer or point of view.

2. **Encourage sharing, not critiquing** – We have all heard the common cliché that there are "no bad ideas in a brainstorm." That's not technically true. There *are* bad ideas, off-strategy ideas, impossible ideas and useless ideas. Unfortunately, they are rarely easy to distinguish in the real time environment of a workshop. For that reason, the best mentality to encourage for all participants is one where everyone commits to sharing new ideas that can be captured rather than wasting time and energy trying to critique an idea in the moment it is shared.

3. **Adopt a "yes and" mindset** – Improv actors always talk about the importance of collaborating with others in a scene by always saying "yes and" instead of "yes but" (its far more negative cousin). This additive approach allows you to build upon what others have shared instead of breaking it down, and it is one of the consistent hallmarks of great and effective workshops as well.

4. **Prepare like a pro** – If you have ever heard the phrase "garbage in, garbage out"—you should know this applies tenfold to workshops. If you have not prepared the right materials, insights and questions before a workshop, you will rarely be able to generate great value. This doesn't necessarily mean spending months on research, but you should have the right background to focus the conversation on the most critical questions.

5. **Recap and summarize** – One of the worst things to do after committing the time and expense to running a workshop is to let everyone in the room leave without summarizing what took place over the time you shared together. It is the role of the facilitator to summarize the conversation, recap any action items and ensure that everyone who spent their precious time participating understands what they collectively achieved and what will need to happen next in order to keep the momentum going.

About the Four Models of Trend Workshops

While the formats and methods you might use in this type of workshop setting are almost endless, I most often use four specific models to help organizations apply trends:

1. **Customer Journey Mapping Trend Workshop** – Building a step-by-step understanding of how your customers interact with you so you can apply trends to each step of the process.

2. **Brand Storytelling Trend Workshop** – Developing a powerful brand story or message designed to resonate with customers based on understanding and using current trends.
3. **Business Strategy Trend Workshop** – Creating a new go-to-market or product-launch strategy or making changes to a business model or revenue model informed by current trends and new competitive situations.
4. **Company Culture Trend Workshop** – Planning your career or optimizing and improving an internal company culture and team based on current trends.

In the original edition of Non-Obvious, each workshop was outlined in detail through four additional chapters. For the sake of brevity those chapters are not included in this edition. If you would still like to read them you can visit www.rohitbhargava/workshops to download a free bonus pdf.

Special Note For Small Teams

Although the following chapters are specifically written from the point of view of having multiple participants in each type of workshop, many of the lessons in these chapters can be easily applied to small businesses individually as well.

It may be tempting to dismiss the value of workshops or even intersection thinking if you happen to be on your own, but I encourage you to give these approaches a chance anyway. Just because you don't have a large group of team members doesn't mean you can't use the benefits of intersection thinking and workshops to power your business. There is never a bad time to break from your normal routine and dedicate time to strategizing for the future.

THE 7 BEST TREND RESOURCES
YOU NEED TO BOOKMARK

Despite the skepticism with which I often approach trend reports from so-called gurus, there are handful of amazingly valuable sources for trend forecasting and techniques that I have drawn upon heavily over the years. Some have already been cited elsewhere in this book, however in the interests of simplicity, I am including a full list of some of my favorite resources below. (*Note:* Several top sources such as Iconoculture have been omitted from this list because most of their research is accessible only to subscribers and not the general public.)

These organizations and individuals publish consistently insightful ideas and forecasts worth paying attention to. Each is on my must-read list every year and never fails to offer several ideas that inform my thinking annually as I prepare the *Non-Obvious Trend Report* – including three new additions from the last edition of the book.

1. **Trendwatching.com (trendwatching.com)**
This is hands-down the most useful trend and forecasting resource in existence. Through a network of thousands of spotters all over the world, this is the one resource that I consistently find insightful, valuable and extremely well researched. There are times, in fact, when seeking sources for a potential trend on my list turns up a very similar idea from Trendwatching.com. Visit their site and subscribe to receive their excellent free monthly

reports. If you work for an organization that can afford it, pay to access their premium service (currently $199 per month) and use it.

2. PSFK (www.psfk.com)

Ever since I first met founder Piers Fawkes at an event more than five years ago, I am consistently impressed with the thinking that he and his team compile on big topics like the future of retail and the future of work. Several of their reports are published in partnership with sponsors, which means they are freely available, but even just browsing their consistently excellent blog will inspire you with new ideas, curated observations and plenty of stories worth saving for later aggregation.

3. *Megatrends* by John Naisbitt

There is a reason why the book about trends and the future has been a bestseller for the past three decades. In the book, Naisbitt not only paints a fascinating future portrait of the world as he saw it back in the early '80s, but he also captures his own time in the mirror from the viewpoint he writes from. Despite the many years that have passed since the book was first published, it remains a valuable read both for the prescience of his ideas and the how he manages to capture the spirit of his time while comparing it to a surprisingly accurate vision of the future.

4. *The Trend Forecaster's Handbook* by Martin Raymond

There isn't really a textbook for trend forecasting, but if there were, this full-color large-format volume from Martin Raymond would come pretty close. It has a hefty price tag (like most textbooks), but the content is beautifully organized and it comes closest to presenting a dictionary-style compilation of everything you can imagine needing to know about trend forecasting. From interviews with top futurists to highly useful sidebars (like how to select and interview an expert panel), this book compiles so much insight that it's worth buying because you'll probably refer to it again and again.

5. Cool Hunting (www.coolhunting.com)

If you have ever been to one of those beautifully authentic farmer's markets where the produce is amazingly fresh, but the organization is a bit haphazard and confusing – then you'll appreciate the value of Cool Hunting. The site has amazing content and is guaranteed to spark new ideas for you anytime you visit, but you'll have to navigate the busy design and minimal organization alongside those sparks of brilliance. If you can find the patience to browse the site instead of searching, though, you will find the content to be completely inspirational.

6. The Cool Hunter (www.thecoolhunter.co.uk)

Despite its name, this site has no affiliation with Cool Hunting. Aside from sharing a compendium of ideas, the structure of the sites couldn't be more different. On The Cool Hunter, all the blog posts are cleanly presented in very specific categories from "Exotic Places" to "Architecture." Each post is highly visual and it is easy to browse from story to story. As a result, the experience of navigating the site is a bit like going to a perfectly organized library and pulling random ideas off the shelf.

7. SlideShare (www.slideshare.com)

Almost every flawed, lazy or overly ambitious trend report I have ever read was one I found on Slideshare.com, so it probably seems like an odd choice to add to my list of must-read resources, but the fact is you can get a lot of great insights on SlideShare. Some of them relate to trend predictions that are of little value, but learning to *see through* them is a valuable skill in itself. Outside of that, there are plenty of deep, insightful presentations that can offer ideas about new industries and markets, or take you inside an unfamiliar subject in a visual and easy-to-read way.

For an online list of all the sources included here, please visit the link below:

WWW.ROHITBHARGAVA.COM/NONOBVIOUS/RESOURCES

ANTI-TRENDS:
The Flip Side Of Trends

From the end of September until the beginning of November, the Piedmont region of Italy is one of the most popular foodie destinations in the world for two reasons. The first are the famous Barolo wines produced from the native Nebbiolo grape and the second reaches its peak during the first week of October, when the town of Alba hosts its annual White Truffle Fair.

Truffles are the favorite decadent ingredient for top chefs and white truffles are the rarest—sometimes costing as much as $2000 per pound. Truffles from Alba are alternately described by chefs as "sublime" and "unlike anything else in the world." The Barolo wines too are considered Italy's best, called the "king of wines" for centuries.

Yet as amazing as these two Piedmont region delicacies seem, there is one critical problem the region can't control: they are never both at their relative prime at the same time – because they requre opposite kinds of weather.

Truffles are best after a wet summer, while wine is best after a dry and hot summer. As a result, any summer cannot be equally good for both wine *and* truffles.

Flip Thinking and Anti-Trends

In this book, I have shared a process for uncovering trends that affect the world around us, and advice on how to use them to power your business and career. Perhaps while reading one of these trends, you thought of an example that seemed to do the exact opposite of what the trend was describing. Or that the impact of one trend might make another less valuable – like the truffles and wine.

Just like Piedmont's delicacies, there is often an opposing force that balances out trends, and it comes from people and companies that see what everyone else is doing and choose to do the opposite. Sometimes we hear it called "flip thinking," a term used most popularly by author Dan Pink. In one instance, he used it to describe a teacher who "flipped" the classroom by assigning math lectures via YouTube video as homework and actually doing the problems together in class.

Flip thinking will always be present, and for every trend someone will usually find an example of the exact opposite. This is not a flaw in trend prediction but rather the opportunity that it routinely presents. Yet it would be natural to wonder: if we have invested all this work into curating and describing trends, how can we be sure they matter when sometimes it seems so easy to find examples of the opposite?

Breaking Trends

Trends are not like mathematical theories. They are describing a behavior or occurence that is accelerating and will matter more and more, but they are not hard and fast rules of culture or behavior. There will always be outliers.

The point of curating trends is to see what others don't, and to predict a future that can inspire new thinking. There is an interesting opportunity, though, that arises from being able to use this truth of "flip thinking" for yourself.

Understanding trends not only empowers you to use them positively, but also to intentionally break them and do the opposite when it's an appropriate way to stand out.

Pablo Picasso famously declared that each of us should aim to "learn the rules like a pro so you can break them like an artist."

The clown in an ice-skating show, for example, often needs to be the most talented in order to execute fake jumps and falls while still remaining under control. Similarly, your ability to know the trends may give you the insight you need to bend or break them strategically.

This is, after all, a book about thinking in new and different ways. So taking a trend and aiming to embrace its opposite certainly qualifies.

AFTERWORD

‎‗•‗‎

"THERE'S NO SUCH THING AS WEIRD FOOD. ONLY WEIRD PEOPLE."

—FERRAN ADRIÀ, chef and molecular gastronomist

Apparently, the world will end on March 16, 2880.

While putting the final touches on this book, I came across a news article about a team of scientists who discovered a 0.3% chance the world will end on that day due to a cosmic collision course between the Earth and a celestial body known only as Asteroid 1950 DA.

The story immediately struck me as the perfect metaphor for the types of predictions we commonly encounter … overblown proclamations with dire consequences and relatively little certainty.

One of my aims throughout this book was to challenge the lazy or obvious trend predictions that are published each year. They are sadly similar to this exaggerated astronomical example in terms of the lack of value they offer us in the present.

A trend is a unique curated observation of the accelerating present.

So this book very specifically *doesn't* offer geopolitical arguments for why Denmark is going to become the world's next superpower by 2050 thanks to wind energy production, or optimistic technology predictions about how self-driving cars will enable virtual-reality tourism during daily commutes.

I know those kinds of predictions are sexy, and some might even come true. Unfortunately, they also include a lot of uncertainty. Getting better at observing reality means preparing for the future should involve far less guesswork.

Curating trends is about seeing the things other don't. Yet it is also more broadly about a mindset that encourages you to be curious and thoughtful. It is about techniques that help you move from trying to be a speed reader to being a speed *understander*, as Isaac Asimov would say.

I believe the future belongs to those who can learn to use their powers of observation to see the intersections between industries, ideas and behaviors and curate them into a deeper understanding of the world around us.

I'm not saying that type of thinking can save us from an asteroid which may strike 867 years from now – but it can definitely change the way we approach our lives and our businesses in the present.

Preparing for the future starts with understanding *today*, as it always has.

ACKNOWLEDGMENTS

Every author says that writing a book is rarely a solitary act. I have to disagree.

Along the past five years of journeying through the publishing industry—I have written books for large publishers as an author under contract, and I have self published short ebooks written alone in a couple of weeks.

Some come faster than others—and require a different team to put them together. Of them all, this book was the most complex, requiring more than a year's worth of research, writing and curation. The concept for the book was five years in the making, and the inspiration to write it came directly from the many people who have read one of my Non-Obvious Trend Reports and decided to get in touch and interact with me directly. This sixth edition of the report (and second version of the full book) was my chance to hone the idea even further, and offer even newer thinking.

As much as anyone, this book is for them—and if you happen to be one of them I want to thank you first.

Beyond this broad group, there are also some individuals who helped with various stages of getting this book ready for publication and deserve my specific thanks:

First of all, to Matthew for being a sounding board on the editorial process and choosing to take on the editing of a project like this even though you've clearly moved on to bigger and better things.

To Herb for helping me navigate the ins and outs of the publishing industry and making exactly the kinds of connections that help a small independent publishing house with just a few authors grow to become something even bigger.

To Christina for her careful reading of an initial manuscript and fast work to make the words and ideas better without needing much space or time within which to do it.

Jeff, Kelly, Torrey and the entire design team at Faceout for understanding the concept of the book, working to translate that into a beautiful cover design, and being overall pleasant people to work with.

Rich for being a great partner, always working under a crazy timeline and still getting things done like a pro.

To my wife Chhavi, who continually manages to share interesting ideas, challenge me to reinvent my thinking, and cheerfully deal with a writing process that requires me to sometimes disappear to finish off chapters and "visualize" ideas by spreading my notes across entire rooms of the house. It is easy to write books and share ideas when you are married to someone who inspires you.

And finally, to my boys Rohan and Jaiden for remaining curious enough about the world to motivate me to observe more, judge less and always listen with both ears.

From time to time, we all need a reminder like that.

NOTES, REFERENCES, & CREDITS

The preparation of each edition of the Non-Obvious Trend Report involves consulting hundreds of publications, interviewing dozens of experts and reviewing more than 50 books each year. Rather than provide an exhaustive list of links here – I have created an online list of references for each trend with live links to each source. Where personal interviews were conducted, those have been individually cited within the relevant chapters and are not included separately in the reference section.

To see and download a full detailed page index to all the individuals, companies and concepts cited in this 2016 edition of the book, or to follow any of the links to sources cited and read the full articles, you can use the link below:

WWW.ROHITBHARGAVA.COM/NONOBVIOUS/RESOURCES

THE PAST YEARS' NON-OBVIOUS TREND REPORTS

(2011–2014)

OVERVIEW:
How to Read These Past
Trend Reports

———

"THE EVENTS OF THE PAST CAN BE MADE TO PROVE ANYTHING IF THEY ARE ARRANGED IN A SUITABLE PATTERN."
—A. J. P. Taylor, historian and journalist

There was a moment several years ago when I was on stage after having just presented one of my trend reports and a gentleman stood up to ask me a question. "It must be easy," he started "to publish your trend report when you get to change them every year. How do you know whether any of them were actually right?"

His question was a fair one. After all, there is plenty of evidence to suggest experts routinely miss predictions and are often just plain wrong. What makes my method or the past trends any different? Of course, every author thinks his book is brilliant, just as all parents imagine their child to be a genius. What is the truth?

In this section, you'll see a candid, unedited review of every one of my previously predicted trends from the first four years of the *Non-Obvious Trend Report*. While some of the descriptions have been edited for space considerations, none of the intentions or meanings have been updated or revisited.

Instead, each trend is accompanied by my own Trend Longevity Rating, which aims to measure how much the trend, as originally described, still applies or has value today in 2016. Predictably, the 2014 trends fared better than the 2011 trends, but the process of going backward and taking an honest look at past research was illuminating for me, and I hope it will be for you as well.

The 2015 trends each are covered more thoroughly through the expanded updates for each in Part III.

In assessing these past trends, my aim was to treat them in as unbiased a way as possible, and where something was wrong or not quite right, I tried to assess and grade it truthfully. For each trend report, there is also a link at the end of the corresponding appendix where you can go back and see that full trend report with no edits, as it was originally presented.

It may be a hard line, but I have done my best to draw it authentically and without embarrassment or defensiveness. If there is anything that has helped me get better at doing this year after year, it's the act of reviewing, grading and critiquing past trends—especially after some of them turn out to be not quite right. I hope you enjoy this journey back in time and the ideas it sparks for which trends stood the test of time and which didn't.

APPENDIX A: 2011 Trends

THE BACKSTORY

The first edition of the *Non-Obvious Trend Report* was inspired by five years of blogging. I released it exclusively in a visual presentation format and heavily featured marketing and social media trends that I had written about throughout 2010. The trends were far more limited in scope than later editions of the trend report and featured less description and less actionable advice. They were also not separated into subcategories, but instead presented as a full list of 15 marketing and social media trends that mattered. Each trend featured a short description, along with some quick tips for brands on how to use the lessons in the report to power their marketing strategy.

RETROSPECTIVE – HOW ACCURATE WAS THIS REPORT?

The report was one of the first to predict the rise in importance of content marketing through curation and also predicted the rapid growth of real-time customer service through social media. It analyzed the increasing number of marketing campaigns featuring employees as a sign of corporate humanity, and introduced the idea of how social media was making unreachable celebrities more connected and approachable. Overall, there were relatively few big misses or trends that completely imploded or reversed themselves. The biggest idea from the report was undoubtedly the first trend *Likeonomics*, which ultimately inspired me to write a book of the same name (released in 2012) to build the idea out further.

THE 2011 TRENDS: RECAP AND ANALYSIS

1. Likeonomics

Brands, products and services succeed by being more human, mission driven and personally likeable through their policies and people, gaining an advantage over less-human competitors.

Examples Used: Ford Explorer Facebook launch and Innocent Drinks

2016 Trend Longevity Rating: A

The fundamental truth of human relationships underlying this trend continues to grow in business each year as more brands focus on being more human, building personal connections with customers and trying to be more consistently likeable.

2. Approachable Celebrity

As social media allows direct access to previously unreachable celebrities, politicians and professional athletes, we increasingly see their real personalities (for better or worse) and can engage with them as real people.

Examples Used: Cisco's "Do You Flip?" campaign and tweeting celebrities

2016 Trend Longevity Rating: A

This direct connection to celebrities has continued to grow as YouTube creates more celebrities who have huge personal followings, and notable people from all industries continue to share their real personalities and opinions through social media without filters or PR spokespeople.

3. Desperate Simplification

Information overload causes consumers to desperately seek simplicity, leading them to aim for more balance through reduction activities like de-friending and actively seeking out new products and sites to help them simplify everything.

Examples Used: iPod, Tumblr, Animoto, Amazon, and Path

2016 Trend Longevity Rating: B-

While "infobesity," as information overload is increasingly being called, continues, the desperate need for simplicity has given way somewhat to more tools that focus on optimizing or curating instead of just culling friendships or content. As a result, this trend continues to matter, but the level of desperation from consumers doesn't have the same intensity it once did in past years.

4. Essential Integration

Marketers' biggest problem continues to be integrating efforts, which can be highly difficult and lack good examples, yet the biggest successes of the past year, in terms of award-winning marketing programs, feature a new level of integration that is still rare in the marketing world.

Examples Used: Old Spice Guy and Best Buy's Twelpforce

2016 Trend Longevity Rating: B

Over the past four years, integration has become an even greater issue for marketers and one that most struggle with on a daily basis—yet there are also more tools and platforms enabling this to happen more easily. This makes it still a trend that matters, but one that is less urgent, problematic or lacking in solutions. The problem, in other words, has become far more fixable.

5. Rise of Curation

Brands increasingly use curation as a much-needed filter to help find and bring together useful or entertaining content in an effort to win more trust and attention from consumers.

Examples Used: Paper.li custom newspapers and the Pharma and Healthcare Social Media Wiki

2016 Trend Longevity Rating: A

The past four years have delivered an even bigger explosion in content. The algorithms are getting smarter but are not yet smart enough to collect content into truly meaningful arrangements. As a result, curation has become an even bigger part of the content marketing strategy for brands, as well as a method for individuals to share their expertise or passion about any topic online.

6. Visualized Data

To make sense of a real-time stream of information on any topic, more and more event managers, news organizations and brands are turning to visualization as a way to leverage their data, better understand it and tell a clearer story.

Examples Used: The 52nd Annual Grammy Awards and CNN's Magic Election Wall

2016 Trend Longevity Rating: B

While data visualization is still frequently used, the widespread overuse of infographics over the past several years has weakened the focus on visuals as a way of using data to tell stories. Instead, more companies are combining the idea of visualization with better user interfaces, gamified design and narrative data storytelling to broaden their methods for getting value out of analyzing data and making it more shareable.

7. Crowdsourced Innovation

Brands turn to crowdsourced platforms to collect ideas from consumers in exchange for the reward of recognition, financial earning and simply being heard by the brands they purchase from every day.

Examples Used: My Starbucks Idea and Kickstarter

2016 Trend Longevity Rating: B

With the growth of Quirky, Kaggle and other platforms for everything from idea generation to problem solving, this trend has certainly continued to grow. My original definition was narrow and focused on brands and consumers, but this has given way to larger ecosystems and marketplaces that exist today with only limited brand support as well as new models for brands to incubate startups.

8. Instant PR & Customer Service

Real-time contact becomes essential as communications teams focus on instant PR to manage social crises and augment customer service with methods for dealing with problems in the here and now.

Examples Used: JetBlue's big media hit and Zappos' Golden Philosophy

2016 Trend Longevity Rating: A

When I first wrote this trend, the idea of customer service through social channels was mostly driven by negative situations and the need for instant PR. Over the past several years, this has exploded into social customer care, a field that almost every large business is investing dollars and time in to figuring out how to do right. In 2016, many more businesses are investing in this type of "omnichannel" care wherever and whenever a consumer wants.

9. App-fication of the Web

As more innovative apps let consumers bypass the web for transactions and leisure, a large number of activities from online banking to online shopping will shift to apps instead of the web.

Examples Used: Flipboard "The Web Is Dead. Long Live the Internet" from *Wired* magazine.

2016 Trend Longevity Rating: C-

There is no denying that the prevalence of apps has grown dramatically over the past several years, but idea of "app-fication," where everything is done through apps, has not quite come to pass. Instead, responsive design and the growing functionality of mobile platforms vs individual apps makes this trend far less important.

10. Re-Imagining Charity

Brands and entrepreneurs create innovative new models for social good, reinventing how people can do everything from donating money to sharing time and specific skills.

Examples Used: Jumo and Yoxi.tv

2016 Trend Longevity Rating: B

The year when I first spotlighted this trend was one where the pace of growth in how nonprofits and charities were using digital tools was explosive. This speed has slowed somewhat as many of these same organizations shifted from doing something completely new online to focusing on how to optimize their efforts and gain better results. The innovation is coming from small changes.

11. Employees As Heroes

Brands of all sizes aim to demonstrate their humanity by putting a spotlight on employees as the solvers of problems and creators of innovation. Organizations feature employee stories as anchor points to describe what the company does in the world.

Examples Used: Intel's "Sponsors of Tomorrow" campaign and IBM's Smarter Planet initiative

2016 Trend Longevity Rating: B

The past few years have added several large brands to this trend beyond the (mostly) tech companies like Intel and IBM that I initially featured. Yet the hero aspect of it has dissipated somewhat as brands start to take a softer and more realistic approach to spotlighting employees. Those same employees are still an important and human part of the brand story, but they are presented more often now in terms of how hard they work, what value they bring to customers and why they are passionate about what they do – rather than as world changing heroes.

12. Locationcasting

More consumers choose to broadcast their locations, enabling brands to tailor messages to a specific location and create more opportunities to engage their customers in real life.

Examples Used: Foursquare, Gowalla and Scvnger.com

2016 Trend Longevity Rating: A-

Mobile marketing is growing rapidly, as are methods for geotargeting offers for customers. While this has not become a commonplace activity, location based marketing continues to gain acceptance and is starting to show signs for potential big growth.

13. Brutal Transparency

Aggressive honesty will lead to edgier (and more effective) marketing as brands reveal an unexpected aggressive honesty that consumers welcome.

Examples Used: Domino's Pizza's "Oh Yes We Did" campaign and Southwest Airlines' policy to eliminate baggage fees

2016 Trend Longevity Rating: A

The growth of social platforms and increase in content marketing is allowing brands to share more honest truths about every aspect of their business than ever before. Combined with that, customer expectations are growing around the basic level of transparency they expect and brands need to meet the demand—and in 2016 more of them will.

14. Addictive Randomness

Brands will increasingly use the addictive power of random content to engage consumers and this will lead to more consumer-generated campaigns where people can add content to a central archive that anyone can browse.

Examples Used: Red Cross' "Why the Heck Should I Give?" campaign and PostSecret.com

2016 Trend Longevity Rating: C

This principle still applies in a limited scope to campaigns featuring a random sort of interface or user experience, however it never quite became large enough to be truly considered a trend in its own right.

15. Culting of Retail

The best retailers create a passionate following of users who not only buy products they like, but also rave about their experiences so completely that they will inspire a significant portion of their social networks to try the experience for themselves.

Examples Used: Groupon and Gilt

2016 Trend Longevity Rating: A-

If anything, the rise of social media has enabled this culting of retail to happen even more frequently. New boutique services and websites pop up nearly every day, and the ones that survive rely on their most enthusiastic customers, whose willingness share their brand passion online influences others to become customers as well.

Want to read the original 2011 Report for free?

Visit www.15trends.com to read and download the full report.

APPENDIX B: 2012 Trends

THE BACKSTORY

This second year of the trend report featured a broader look at business beyond marketing and brought together the worlds of corporate marketing, charitable causes, the marketing of death and more. Like the first report, it was only released exclusively in visual presentation format online. This report tackled the sensitive yet emerging field of the digital afterlife of loved ones who have passed on, as well as the rising sense of social loneliness that people felt. In contrast to my 2011 report, the theme of this report moved a little further away from marketing campaigns and took a more human tone as many of the trends featured cultural or consumer-based trends instead of those inspired by what brand marketers were already doing.

RETROSPECTIVE – HOW ACCURATE WAS THIS REPORT?

The 2012 report had a few big hits and several big misses. The overall trends that centered on the growth of humanity in companies and consumers worked out well. This report was one of the first to explore the potential of big data to impact everything from optimizing supply chain logistics to measuring and quantifying every aspect of our lives. On the flip side, the trends that made bigger bets on niche concepts like *Pointillist Filmmaking* or *Social Artivism* did not quantifiably catch fire, either in adoption or in the behaviors they described.

THE 2012 TRENDS: RECAP & ANALYSIS

1. Corporate Humanism

Companies find their humanity as they create more consumer-friendly policies and practices, spending more time listening to customers and encouraging employees to more publicly represent their companies.

Examples Used: Aviva, Ally Bank, Domino's Pizza and Best Buy

2016 Trend Longevity Rating: A

If there is one trend that perhaps describes the past decade of corporate evolution, it is this one. Every year there are new signs of how companies are finding their humanity and avoiding the facelessness that once used to be a hallmark of business – so much so that this once "non-obvious" trend has now become fairly obvious to most.

2. Ethnomimicry

Ethnographic analysis of how people interact in the real world inspires new social tools or products that mimic human behavior and social interaction, and fit our lives.

Examples Used: Google+, Emotion Lighting and Microsoft Kinetic

2016 Trend Longevity Rating: A

I am keenly aware that any trend which used Google+ as an example can't be scored particularly high as a matter of principle, however this idea of companies watching human interaction in the real world and tailoring products and services to mimic those behaviors is still a common design principle and frequently results in valuable and useful products or services. In 2016, the trend will see a resurgence as the link between ethnographic research and product development continues to get even stronger.

3. Social Loneliness

Despite online social connections, people feel a real-world sense of loneliness, causing them to seek deeper friendships instead of many superficial ones. As a result, people seek new ways of knowing friends beyond their latest tweet.

Examples Used: Toyota Venza's "This Is Living" campaign and Couch-surfing.com

2016 Trend Longevity Rating: B

This sense of social loneliness is still present with interactions online, and it is a concern particularly for teens and adolescents, but there is far greater awareness of the issue along with more innovation from startup products and services that connect the digital world more deeply with the real world.

4. Pointillist Filmmaking

Named after the painting form using millions of dots to create larger images, this trend describes a form of collaborative filmmaking where are large number of short clips are merged together in order to tell a broader story through video.

Examples Used: Mont Blanc's Beauty of a Second Challenge and One Day on Earth

2016 Trend Longevity Rating: D

This trend was an example of an overly fancy concept that ended up being too limited in scope to really become an impactful trend over the long term. The experience of writing this and reviewing it years later, though, was a perfect lesson in the importance of making sure that an idea is big enough to truly accelerate in subsequent years. This one was not.

5. Measuring Life

A growing range of tracking tools offer individualized data to monitor and measure all areas of your life to allow you to track your own health, measure your social influence and set goals.

Examples Used: Jawbone Up and Klout

2016 Trend Longevity Rating: A

What was a big idea back in 2012 is now mainstream and rather obvious as new wearable devices are seemingly launched every week. While much of that growth to date has been in the areas of health and fitness, the coming year will bring more life tracking tools for everything from what we drink to measuring the air we breathe.

6. Co-Curation

Curation gets more collaborative as amateurs and experts combine forces online to add their unique points of view and bring together multiple angles of every issue.

Examples Used: Storyful & Futurity

2016 Trend Longevity Rating: A

Curation continues to be one of the biggest trends in online content and this idea of co-curation and the central role of collaboration as a part of curation activities online will experience a resurgence in 2016. Fueled by tools that make it easier for curators to work together, we will see more examples of collaboration aiming to improve the content we digest every day.

7. Charitable Engagement

More charities rethink their focus on quick donations and instead actively promote participation through gaming and other methods of behavioral engagement.

Examples Used: WaterForward.org and Jamie Oliver's Food Revolution

2016 Trend Longevity Rating: B-

While charities and nonprofits continue to find more ways to engage donors proactively in their efforts, this trend predicted a dramatic shift in the industry that hasn't become quite so pronounced. More platforms to allow for convenient donation collection and the ease of online publishing actually led more smaller nonprofits to focus on the fundraising side of the equation for the short term, and on engagement in the longer term.

8. Medici Marketing

Inspired by the book *The Medici Effect*, this trend describes how thinking from multiple disciplines is combined to make marketing more engaging, creative or useful.

Examples Used: The Creators Project and Albam's *Factories* book

2016 Trend Longevity Rating: B

The name was a bit limiting to describe the scope of this trend, however the idea that marketing is becoming more of a melting pot for people from nontraditional backgrounds including journalism and art certainly has continued throughout the last several years and for the foreseeable future.

9. Digital Afterlife

Over the past year, more companies have started to focus on the digital afterlife, creating tools, education and services to help manage all the data that loved ones leave behind after they die.

Examples Used: 1000memories.com (since acquired by Ancestry.com) and Aftersteps.com

2016 Trend Longevity Rating: B

This is the perfect type of frustrating trend prediction, that always seems to be on the cusp of emerging as a mainstream idea but never quite makes it. Over the past several years, there is always a steady drumbeat of stories and attention on this idea of the digital afterlife, but it rarely translates into something bigger.

10. Real-Time Logistics

Tech-savvy businesses use real-time conversation in social media to generate insights that help with supply chain and logistical planning to eliminate wastage and maximize profits.

Examples Used: Walmart Labs and SAP's social supply chain

2016 Trend Longevity Rating: A

Supply chain software continues to get more and more sophisticated as large retailers and other distributors continue to implement new tools to get better forecasts and leverage social conversation data to run their businesses better. In 2016 expect to see big investment and more visible "hero style" case studies from brands in this space.

11. Social Artivism

The intersection between art and activism known increasingly as *artivism* starts to get social as more artists see social tools as a way to reach more people and create greater social impact.

Examples Used: Artivist Film Festival and the Estria Foundation's Water Writes Project

2016 Trend Longevity Rating: B

Art is still used frequently for activism and social media continues to amplify it, but this trend never accelerated beyond several interesting examples. Even today, there are examples of this same principle, but not enough to make this a top-rated trend.

12. Civic Engagement 2.0

A growing range of digital tools allows people to engage more actively with local governments on everything from reporting potholes to offering suggestions for improving their communities.

Examples Used: CitySourced and Give a Minute

2016 Trend Longevity Rating: B+

Though civic engagement hasn't quadrupled year after year, these tools to allow for deeper citizen engagement continue to grow and be adopted by more and more people. Though there hasn't yet been mass consolidation or a tipping point in usage, a growing number of tech-savvy cities are leading the way to help this trend continue to accelerate into the mainstream.

13. Tagging Reality

Better-quality mobile cameras allow developers to create tools that can tag any object in reality to unlock interactive content.

Examples Used: Layar and Sony SmartAR

2016 Trend Longevity Rating: C

This was a perfect example of the type of trend that may have been better explored as an element of a broader trend. Alone, it described a few isolated efforts, but over the course of several years, the trend never quite accelerated as quickly as I first described.

14. ChangeSourcing

Crowdsourcing itself is evolving beyond information sharing to a point where people can use the collaborative power of the crowd to achieve personal, social or political change.

Examples Used: Self-reported clinical trials and Peerbackers.com

2016 Trend Longevity Rating: B

The basic idea behind this trend was focused on how crowdsourcing was moving beyond information and into action as people tapped the power of crowds to achieve real things. This trend continued with multiple new sites and efforts using it in past few years.

15. Retail Theater

In the coming year, more retail stores will create unique experiences using the principles of theater to engage customers with memorable experiences.

Examples Used: Puma Creative Factory and Villa Sofa

2016 Trend Longevity Rating: A

Over the past several years, retailers have tried to get even more theatrical to combat the dangers of showrooming and the rise of online retail. If anything, this is making retail experiences even more interactive and dramatic than before.

Want to read the original 2012 Report for free?

Visit www.15trends.com to read and download the full report.

2013 NON-OBVIOUS TRENDS OVERVIEW – SUMMARY

WHAT IS A TREND?
A trend is a unique curated observation about the accelerating present

CULTURE & CONSUMER BEHAVIOR - Trends in how we see ourselves and patterns in popular culture

Optimistic Aging

Human Banking

MeFunding

MARKETING & SOCIAL MEDIA - Trends in how brands are trying to influence and engage consumers

Branded Inspiration

Backstorytelling

Healthy Content

MEDIA & EDUCATION - Trends in content and information impacting how we learn or are entertained

Degree-Free Learning

Precious Print

Partnership Publishing

TECHNOLOGY & DESIGN - Trends in technology innovation and product design impacting our behavior

Microinnovation

Social Visualization

Heroic Design

ECONOMICS & ENTREPRENEURSHIP - Trends in business models, startups and careers affecting the future of work or money

Hyper-Local Commerce

Powered By Women

Shoptimization

* Note – The categories above were not included in the 2013 Report and were curated afterwards. In addition, the final 15 trends featured above omit three bonus trends which failed to produce ongoing impact over time: Audio Tagging, Friend Sourced Travel, and Method Consulting.

APPENDIX C: 2013 Trends

THE BACKSTORY

In the third year of producing the trend report, the level of detail exploded as my full report went from about 20 pages to more than 100. The report featured more examples, more analysis—and more trends (with 3 bonus trends added to the usual 15).

The report was still delivered primarily in a visual presentation format, but this year there was an accompanying ebook available for sale on Amazon featuring not only the trends, but also suggestions on how to put them into action.

This third edition ebook was an immediate best seller on Amazon, remaining the number-one book in the market research category for eight straight weeks after launch and was viewed more than 200,000 times online. The clean visuals, level of detail and growing reputation for the annual report also resulted in plenty of sharing and comments online as well.

RETROSPECTIVE – HOW ACCURATE WAS THIS REPORT?

Developing the trends for 2013 was a more deliberate process requiring more research and a higher standard of proof before including any particular trend in the report. Topics featured in the 2013 report included the future of print publishing, the rise of women in business, authenticity in the banking sector, hyper-local commerce and the evolution of the travel industry. From these, there were several that received my own top longevity rating two years later as early predictions of large shifts in marketing and business.

THE 2013 TRENDS: RECAP & ANALYSIS

1. Optimistic Aging

A wealth of content online and new social networks inspire people of all ages to feel more optimistic about getting older.

Examples Used: YourEncore and Intent

2016 Trend Longevity Rating: A

When it comes to aging, there are more reasons for optimism than ever. Technology gets better at offering mobility and predictive interfaces, while overall health services and living options continue to improve. In 2016, the optimism will drive entirely new industries and continue to transform existing ones.

2. Human Banking

Aiming to change years of growing distrust, banks finally uncover their human side by taking a more simple and direct approach to services and communication

Examples Used: Ally Bank, FoundersCard, Zuno Bank, the IRS form redesign, Simple, BillGuard, and Project Catalyst

2016 Trend Longevity Rating: A

Every new financial crisis or data breach underscores the importance of more human interactions between us and our financial institutions. Continued consumer distrust of the entire industry means that more banks and financial services groups will be considering how to use this trend in 2016.

3. MeFunding

Crowdfunding evolves beyond films or budding entrepreneurs to offer anyone the opportunity to seek financial support to do anything from taking a life-changing trip to paying for a college education.

Examples Used: Upstart, GoFundMe, GiveForward, Takeashine,

GiveCollege and Indiegogo

2016 Trend Longevity Rating: B-

While the many sites featured as part of this trend remain available for people to use, the trend still has not exploded the way I predicted. This is one of those ideas that sees a steady stream of attention and usage but never accelerates beyond a niche idea.

4. Branded Inspiration

Brands use awe-inspiring moments, innovative ideas and dramatic stunts to capture attention and demonstrate their values to the world.

Examples Used: RedBull Stratos, Toyota 100 Cars for Good and Nature Valley Trailview

2016 Trend Longevity Rating: A

Driven by 2013 being a watershed year for brands to use big moments for inspiration, the trend continues with large investments into social movements from brands like Dove, and social experimentation in bringing people together, like efforts from Coca-Cola. With Always brand winning top honors at this past year's Cannes awards for their branded inspiration campaign #likeagirl, more brands will move and try to create their own similarly inspirational campaigns in 2016.

5. Backstorytelling

Organizations discover that one of their greatest assets to inspire loyalty can come from taking people behind the scenes of their brand and history through storytelling.

Examples Used: Land Rover, Ford, CustomInk and McDonald's Canada's Our Food. Your Questions website

2016 Trend Longevity Rating: A

As social platforms splinter but also grow in popularity, the opportunity for brands to share their backstory in multiple ways continues to grow. Add this to the rising consciousness of consumers about the ethical business practices of companies and this trend will to continue to matter in 2016.

6. Healthy Content

Healthcare organizations feel pressure to create more useful and sub-stantial health content to satisfy increasingly empowered patients who have become unreachable through pure marketing or advertis-ing messages.

Examples Used: Diabetapedia, the CDC's response to the year's meningitis scare, the Cleveland Clinic's Health Hub and Boehringer Ingelheim teaming up with PSFK

2016 Trend Longevity Rating: B-

In the healthcare industry, content continues to be golden because empowered patients gain more confidence and increasingly turn to the web before seeking information from other sources – however this content is being balanced with an industry-wide shift to functionality, usability and new ways to leverage data.

7. Degree-Free Learning

Quality of e-learning content explodes as more students consider alternatives to traditional college educations.

Examples Used: CreativeLive, Uncollege, [E]nstitute, Fluent in 3 Months and Soundslice

2016 Trend Longevity Rating: B+

Learning and higher education are simultaneously changed by this growth of people who choose to learn new skills and industries without seeking a degree to display at the end of it. While this will not overtake traditional degree-granting programs in 2016, it continues to gain in popularity.

8. Precious Print

Thanks to our digital-everything culture, the few objects and moments we choose to interact with in print become more valuable, personal and emotional.

Examples Used: Esopus, Monocle, *NewsWeek*, Paper Because, Moo Luxe cards, *Star Trek Federation: The First 150 Years* by David Good-man, Moleskine notebooks, Wantful

2016 Trend Longevity Rating: A

As digital tools and interfaces get more popular, more experiences are moving to the digital sphere and fewer remain in print. Even so, the basic human behavior outlined in this trend—that we place even more value on the things that are printed and which we can hold in our hands because they are so much more rare—continues year after year.

9. Partnership Publishing

Aspiring authors and publishing professionals team up to create a new do-it-together models of publishing.

Examples Used: Net Minds, Mindvalley, Paper Lantern Lit, and The Domino Project

2016 Trend Longevity Rating: B+

This do-it-together approach to continues to accelerate as the entire industry maintains its rapid pace of innovation. The trend also inspired the creation of the entity behind this book – Ideapress Publishing. In 2016, more of these types of joint ventures will continue to fracture and reinvent the publishing landscape.

10. MicroInnovation

Thinking small becomes the new competitive advantage as slight changes to features or benefits create big value.

Examples Used: Toyota Easy-Fill tire alert, Mercedes-Benz Magic Vision wipers, Ford Liftgate, Apple iPod and Universal Lubricants

2016 Trend Longevity Rating: A

This trend has accelerated dramatically in recent years as more brands adopt a lean startup mentality that encourages them to make incremental changes to products in ways that can deliver big value.

11. Social Visualization

Going beyond data, new tools and technologies to let people include visualizations as part of their social profiles and conversations online.

Examples Used: The new MySpace, Infusd, Coca-Cola's new website and Cowbird

2016 Trend Longevity Rating: A

Visual interfaces continue to be commonplace and popular. This trend has grown so fast that it clearly no longer really qualifies as "non-obvious." Its popularity and growth give it a top rating in this recap of trends that will continue to matter in 2016.

12. Heroic Design

Design takes a leading role in the introduction of new products, ideas and campaigns to change the world.

Examples Used: Stanford Design for Change Center, Project H Design, Kony2012, LifeStraw, Information Blanket, ChangeMakers ColaLife and "The Wire" from Frog Design

2016 Trend Longevity Rating: A

Thanks to an intersection between this trend and increased crowd-funding, ideas for heroic design products can not only be funded and supported online, but they also have increasing opportunities for media exposure in a consumer world more engaged with and hungry for amazing business stories.

13. Hyper-Local Commerce

New services and technology make it easier for anyone to invest in local businesses and buy from local merchants.

Examples Used: Square, GoPayment, MobilePay, Paypal Here, Shopify, Popularise, Fundrise, Goodzer, Sears Local and Peixe Urbano

2016 Trend Longevity Rating: A

Whether you examine this trend in relation to the growth of local commerce or as fueled by investment and interest in mobile commerce platforms and experience, the fact is consumer experiences continue to become more local and focused on customization and personalization from brands of all sizes. This trend is likely to continue well into 2016.

14. Powered by Women

Business leaders, pop culture and groundbreaking new research intersect to prove that our ideal future will be led by women.

Examples Used: The Athena Doctrine by John Gerzema and Michael

D'Antonio, The Girl Effect, Girls Who Code, WIT, *Fast Company's* Influential Women In Technology list, *Brave* the movie, *The Hunger Games* movies, *Twilight* movies and *Revolution* TV series

2016 Trend Longevity Rating: A

There is no denying the role of women in business, culture and politics has grown year after year. Today there are more female leaders, role models and celebrated citizens than ever before—and it is a wonderful thing. This is one of those world-changing trends that we should all hope continues to accelerate every year, and certainly will throughout 2016.

15. Shoptimization

New mobile apps and startups let consumers optimize the process of buying everything from fashion to medical prescriptions.

Examples Used: Slice, Dashlane, ShopSavvy, GoodRx, Rent the Runway, Wish Want Wear, Le Tote, CardStar, Perx, Keyring and Macy's in-store GPS

2016 Trend Longevity Rating: A

Thanks to increasing competition among retailers and a rising tide of new productivity tools online, the task of optimizing each of our shopping experiences continues to be a top priority for all types of brands.

Want to read the original 2013 Report for free?

Visit www.15trends.com to read and download the full report.

2014 NON-OBVIOUS TRENDS OVERVIEW – SUMMARY

WHAT IS A TREND?
A trend is a unique curated observation about the accelerating present

CULTURE & CONSUMER BEHAVIOR - Trends in how we see ourselves and patterns in popular culture

Desperate Detox

Media Binging

Obsessive Productivity

MARKETING & SOCIAL MEDIA - Trends in how brands are trying to influence and engage consumers

Lovable Imperfection

Branded Utility

Shareable Humanity

MEDIA & EDUCATION - Trends in content and information impacting how we learn or are entertained

Curated Sensationalism

Distributed Expertise

Anti-Stereotyping

TECHNOLOGY & DESIGN - Trends in technology innovation and product design impacting our behavior

Privacy Paranoia

Overquantified Life

Microdesign

ECONOMICS & ENTREPRENEURSHIP - Trends in business models, startups and careers affecting the future of work or money

Subscription Commerce

Instant Entrepreneurs

Collaborative Economy

* Note – The categories above were not included in the 2014 Report and were curated afterwards.

APPENDIX D: 2014 Trends

THE BACKSTORY

This fourth edition of the *Non-Obvious Trend Report* was expanded in several ways from previous reports. The first and most visible change was that the report featured five categories for trends for the first time instead of simply listing 15 in random order. Those categories are the same as the ones used in the 2015 and 2016 reports.

In addition, the report featured deeper examples, more actionable advice and a new visual look that spotlighted each trend more deeply and encouraged people to learn more about each one. The overall report was more than 160 pages.

In an effort to build visibility, in 2014 I also made the vast majority of the report freely available online rather than moving it to an ebook available for sale on Amazon. The result was wider distribution of the report, and greater use of the corresponding ebook among those who needed to implement and put the trends into action. This report was the first where my focus started to go beyond simply sharing the trends and more to how they could be used in business by leaders.

RETROSPECTIVE – HOW ACCURATE WAS THIS REPORT?

As the reports get more recent, the number of trends which are still applicable to business today increases. As a result, I was tempted not to go through the process of rating each trend because the time since they were published is so short, but I decided there is value in reviewing them, so you will find the same analysis of the 2014 trends in the following pages.

THE 2014 TRENDS: RECAP & ANALYSIS

1. Desperate Detox

Consumers try to more authentically connect with others and seek out moments of reflection by intentionally disconnecting from the technology surrounding them.

Examples Used: Nomophobia, Camp Grounded, Human Mode app, *Fast Company*'s #unplug hashtag, Belize and FOMO

2016 Trend Longevity Rating: A

Technology is only becoming more omnipresent in our lives, making this trend one that continues to grow in 2016.

2. Media Binging

As more media and entertainment is available on any device on demand, consumers binge and are willing to pay extra for the convenience.

Examples Used: Breaking Bad TV show, *Beyoncé* album release, Netflix, telecom data plans, *House of Cards* TV show and Pocket app

2016 Trend Longevity Rating: A

Streaming options continue to expand and consumer behavior follows. Additionally in 2016 and early 2017 more networks will be experimenting with on-demand direct access making this a macro trend that will continue.

3. Obsessive Productivity

With thousands of life-optimizing apps and instant advice from social media–savvy self-help gurus, becoming more productive has become the ultimate obsession.

Examples Used: Narrative, Swiftkey, Manhattan Disney moms and Coffitivity

2016 Trend Longevity Rating: A

Last year brought plenty of new bestselling books talking about optimizing your life, hacking your daily chores and saving time. To say people

continue to obsess over their own productivity is becoming an understatement. In 2016, this obsession will continue to be catered to by new startups, products and services.

4. Subscription Commerce

More unexpected businesses and retailers use subscriptions to sell recurring services or products to customers instead of focusing on the one-time sale.

Examples Used: Adobe Creative Cloud, Amazon Prime, Oyster Books, Pleygo.com, Moviepass, Trunk Club, Bulu Box, Birchbox, Carnivore Club, Love with Food and Shoe Dazzle

2016 Trend Longevity Rating: B+

More industries and brands turn to the lessons of subscription commerce, but the more powerful effect of this trend will come from how subscription-based models that were launched in the past few years grow and receive more attention in 2016.

5. Instant Entrepreneurs

Better support, incentives and tools mean anyone with an idea can launch a startup knowing that the costs and risks of failure are not as high as they once were.

Examples Used: LegalZoom, coworking spaces, Strikingly, Bitcoin mining, StockLogos.com and Startup America

2016 Trend Longevity Rating: A

The shift in many industries from full-time employee to entrepreneur continues to take shape as top professionals continue to branch out on their own.

6. Collaborative Economy

New business models and tools allow consumers and brands to use sharing and collaborative consumption for new ways to buy, sell or consume almost anything.

Examples Used: Crowd Companies, Heineken Ideas Brewery, GE's partnership with Quirky and Patagonia's partnership with Ebay

2016 Trend Longevity Rating: A

While growing last year, the shared or collaborative economy has become one of the more obvious trends anyone could point to today, a symbol of its continued rapid acceleration. In 2016, greater investment and initiatives from large brands will continue to propel this trend toward dominance in the coming year.

7. Branded Utility

Brands use content marketing and greater integration between marketing and operations to augment promotions with real ways to add value to customer's lives.

Examples Used: Content Rules by Ann Handley and C. C. Chapman; *Ctrl Alt Delete* by Mitch Joel; *Jab, Jab, Jab, Right Hook* by Gary Vaynerchuk; *Weber's Way to Grill* by Jamie Purviance; Charmin's Sit or Squat website and KLM's Wanna Gives

2016 Trend Longevity Rating: A

As content marketing continues to dramatically change the way that marketers communicate with their audiences, there have been dozens more examples of brands using this trend across 2015 and the trend will continue.

8. Lovable Imperfection

Consumers seek out true authenticity and reward minor imperfections in products, personalities and brands by showing greater loyalty and trust.

Examples Used: Jennifer Lawrence, Domino's Artisan Pizza, McDonald's Egg White McMuffin, *Despicable Me* and MegaMind

2016 Trend Longevity Rating: A

The impact of this trend was so powerful in business across the year following its initial publication, that my 2015 trend of Unperfection relates directly to this one and continues to gain widespread attention and discussion.

9. **Shareable Humanity (Marketing & Social Media Trend)**

   Content shared on social media gets more emotional as people share amazing examples of humanity and brands inject more of it into communications efforts.

   Examples Used: Mashable stories, Kikkoman and Hopemob,

   2016 Trend Longevity Rating: B

   This was one of the trends from the previous year that was negatively affected by the fatigue some media consumers are starting to experience from overly dramatic media stories and clickbaiting headlines. Though we continue to find human stories irresistible to read and share, overuse is shifting the way we consider what we share and when we share it.

10. **Privacy Paranoia**

    New data breaches are leading to a new global sense of paranoia about what governments and brands know about us—and how they might use this big data in potentially harmful ways.

    Examples Used: DuckDuckGo, Lendup.com, Cloaking, International Data Privacy Day and "The Deep Web" from *Time* magazine

    2016 Trend Longevity Rating: B-

    As more tools enter the market to help consumers protect their information and take back control of their privacy, this paranoia is shifting to empowerment – and despite warnings daily in the media, the paranoia of 2014 is giving way to a dangerous complacency about how our data is collected and who can see it.

11. **Microdesign**

    As communication becomes more visual, design gains respect and integrates into business. Demand for design skills also explodes, leading to easier access to bite-sized chunks of design expertise.

    Examples Used: Candy Crush, Infogr.am, Visual.ly, PicktoChart, *Microinteractions* by Dan Saffer, Swiftly and Over app

    2016 Trend Longevity Rating: A

    The need for design expertise in every corner of business continues to grow, and this trend is still an important one for any type of organization to consider when building a team in 2016.

12. Overquantified Life

As big data leads brands to overload data with cute infographics and superficial analysis, they add more confusion about what all this data really means, and how it can inform decisions in real life.

Examples Used: Kred, Klout, Jawbone, Fitbit and Google Glass

2016 Trend Longevity Rating: B

Connecting all the data we collect on ourselves in a meaningful way continues to be a challenge, however, consumers are feeling less overquantified and more in control of this data and comfortable with how to selectively read it.

13. Curated Sensationalism

As the line between news and entertainment blurs, smart curation displaces journalism as content is paired with sensational headlines to drive millions of views.

Examples Used: Buzzfeed, Upworthy, *Forbes*, ThunderClap and SunnySkyz

2016 Trend Longevity Rating: A

Media continues to deliver over-the-top headlines and sensationalism that continue to negatively affect consumer trust in media. Despite growing consumer skepticism, 24 hour news cycles and everyday social tragedy have made this type of sensationalism a device today's media is completely addicted to using in the industry-wide race to chase clicks and impressions rather than to tell stories worth sharing.

14. Distributed Expertise

The idea of expertise itself shifts to become more inclusive, less academic and more widely available on demand and in real time.

Examples Used: Plated, Contently, Vikram Patel, Kaggle, Pop Expert and Clarity.fm

2016 Trend Longevity Rating: A

Learning through experts online in many formats is still a big trend and one that is powering some of the fastest growing learning platforms online today (including many profiled in this original trend).

15. Anti-Stereotyping

Across media and entertainment, traditional gender roles are being reversed, assumptions about alternative lifestyles are being challenged and perceptions of what defines anyone evolve in new ways.

Examples Used: "Lean Out" from *Bloomberg Businessweek*, Hasbro Easy Bake Oven, *In A World* … the movie, the Bic for Her pen firestorm, Tide laundry, *Delusions of Gender* by Cordelia Fine, *A Call to Action* by Jimmy Carter and *Whistling Vivaldi* by Claude Steele

2016 Trend Longevity Rating: A

The shifting of gender roles continues to be a big opportunity for brands to get their messaging right, or wrong, when it comes to speaking to these diverse groups through marketing and communications.

Want to read the original 2014 Report for free?

Visit www.15trends.com to read and download the full report.

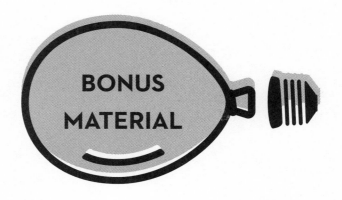

BONUS
MATERIAL

EXCLUSIVE
ADDITIONAL
CONTENT

BONUS MATERIAL

EXCLUSIVE ADDITIONAL CONTENT

ARTICLE:
"How to Create a Brand Story"

This article was first published on my blog and inspired by a session I facilitated with GE Chief Marketing Officer Beth Comstock at the Future of Storytelling Conference. We collaborated to host three such sessions throughout the day for participants from a variety of industries, and the topic was the art of brand storytelling. The following is my recap of those sessions, along with five specific takeaways that came from it which are sure to help anyone trying to craft a more compelling brand story of their own.

Yesterday I heard the same story three times in a row, and it was illuminating.

Outside the well scripted confines of Manhattan every year, an epic event called The Future of Storytelling brings together designers, technologists, builders and brand marketers to ask the most fundamental question facing any creator: how do you tell a story that people will care about? I was fortunate to participate in this year's event, which gathered spoken word poets, a master perfumer, a world renowned magician and many other unexpected characters to discuss and question the future of the art of storytelling itself.

At an event like this, injecting a conversation about "corporate storytelling" might seem a bit unambitious. After all, how interesting could marketing be when you are literally following a presentation about the first human in history who is aiming to actually become a cyborg by implanting an antennae in his brain that allows him to "hear colors."

Thanks to the cruel fate of the agenda, I found myself getting ready to moderate my session that day facing this exact challenge. Thankfully, I had been paired with one of the few people in the world of marketing and business who had the gravitas to pull it off: General Electric CMO Beth Comstock. Over the course of our three hour long moderated roundtable discussions with about 25 people per session, we debated everything from how brands might work with creators to why so much of "content marketing" is so tragically forgettable.

Over the course of those three hours – I captured some of the most powerful insights that arose from our collaborative discussion and my share them in the list below. Together, they capture insights and practices from one of the most forward thinking brands in the world at using corporate storytelling to make a lasting emotional connection with audiences around the globe.

1. Develop "Story Archaeologists."

The brilliant thing about archaeologists is that they don't create history, they only discover it and help us find the meaning behind it. Similarly, there are so many stories that brands have already behind the way they make the things they make. If you can simply get better at finding them more consistently, you can often unlock a hidden treasure of stories that are waiting to be shared.

2. Be A Participant, Not A Patron.

We expect a certain behaviour of our patrons – particularly when it comes to the Arts. The most obvious way for a brand to support a story is simply to sponsor it. Yet slapping a "Presented by" logo on a piece of storytelling produced by someone else is never the same as true storytelling. Instead, great storytelling requires you to be a participant and take a leap of faith to produce something.

3. Make The Invisible Visible.

When you make big intimidating world shifting products like a jet engine – it can be easy for the individuals behind it to lose their sense of purpose. The end product is often invisible to them. Yet if you can bring that engineer to the first flight of the aircraft using that engine, or connect the designer of the new MRI machine to the cancer patient who ends up using it then you can make the impact of what they do come to life. Those situations create amazing stories because you make the invisible impact of their work visible.

4. Hire People Who Are "Story Culture" Fits.

All storytellers are not created equal and the thing that separates them is passion. A great storyteller for GE must also love science and have curiosity. Without that combination of passion and curiosity, the beauty of the stories that GE might authentically tell could be lost. Great and visual storytelling isn't about hiring the hottest agency to reshape an image and to make a brand "cool." Instead, it's about embracing the inner geek and being true to yourself.

5. Create Wearable Meaning.

The thing that connects people is other people. We tend to think about meaning sometimes in the same way as logic. It has meaning as long as it makes sense. But they are not the same. When a story has true meaning, you connect with it so authentically that you would literally wear it. You would produce a t-shirt, put it on, and never take it off. Perhaps the biggest opportunity for corporate storytelling is to create and evangelize this type of meaning.

The Bottom Line:

Of course, over the span of the day our conversation branched into many different categories and the participants (who I am in the process of curating to list here) offered many other useful ideas. Ultimately, as one participant put it, the key for corporate or brand storytellers is to move beyond history to heritage – because a history is just a list. A heritage is something you can be proud of – and that is worth finding a way to share because people will connect with it and learn from it. Even if they end up hearing it three times in a row.

ARTICLE:
"Why Indian Drivers
Make Better Leaders"

A central lesson through the first part of this book was all about honing your powers of observation. Based on the streets of India, this article offered the point of view that real leadership takes a skill that every Indian driver has already learned... how to communicate in the midst of chaos.

If you have spent any time in a car in India, you know there is a system that helps to create order out of chaos on Indian roads.

That uniting force isn't some magical technology or better signage. Indian drivers, quite simply, are more attuned to the movements happening around them. They communicate with each other to negotiate how to navigate tricky situations. They honk to announce their intention to move through an intersection, and use hand signals and eye contact to describe their intent. Traffic is more congested, but it moves with purpose. And the drivers are, in short, not oblivious.

Drivers in America are the exact opposite.

American drivers rarely communicate with each other unless it is to express angry disbelief at one another's stupidity. They buy increasingly luxurious sound proof cars to insulate themselves from the road. This in car technology offers all kinds of escapes from the "horror" of actually driving and paying attention to driving. The result is predictable.

Most US drivers pay little attention to one another and simply believe that following the traffic signs and traffic rules will be enough. Sadly, they are often wrong - leading to accidents or injury.

So what does any of this have to do with leadership or trends?

Imagine if you treated your approach to your team the same way Americans approach driving. You could surround yourself with the best technology, avoid interacting on a genuine face to face level with anyone, and rely on the "rules of the road" to help you get to where you want to go. How effective do you think that would be?

Instead, real leadership means picking your head up instead of putting it down. It means communicating more than anger.

The most effective leaders make a commitment to learning through conversations. They are not observationally or conversationally lazy. Instead, they are curious, observant and realize that real insight comes from listening, not speaking.

The good and bad news is that there is more conversation than ever before. Of course there are the people right in front of you or those you interact with on your team. But the Internet is also a goldmine of public conversation on social media and it is ready to be mined.

What are people talking about and why are they talking? What could you learn by interacting directly with them?

For example, Benetton India Managing Director Sanjeev Mohanty is rapidly creating a reputation for transformation by paying attention to trends and conversations. He reportedly chooses several customer emails every day to respond to directly. Customers are stunned to get a response from a top leader - and he gets the benefit of direct customer feedback. Win-win.

The point is, all of this insight is sitting online, and people are hungry for these types of connections from leaders. You just need to make a commitment to get better at observing and interacting.

It is easy to think that becoming a better driver is learning the rules of the road. What if the real key is slowing down, paying attention to what is happening around you and actually communicating with your fellow humans?

You know ... like they do in India.

READER Q&A:
12 Questions with the Author

One of the best things about speaking at events around the world is having the chance to speak with real people about the ideas in this book. This is a Q&A featuring some of the most common or interesting questions I have been asked so far in person, online or through interviews – only slightly reworded to improve their clarity ...

Q1: ***You say in the book that "it's never been a better time to be an employee." Do you really believe that?***

A: This is a point that is easy to disagree with if you happen to be out of work or struggling. I do believe, though, that the time we are in now is one that is better for many employees. We have awards given to companies for being the "best places to work." Millennials in the workforce are bringing a new expectation of moving from company to company rather than staying at one company for decades. As a result, companies seeking the best people need to find more ways to compete to keep their people. When companies compete to keep employees, work places and the employee experience gets better.

Q2: *Why is it so important to offer catchy names for trends and isn't that just another form of "future babble" that you advise us all to avoid?*

A: The real problem with "future babble," as Dan Gardner described it in his book which I cited is that experts who predict the future can be unwilling to admit any sort of mistakes. The babble, therefore, actually comes more from mistaken predictions and stubborn refusals to evolve thinking. I do love developing interesting names for trends to help them stand out, but I also work hard not to become emotionally attached to the trends or defensive of anyone who has an alternative viewpoint to share. That's ultimately the responsibility I think any of us have to curating trends. We must be comfortable enough to see another point of view – and admit mistakes when we make them.

Q3: *Some of the trends in this year's report (as well as some previous trends) seem to contradict one another. How do you think about or handle trends that seem contradictory?*

A: I know some people read the book and want to see the trends as a whole, but every year there are contradictions. Why? The main reason is because the world is contradictory too. Products compete for contradictory audiences. Individuals are influenced in contradictory ways. People are different. So the way to approach trends is not to say that they all point to one view of the world. Rather, what I hope people take away from the book is that there is plenty of meaning and acceleration between each trend … even if they happen to describe slightly different and contrasting observations about the world around us.

Q4: *One theme across several of your trends this year has to do with our shrinking attention spans. Do you think humans as a whole are getting dumber and less able to focus on anything for an extended time?*

A: Well not necessarily dumber, but certainly more distracted! Yes, the shrinking attention span is a major challenge for any of us – but I think people do still want to consume content in longer formats. They are, however, more selective with the content they will devote this additional attention to. What that really means is that we each need to get better about giving people that "glanceable" snapshot of our story to entice them to spend more time with it either in the moment, or later when they have more time.

Q5: *Can anyone (not just business people) identify trends? And if so, how might they use these insights in their daily life?*

A: Yes, after leading dozens of workshops now and teaching thousands of people across the last six years about trends and predicting the future, I have found that anyone can learn to put the five habits of trend curators to work in their own lives. Beyond trends though, one of the most surprising things about these skills is how applicable they are for the rest of our lives. Being more curious, observant or thoughtful – for example, can lead you towards appreciating the people in your life or gain a greater understanding of the world around you. Even if it happens to have nothing to do with business.

Q6: *Every day I feel like I see a little more marketing targeting me directly and using more persistent personalization to sell me something – like those ads that follow me around the Internet promoting whatever product or site I was browsing earlier. Is that really "reluctant" marketing?*

A: This is a fair point – it probably isn't! When you consider how frequently companies are using the big data they have collected to tailor more specific and potentially intrusive marketing messages, it hardly seems reluctant. Yet this trend was meant to focus on the idea that marketing now encompasses more than just promotion. Brands are trying to answer questions through content, build better experiences and create more engagement online and offline – so the time spent on this direct outbound type of marketing is becoming a smaller piece of the overall marketing mix.

Q7: *If it is getting close to the end of the year and I know you do your trend predictions annually, should I just wait for next year's report?*

A: At the beginning of every year when the new trends come out, there does tend to be quite a bit of buzz and excitement because they are new. The thing about my reports, though, is that some trends take more time to develop so there is still value in the trends identified for any year and the reason I revisit them each year. The interesting thing that happens over time with these "non-obvious" trends is that they start to become more obvious because more people pay attention to them and they become a more common fixture in conversations about business and the world. When I first wrote about the "Power of Women" trend a few years ago, for example, it was just emerging. Today the rapid acceleration and impact of women on culture and the workplace is a known fact. Knowing about and using the trends from this year into next year, no matter when you pick up the book, will always have value in the moment. Some trends just might have increasing value over time since they are first introduced.

Q8: *I have seen you in several interviews reject being called a "futurist." Why is that a term you don't think describes what you do?*

A: I know many futurists, admire them and consider several to be close friends. What they do, though, is quite different than my approach. They see the future in terms of technology and cultural advances over wider spans of time. They look at how these shifts will affect entire nations and populations. And they tend to be more focused on macro shifts in society. My approach, instead, is much more about short term behavioral shifts and how they specifically impact *business* in what we buy or sell. Their approach is valuable for governments, and large multinational organizations seeking to understand big shifts that may challenge their business 15 years from now. My approach is far more focused on near term shifts and what it means for your strategy over the next year.

I find it interesting to look at what will happen in 20 years. I find it more useful and actionable to focus my curated trends only on the upcoming year.

Q9: *You have said in interviews that writing a book usually takes you about a year. Is that really how long it takes – and how does that break down for you in terms of writing versus research?*

A: Now that I have done it four times with full length books (and once with a shorter ebook), I can safely say that the time frame for me is one year to produce a book. For every book, I use a storyboarding technique to map out the flow of the book, then write it in sections to be assembled and edited later. The process, though, varies greatly based on the type of book. *Personality Not Included,* my first book, was heavily based on my own experiences and so the writing was the hard part. *Likeonomics* required a lot of story research and writing + rewriting to tell those stories effectively. *Non-Obvious* is very research oriented where the majority of my time was spent doing interviews, collecting and curating information, and then bringing the arguments for each trend together.

Q10: *You shared in the book that you don't look at trends specifically by industry, but some of your trends like "E-mpulse Buying" seem fairly industry focused. Wouldn't it be more useful to break down your trends by industry?*

A: This is a question I get often and I appreciate that making trends relevant for a particular industry is really important. In fact, one of the first things I do whenever I deliver a keynote or workshop is some level of customization of the trends for a particular industry. One of the fundamental beliefs of my system and the Haystack Method, though, is that real insights come from the process of intersecting industries. Too often we spend all our time just comparing ourselves with others in our industry. Real innovation has to come from outside of industry silos and from people willing to learn from unexpected sources. Learning to think different, as I promise in the subtitle of the book, involves taking a broader view of the world.

Q11: *How do you use these trends in your own business?*

A: Well, aside from the obvious fact that helping companies use the trends in their business is a large part of what I do, the trends have also impacted the way I think about the consulting and speaking work that I do as well. "Mainstream multiculturism", for example, has helped me think of my audience differently in terms of being able to connect with them from the stage. "Disruptive Distribution" has been a central factor in some of the new publishing initiatives I have launched to help promote and sell this book. So the trends relate to my business in many ways – and I am always trying to put them into action to power my own thinking even more.

Q12: *How do these trends work outside of America? Are they really useful for an international audience?*

A: About a dozen times a year, I travel outside of the United States to share these trends with a global audience. They do work internationally – and a big part of the reason is the outlook I aim to bring to them. In the pages of this book are stories from the streets of India and an opening story from a quirky museum in Norway. The idea with all of it is to focus on looking at trends and predicting the future as a skill that focuses on human behavior rather than the latest and greatest startup that has captured the interest of early adopters in America. I work hard each year to make sure that the trends I share are widely applicable to many cultures and countries.

Have more questions? You can always submit another question or just let me know what you think by visiting www.nonobviousbook.com.

INDEX

bite-sized content, 225
Blackish (TV show), 111
blogs/blogging, 27–28, 37–38
Bloomberg News, 188
Blue Apron meal service, 165
BMW Performance Driving School, 195
Boing Boing, 70
Bolthouse Farms, 232
books, as idea sources, 39
brainful vs. brainless media, 21
Brain Pickings (Popova), 29, 171
Branded Benevolence trend
defined, 190
how to use, 191–192
2016 perspective, 190–191
who should use, 191
Branded Inspiration trend, 270
Branded Utility trend
added learning material, 107–108
with apps, 106–107
defined, 104
how to use, 108–109
magazine brands, 105–106
overview, 104–105, 279
who should use, 108
why it matters, 108
Brand Storytelling Trend Workshop, 237
breaking trends, 242
broad predictions with trends, 11–12
BroApp, 165
Brockman, John, 22
Brooks, David, 164
Brown, Tim, 154
Brutal Transparency trend, 47, 258–259
bucket lists, 85
building industry marketing, 92–93
business incubators, 156–157
Business Marketing Association conference
(2012), 93
business models, 45
Business Strategy Trend Workshop, 237
BusinessWeek magazine, 12, 80, 114, 230

C
campaign strategy collection, 41
Cannes Lions International Festival of
Creativity, 197
Carnival Cruise Lines, 118–119
Caterpillar company, 91–92
Cebu Pacific, 67
Center for Advanced Studies in Adaptive
Systems (CASAS), 82

Center for Restorative Breast Surgery, 185
Center on Aging & Work at Boston College,
81
Centre for Open Data Enterprise, 142
Century Fox Home Entertainment, 133
challenging predictions, 244–245
Change By Design (Brown), 154
ChangeSourcing trend, 31, 265, 267
charitable engagement trend, 263
Cheng, Lily, 174
civic engagement 2.0 trend, 265
ClassDojo app, 174
The Click Moment (Johansson), 233
Clouds Over Sidra (film), 135
Coca-Cola company, 158, 232
Co-Curation trend, 263
Collaborative Economy trend, 278–279
collider data, 142
Comcast, 67
commenting on blog, 27–28
Company Culture Trend Workshop, 237
Comstock, Beth, 89, 287
confectionary brands, e-impulse buying
trend, 64–65
Confectionary News, 65
Consumer Electronics Show, 219
consumer-owned data, 219
content building for moods, 204
Content Marketing Institute (CMI), 92
content studio explosion, 157–158
thecoolhunter.co.uk, 240
coolhunting.com, 240
corporate entrepreneurship, 155
Corporate Humanism trend, 261
Coulton, Jonathan, 100
Coursera platform, 99
Crain Media, 157
Crispin Porter + Bogusky (CP+B), 232
Crowdsourced Innovation trend, 256
Ctrl Alt Delete (Joel), 105
Culting of Retail trend, 259
curated compilations, 22
curated health data, 145–147
Curated Sensationalism trend, 281
Curationism (Balzer), 18
curationism, rise of, 18–19
curators of the mind, 171–172
curiosity.com, 216
curiosity in trend curation, 20–22, 34
current popularity and trends, 11
Customer Journey Mapping Trend Workshop,
236

defined, 181
how to use, 182–183
2016 perspective, 181–182
who should use, 182
experiences vs. promotion, 197–198
Experimedia trend
defined, 205
how to use, 207
2016 perspective, 205–206
who should use, 206
explaining the world to children, 26
Eyal, Nir, 53, 54

F
Facebook
aggregating, 41
digital personal assistants, 174
distribution of services, 220
female executives, 129
online "hot zones," 65
social media campaigns, 66
virtual reality technology, 134
facial coding software, 102
fantasy football, 215
Farhang, Omid, 232
Fascinate (Hogshead), 96
Fast Company magazine, 100
Fathom cruises, 118–119
Fawkes, Piers, 239
fear of wastage, 94–95
fickleness in trend curation, 25–27, 34
fierce femininity, 129–130
Financial Technology startups, 220
fixed mindsets, defined, 16
Flappy Bird game, 52–53
flip thinking and anti-trends, 242
focus groups and virtual technology, 137–138
focus of attention, 234
folder storage for ideas, 40
food delivery observation, 25
Food Institute, 165
Food Network, 89
Forbes, 157
Ford Motor Company, 137
Ford Research and Innovation Center, 159
Founding Farmers, 222
four models of trend workshops, 236–237
Fowler, Jim, 99
Free Code Camp, 121
Fresh Direct groceries, 172
Fresh off the Boat (TV show), 111–112
Frog Design agency, 152, 154

fundamental message in B2B marketing, 94
The Furrow magazine, 106
Future Babble (Gardner), 55–56
The Future Laboratory, 231

G
game-changing products, 230
gamification, 53
Gamified Learning trend, 53–54
Gardner, Dan, 55–56
Garvin, David A., 155
Gates, Bill, 28
gathering step in Haystack Method, 38–40, 52–53
gaze tracking technology, 97–98
Gear VR, 134
gender blending, 130–131
General Electric, 89–90
Generation Me, 163
genetically modified organisms (GMOs), 76
genius bars, 195
Getty Images, 128
Gilbert, Dan, 207
Glanceable Content trend
defined, 199
how to use, 201
2016 perspective, 199–200
who should use, 200
global consumer behavior, 69
Glynn, Ian, 30
Goldberg, Andy, 89–90
GOOD DESIGN award, 83
GoodRx, startup, 43
Google product launches, 118
Google's keyword analysis tools, 201
Grand View Research, 83
Grossman, Pam, 128
grouping of ideas, 41–42
growth mindsets, defined, 16–17
Gundotra, Vic, 182
Gurin, Joel, 142

H
Haas School of Business (UC), 56
habit-forming products, 53
Hallmark cards, 206
Handley, Ann, 105
Hanley Wood, 92–93
hard data and trends, 11
Harford, Lexxie, 184
Harley-Davidson motorcycles, 131
Harvard Business Review, 155

Sysco Corporation, 88–89